LEARN JAPANESE
WITH MANGA
AN INTERMEDIATE SELF-STUDY LANGUAGE GUIDE
Volume Two

Marc Bernabé

TUTTLE Publishing

Tokyo | Rutland, Vermont | Singapore

Marc Bernabé, the author of the two-volume course *Learn Japanese with Manga*, is a manga and anime translator who teaches Japanese language and etiquette courses for non-Japanese. He is the co-founder of the manga- and anime-specialized translation agency Daruma Serveis Lingüístics SL and the Japan culture center Espai Daruma. He has also published several Japan-related books.

Ken Niimura is the illustrator of the manga story ***Kage***, co-written with Marc Bernabé. A Spanish-Japanese cartoonist and illustrator, he has a unique style informed by his international background. He has worked with clients such as Amazon, Google, McDonald's, Marvel Comics, Apple, L'Oreal, DC Entertainment, Shogakukan, Slate, The Apatow Company, Tezuka Pro, Image Comics, Kodansha and NHK Broadcasting Station among others. His book *I Kill Giants*, written by Joe Kelly, won the International Manga Award and was adapted into a film in 2019 starring Zoe Saldana. His series *Umami* earned him an Eisner Award to the Best Digital Comic. Ken Niimura's work has been translated into twelve languages. He lives and works between Japan and Europe. **www.niimuraweb.com**

Other illustrations in volume 2:
Studio Kōsen
Xian Nu Studio
Gabriel Luque

Translation: **Olinda Cordukes**

Table of Contents

Introduction

It is possible that some readers, not acquainted with the manga and anime world, will wonder why Japanese manga comic strips have been chosen to illustrate the lessons in these two volumes of books *Learn Japanese with Manga*.

The first reason is that the lessons that make up this course were originally published in a well-known Japanese comic book and anime magazine in Spain. When the magazine's editor-in-chief at the time asked me to produce a monthly Japanese course, I thought this should somehow be in line with the general subject matter of the magazine. Drawing inspiration from the lessons in the now defunct American magazine *Mangajin*, where every month a linguistic subject was explained using manga as examples, I managed to find a formula, which involved developing a course in Japanese with a fixed structure. This structure consisted of a page of theory with vocabulary and grammar tables and a page of examples taken directly from Japanese manga, to illustrate and expand what had just been explained. To my surprise, the idea worked perfectly well, allowing the course to be published without a break for thirty issues of the magazine (almost three years). All this allowed for the publication of these books, a largely improved compilation of the contents in the magazine.

The second reason we use manga to teach Japanese in these two volumes is because manga is a big phenomenon, not only in Japan, but throughout the world. Manga, with its enormous subject variety, is an ideal window through which to observe Japanese society and its mentality.

The word *manga* literally means "spontaneous and meaningless drawings." By extension, the West has adopted this word with the meaning of "Japanese comic-book." However, the popularity of manga in Japan is incomparable to similar genres in Western countries. If a comparison must be made, the manga phenomenon could possibly meet its match in the movie industry. A successful manga author is able to charge a real fortune and, in fact, the best-known authors are among the wealthiest people in Japan.

Here are some facts you may not know about the Japanese manga industry:

a) The sales value of comics, or manga, in Japan was estimated at almost 676 billion Japanese yen in 2021, up by more than 10 percent compared to the previous year. The market size increased for the fourth year in a row (*Annual Report on the Publication Market 2022*).

b) Weekly manga magazines and manga serials have amazing sales figures in Japan. The manga series *Jujutsu Kaisen* (lit. "Sorcery Fight") sold approximately 30.9 million volumes in Japan from November 2020 to November 2021, making it the best-selling manga series in the country during that time period (statista.com).

c) In Japan there are manga of all genres, for all ages and social strata, including children, teenagers, older women, laborers, office workers, etc. There are even erotic and pornographic manga.

In Japan manga tend to be published initially in thick and cheap weekly magazines, in the form of serials of about twenty pages per episode. When a weekly series is successful, it's usually then compiled in a volume of about two-hundred pages called a 単行本 *tankōbon*. This ecosystem is maintained in digital form. Actually, in 2021, the digital manga market size was already almost double than the traditional printed book market.

All in all, manga is a very important phenomenon in Japan. Through these comic books—with a degree of caution and an analytical spirit—we can study not just the Japanese language but Japanese culture and idiosyncrasies too!

Be sure to read through the next section carefully to get an idea of how this method works and how this two-volume course is structured. I hope *Learn Japanese with Manga* will help you to learn about Japanese language culture. It is a great honor for me to be your **sensei**.

How to use *Learn Japanese with Manga*

This two-volume series is designed for the self-study of the spoken, colloquial Japanese used in manga, so that you will be able to understand a Japanese comic book or anime series in the original, with the help of a dictionary.

With the focus on the informal oral language of manga, you will study many aspects of Japanese not usually taught in conventional courses or textbooks. Difficulty increases as the lessons progress, so I recommend studying the lessons in order, starting with Volume 1, and moving on to the next lesson only when you are familiar with the contents of the previous lessons.

The Volume 2 course

Volume 1 consists of lessons 1–35, and this Volume 2 contains lessons 36–60. The content of the lessons in Volume 2 builds on what was taught in Volume 1, so I recommend completing the Volume 1 course of study before starting with this book. However, you can still study the lessons in this book even if you haven't studied Volume 1, as long as you have mastered the basics of elementary level Japanese grammar, including the hiragana and katakana alphabets.

As in Volume 1, each chapter in Volume 2 is divided into the following sections:

a) **theory:** a detailed explanation of the lesson's subject matter often with grammar or vocabulary tables which help summarize and reinforce what has been explained.

b) **manga examples:** from real Japanese manga, to illustrate and expand what has been explained in the theory pages. The system used to analyze each sentence is the following:

> **Chiaki:** ただいま川井(かわい)が参(まい)りますので…
> *now Kawai SP come because . . .*
> Kawai will come right away . . .

First line:	exact transcription of the original Japanese text including ***furigana*** (hiragana transcriptions that give the Japanese reading of the kanji).
Second line:	literal translation, word for word. (The meaning of abbreviations such as **SP** and others can be found in the glossary on page 7.)
Third line:	translation of the text into natural-sounding English.

c) **exercises:** these are always related to the lesson's subject matter, and the answers can always be obtained or deduced from the content of the lesson they belong to. The answers to the exercises can be found online by following the link on page 7.

On translations

There are many example sentences throughout the book, as well as many manga examples, with their corresponding word-for-word translations into English. Sometimes, the sentences we offer may not sound very natural, since we have chosen more literal translations for an easier understanding of their formation. Trying to create a more natural English translation of every sentence would be a good exercise: it would help you consolidate concepts, make and in-depth analysis of the Japanese sentence, and think about it as a whole rather than a mere group of words and grammatical patterns.

Online materials

This book comes with comprehensive online materials which can be accessed using the link on page 7:

1 **Answers to the Exercises:** detailed answers to all the exercises included in the book.

2 **Kanji Compilation:** a compilation of 260 kanji characters, with stroke order and example word. The study of these characters is essential to acquire a sound basis for a subsequent, more in-depth study of the language.

3 **Glossary of Onomatopoeia:** a useful reference tool for readers of manga in their original version.

4 **Vocabulary Index:** an index of the Japanese vocabulary words that appear throughout the book, in alphabetical order.

5 **Audio Files:** Key words and sentences recorded by native Japanese speakers to help you achieve authentic pronunciation. Sections of the text that have online audio recordings are indicated by the headphones logo.

6 ***Kage*, Episode 1:** The manga serial ***Kage*** runs throughout this book, an exciting read that will reinforce and consolidate the language points you have been studying. The first of the six episodes was at the end of Volume 1, and is also accessible online for your convenience. I recommend reading Episode 1 before starting Episode 2 on page 60 of this book.

略称集 Glossary of abbreviations

CP: Companion Particle, (who with), for example と

DOP: Direct Object Particle (what), for example, を

DP: Direction Particle (where to), for example, へ

EP: Emphatic Particle. Most end-of-sentence particles state emphasis or add a certain nuance, for example, ね, よ, ぞ, etc.

IOP: Indirect Object Particle, for example, に

IP: Instrument Particle (what with), for example, で

NOM: Nominalizer, a word such as こと or の that is used to turn a group of words into a noun phrase (Lesson 40)

POP: Possessive Particle (whose), for example, の

PP: Place Particle (where), for example, で , に

Q?:   Question particle. Shows that the sentence is a question, for example, か

SBP: Subordinate Sentence Particle. This particle is used as a link between a subordinate sentence and the main sentence, for example と

SP: Subject Particle (who or what), for example, が

SUF: Suffix for a person's name, for example, さん , くん , etc.

TOP: Topic Particle. Shows that the previous word is the topic, for example, は

TP: Time Particle (when), for example, に

To Access the Online Materials:

1. Check to be sure you have an internet connection.
2. Type the URL below into your web browser.
   www.tuttlepublishing.com/learn-japanese-with-manga-volume-2

For support, you can email us at info@tuttlepublishing.com.

Lesson 36 ● 第36課

At a Hotel or Ryokan

You probably remember we arrived in Japan in Lesson 33 of Volume 1: we concluded the lesson just as we left the airport. This lesson is devoted to accommodation and possible situations that can come up at the place where you are staying.

🎧 The booking

Hotels staff probably speak at least a little English. But at some places, like the traditional Japanese-style inns called ryokan, you may need to communicate in Japanese. Let's take the first step, and book a room. **Note:** The suffix 〜付き *tsuki* after a noun means "included," for example, ご飯付き *gohan tsuki* (meal included). The opposite expression, that is, "not included" is 〜なし. For example, 朝食なし *chōshoku nashi* (breakfast not included).

- 今夜、部屋を予約したいんですが I would like to book a room for tonight.
- 一泊、いくらですか？ How much is it for a night?
- 朝食付きですか？ Is breakfast included?
- もう少し安い部屋はありますか？ Do you have a cheaper room?
- その部屋にします I'll take that room.
- お名前と国籍をお願いします Can I have your name and nationality, please?

🎧 Check-in

You're checking in at your accommodation. These sentences will help you:

- ケントと言いますが、予約を入れています My name's Kent, I have a booking.
- チェックインしたいんですが I would like to check in. (Lesson 31)
- 国際ユースホステルの会員証で割引はありますか？ Do I get a discount with my international youth hostel card?
- 部屋を見てもいいですか？ Can I see the room? (Lesson 32)
- 今日から5泊の宿泊ですね You are staying for five nights from today, right?
- 宿泊カードに記入してください Please fill in the registration card. (Lesson 35)

Booking and check-in					
bunk bed	二段ベッド <ruby>二段<rt>にだん</rt></ruby>	no rooms available	<ruby>空室<rt>くうしつ</rt></ruby>なし	reservation	<ruby>予約<rt>よやく</rt></ruby>
to cancel	キャンセルする	price	<ruby>宿泊料<rt>しゅくはくりょう</rt></ruby>	rooms available	<ruby>空室<rt>くうしつ</rt></ruby>あり
cash	<ruby>現金<rt>げんきん</rt></ruby>	shared bathroom	<ruby>共用<rt>きょうよう</rt></ruby>トイレ	x nights	〜<ruby>泊<rt>はく</rt></ruby>
curfew	<ruby>門限<rt>もんげん</rt></ruby>	shared room	<ruby>共同部屋<rt>きょうどうべや</rt></ruby>	with bathroom	トイレ<ruby>付<rt>つ</rt></ruby>き
credit card	クレジットカード	signature	<ruby>署名<rt>しょめい</rt></ruby>	with breakfast	<ruby>朝食付<rt>ちょうしょくつ</rt></ruby>き
double room	<ruby>二人部屋<rt>ふたりべや</rt></ruby>	single room	<ruby>一人部屋<rt>ひとりべや</rt></ruby>	with shower	シャワー<ruby>付<rt>つ</rt></ruby>き
nationality	<ruby>国籍<rt>こくせき</rt></ruby>	triple room	<ruby>三人部屋<rt>さんにんべや</rt></ruby>	youth-hostel card	ユースホステルカード

Services

Next, let's interact with the hotel staff, either to ask for a service or how something works.

- <ruby>部屋<rt>へや</rt></ruby><ruby>番号<rt>ばんごう</rt></ruby>は<ruby>２０６<rt>にゼロろく</rt></ruby>です My room number is 206.
- <ruby>３１２<rt>さんいちに</rt></ruby><ruby>号室<rt>ごうしつ</rt></ruby>の<ruby>鍵<rt>かぎ</rt></ruby>をください Can I have the key for room number 312, please?
- <ruby>貴重品<rt>きちょうひん</rt></ruby>を<ruby>預<rt>あず</rt></ruby>けたいんですが I'd like to put some valuable objects away (Lesson 31)
- インターネット（<ruby>WiFi<rt>ワイファイ</rt></ruby>）のパスワードを<ruby>教<rt>おし</rt></ruby>えてください Can you tell me the Internet password, please.
- ロッカーはありますか？ Do you have any lockers?
- <ruby>朝<rt>あさ</rt></ruby><ruby>8時<rt>はちじ</rt></ruby>にモーニングコールを<ruby>お願<rt>おねが</rt></ruby>いします Could I have an 8am morning call?
- ドライヤーを<ruby>貸<rt>か</rt></ruby>してください Could I borrow a hairdryer, please?
- <ruby>お風呂<rt>おふろ</rt></ruby>は<ruby>何時<rt>なんじ</rt></ruby>から<ruby>何時<rt>なんじ</rt></ruby>までですか？ What are the opening hours for the bath?

Requests and problems

Lost keys, broken air-conditioning or heating, noisy neighbors, accidents . . . All kinds of problems can arise in a hotel, and in this lesson we will deal with the most typical.

- すみません、ちょっと<ruby>困<rt>こま</rt></ruby>っているんですが . . . Excuse me, I have a problem . . .
- <ruby>部屋<rt>へや</rt></ruby>の<ruby>鍵<rt>かぎ</rt></ruby>をなくしてしまいました I've lost my room key. (Lesson 35)
- <ruby>鍵<rt>かぎ</rt></ruby>を<ruby>部屋<rt>へや</rt></ruby>の<ruby>中<rt>なか</rt></ruby>に<ruby>忘<rt>わす</rt></ruby>れました I've left my key in the room.
- <ruby>部屋<rt>へや</rt></ruby>がうるさくて<ruby>眠<rt>ねむ</rt></ruby>れません The room is so noisy I can't sleep. (Lessons 32, 35)

- お湯が出ません There is no hot water.
- エアコン・電気・テレビがつきません The air-con / light / TV isn't working.
- 部屋の掃除をしてください Could you clean the room, please?

🎧 Check out

It's time to leave. On checking out, we pay our bill and we say thank you.

- チェックアウトをしたいんですが I would like to check out . . . (Lesson 31)
- お支払いは現金ですか、カードですか？ Will you pay by cash or credit card?
- カードでお願いします Credit card. | 現金でお願いします Cash.
- いろいろお世話になりました Thank you very much for everything.

🎧 Hotel		🎧 Room			
bar	バー	air conditioning	エアコン | 冷房	local call	市内電話
coffee shop	コーヒー ショップ	alarm clock	目覚まし時計	morning call	モーニングコール
elevator	エレベー ター	bath	バス	plug / socket	コンセント
emergency exit	非常口	bed	ベッド	sheet	シーツ
lobby	ロビー	chair	いす	sink	流し
to pay	支払う	door	ドア	sofa	ソファ
reception	フロント	faucet	蛇口	table	テーブル | 机
restaurant	レストラン	fridge	冷蔵庫	television	テレビ
safe	セーフ | 金庫	hairdryer	ヘア ドライヤー	toilet	トイレ
stairs	階段	heating	暖房	toilet bowl	便器
valuable objects	貴重品	international call	国際電話	towel	タオル
x floor	〜階	key	鍵	wardrobe	たんす
room x	〜号室	lamp	照明 | ランプ	window	窓

🎧 At a ryokan

If you are staying at a traditional Japanese ryokan there are certain customs to observe (see Cultural Note, page 12). Check-in takes place in your room, over a cup of tea.

- いらっしゃいませ。靴を脱いでください Welcome! Take your shoes off, please.
- この書類に記入してください Could you fill in this document, please?
- 夕食は七時から八時までです Dinner is from 7 to 8 pm.
- お風呂は１階にありますが、露天風呂もあります The bath is on the first floor, but we also have an open-air bath.
- どうぞ、浴衣を着て、くつろいでください You may put your yukata on and enjoy your stay.
- 食事後に仲居さんは布団を敷きます After dinner, the maid will lay out your futon.

🎧 Ryokan	
女将さん	landlady and owner of the ryokan
お風呂	Japanese-style deep bath
障子	translucent rice paper placed on doors and windows
スリッパ	slippers
畳	tatami mat
仲居さん	parlor maid or waitress
庭	garden
番頭さん	head clerk
ふすま	sliding door used as a partition between rooms
布団	futon
浴衣	light kimono used after a bath or to relax
洋式トイレ	Western style seated toilet
露天風呂	open-air bath, usually a spa
和式トイレ	Japanese-style squat toilet
和室	Japanese-style room

Cultural Note: The Ryokan

The 漢字 *kanji* that make up the word 旅館 *ryokan* give a clear hint about its meaning: travel (旅) house (館). The 旅館 is what we could call a "Japanese-style hotel," radically different in character to Western-style hotels, which are called ホテル in Japanese, an obviously foreign word, indicating that this latter style of accommodation was only introduced to Japan relatively recently.

Picture of a traditional ryokan in Futami, Mie Prefecture
(Photo: M. Bernabe)

In the 旅館, we can enjoy the pleasure of staying at a typical Japanese inn, with all that this involves. We must comply with certain rules, such as taking off our shoes when entering the building, and we have to be willing to take part in traditional customs such as bathing in the お 風呂 *ofuro* (communal bath) with other guests. However, the opportunity to experience the pleasure of sleeping in a typical 和室 *washitsu* (Japanese-style room), wrapped up in a 浴衣 *yukata* (light, dressing-gown style kimono), on a soft 布団 *futon*, placed on a floor covered with elegant 畳 *tatami* mats is well worth it. The only inconvenience is that some 旅館 only have 和式トイレ *washiki toire* (Japanese-style squat toilets). This is, though, changing at a fast pace, and at most 旅館 you can now choose between Western-style or Japanese-style toilets.

Nowadays, many of the most traditional and authentic 旅館 are in rural tourist areas, especially in towns and villages with natural hot springs, such as 箱根 *Hakone* (神奈川 *Kanagawa* Prefecture), 熱海 *Atami* (静岡 *Shizuoka* Prefecture), 別府 *Beppu* (大分 *Ōita* Prefecture), or 有馬 *Arima* (兵庫 *Hyōgo* Prefecture). The Japanese usually combine a stay at a 旅館 with visits to local restaurants or with relaxing hot-spring baths (most of the 旅館 in these areas have their own hot-spring facilities), especially open-air baths, which are called 露天風呂 *rotenburo*. Bathing outdoors, in natural hot water, is an unforgettable experience, especially when surrounded by snow!

Although staying in a 旅館 can be expensive, it is a highly recommended experience—a true immersion in the Japanese ocean of culture. Don't miss it!

🎧 漫画例 Manga Examples

As usual, the manga examples on these pages will illustrate the usage of the language of hotels and inns that we have studied in this chapter.

Manga Example 1: Before checking in

This is a variation of the example sentence on page 8 (ケントと言いますが、予約を入れています *Kento to iimasu ga, yoyaku o irete imasu*), although it has exactly the same meaning. Tanaka introduces himself as a member of Fiction Constructions, and then gives his surname (in Japan the group one belongs to is more important than the individual). He uses the verb 取る *toru* (to take) after 予約 (booking), while we used the verb 入れ (to put) in our example. The overall meaning of the sentences is the same. Also notice the 取ってある used by Tanaka, which we saw in Lesson 35 (〜てある), to refer to an action that is already finished. Also remember the customer is a god in Japan, and receptionists address the customer using the honorific 〜様 (Lesson 15).

Xian Nu Studio

Tanaka:	フィクション建設の田中で予約とってあるんですが。
	Fiction Constructions POP *Tanaka booking take (finished action) (softener)*
	I'm Tanaka, from Fiction Constructions, and I have a booking.
Receptionist:	はい、田中さまですね。
	yes, Tanaka SUF *be* EP
	Oh, yes, that's right: Mr. Tanaka.

Manga Example 2: "Seeing" the room

Studio Kōsen

If we want to see the room before deciding on a hotel, you can use the sentence 部屋を見てもいいですか？ *Heya o mitemo ii desu ka?* Here the bellboy shows the room to some guests who are anxious to start "using" it and gets very embarrassed! **Note:** The construction なっております is a humble form of the verb "to be." We will look at forms like these in Lesson 51.

Bellboy:	こちらがバスとトイレになっておりますから…
	here SP bath CP sink be (formal) because...
	And here are the bath and the toilet, so . . .

Manga Example 3: The fearsome bill

J.M. Ken Niimura

This example shows how to check out and pay the bill. The receptionist uses the verb 含める to say that the price (代 *dai*) for last night's (昨晩 *sakuban*) meal (お食事 *oshokuji*) has been included in the bill. He also uses the *-te* form (Lesson 35) to link the two clauses "including last night's meal" and "the total comes to 57,850 yen." The guest says he will pay (支払う) by credit card (カードで). By the way, don't worry! A regular hotel in Japan is in no way as expensive as the one in this example!

Receptionist:	昨晩^{さくばん}のお食事代^{しょくじだい}を含^{ふく}めまして、５７８５０円^{ごまんななせんはっぴゃくごじゅうえん}です。
	last night POP meal price DOP include, 57,850 yen be
	Including last night's meal, the total comes to 57,850 yen.
Guest:	ああ、支払^{しはら}いはカードで…
	oh, payment SP card with . . .
	Oh, I'll pay by credit card . . .

Manga Example 4: Asking for something at reception

The guest calls reception (フロント) to ask for a can opener (缶切り **kankiri**). The woman uses a casual style of speech indicating that as she is staying in a suite, she feels superior to the staff. The polite sentence would be 缶切りをお願いします **kankiri o onegai shimasu**.

Typical things we can ask for might be a hairdryer (ドライヤー), soap (石けん **sekken**), or a towel (タオル).

Gabriel Luque

Guest: …カン切りお願い… そ、２９０３のスイートよ

. . . can opener please . . . that's right, 2903 POP suite EP

Bring me a can opener, please . . . Yes, it's suite #2903.

Manga Example 5: Welcome to the ryokan

In this example the ryokan landlady introduces herself as ここの女将 **okami** (the landlady here). The kanji 女将, literally "woman-leader," (i.e., "boss") is called an **ateji** or "arbitrary kanji": the reading of the kanji doesn't agree with the pronunciation it should have (じょしょう). The 女将さん greets us with いらっしゃいませ, a word used to welcome guests at a commercial establishment (Lesson 27). She speaks formally, using the verb でございます (formal equivalent of です), and the formal sentence structure "お + verb root + する" Notice, too, how she uses the invitation form -**ō** (Lesson 34).

Xian Nu Studio

Landlady: いらっしゃいませ。私 ここの女将 でございます

welcome. I here SP landlady be (formal)

Welcome, I'm the landlady of this ryokan.
お荷物 お持ちしましょう

bags pick up (invitation)

Let me take your bags.

Manga Example 6: Fully booked

The guests arrive at the 旅館 *ryokan* late, and ask the 女将さん *okami-san* if any rooms are available. She says all rooms are taken, using the word 満室 *manshitsu* (満 full, 室 room), and then says *all* (どこも) are "not empty" (空いてない *aitenai*). In Japanese, repeating the same idea in two different ways in one sentence is common.

J.M. Ken Niimura

Landlady: すみません、今日はもう満室でどこも空いてないんですよ。

I'm sorry, today SP *already full all empty not be*

I'm sorry, but today all the rooms are full and there are no openings.

Manga Example 7: In the communal bath

Communal baths are found in 旅館 *ryokan*, in 温泉 *onsen* (hot springs) or in a 先頭 *sentō* (public bath) and have several big bathtubs where people can soak together. Be sure to soap and rinse in the shower before getting into the bath! In the text of this manga Shinji uses the permission form 〜てもいい, which we studied in Lesson 32.

Xian Nu Studio

Kenji: うわ〜っいろんなおふろがある〜！

wow! several bathtubs SP *are!*

Wow, there are plenty of bathtubs!

Shinji: 好きな所に行っていいよ

like place go (permission) EP

You can go to any one you like.

Exercises 練習

1 Write the following words and phrases in Japanese: "price," "to cancel," "rooms available," and "breakfast included."

Translate the words: 署名〔しょめい〕, バス, 階段〔かいだん〕, クレジットカード, レストラン and 〜泊〔はく〕. **2**

3 Write in Japanese the sentence: "What is the price for a night?"

Translate: お支払〔しはら〕いはカードですか、現金〔げんきん〕ですか？ **4**

5 Give the Japanese words for at least five objects you can find in a hotel room.

Go to the hotel reception and ask for a morning call at 7am. **6**

7 Go to the hotel reception and complain about there being too much noise and not being able to sleep.

What exactly is a 浴衣〔ゆかた〕 and in which situations do you use it? **8**

9 Translate: いらっしゃいませ！ 京都 旅館〔きょうとりょかん〕へようこそ。 靴を脱〔くつ・ぬ〕いでください。 (京都 Kyoto; ようこそ welcome)

Translate: "You can get in the bath you prefer." (入〔はい〕る to get in) **10**

— **Answers to all the exercises can be found online by following the link on page 7.** —

Particles (1) wa / ga / mo

In Lesson 16 we had a quick look at grammatical particles, and in this chapter we will study them in greater detail. Let's begin with は , が and も .

Topic particles

Let's clarify what we mean by the grammatical concept "topic." The dictionary definition of "topic" is: "a subject written or spoken about." Consider the following two sentences: "John is eating the bread," and "The bread, John is eating it." The topic in the first sentence is John, who is eating the bread. In the second sentence the topic is the bread that John is eating. In English, the topic is usually the grammatical subject of the sentence (as in the first sentence), and sentences like the second one are somewhat unnatural, or they belong to the spoken language. But in Japanese the topic doesn't always coincide with the grammatical subject.

🎧 The particle は

The particle は , (read ***wa*** and not ***ha*** when used as a grammatical particle), indicates the topic of a sentence. As the topic is usually the grammatical subject, it is often mistaken for the subject particle; but it isn't. So, commit this concept to memory: は = topic particle.

- この太郎は学生です
  "Talking about this Taro," he is a student. (This Taro is a student.)
- この学生は太郎です
  "Talking about this student," he is Taro. (This student is Taro.)

Notice these two sentences are similar but have different connotations. In the first, the "topic" we are talking about is 太郎 ***Tarō***, whereas in the second one it is 学生 ***gakusei***.

🎧 Basic usages of は

The simplest structure using は is "X は Y です"

- 花子は学生です "Talking about Hanako," she is a student. (Hanako is a student.)
- 大学はつまらないです "Talking about university," it's boring. (University's boring.)

The basic rule for は is that we use it to offer information the person we are speaking to already know, for example identifiable names, such as sun, star or fire, or generic names, such as house, truck or cat. Look at the categories and examples below:

- **Information that has just been given:** 池に亀がいます。亀はのろいです
  There is a turtle in the pond. The turtle is slow.
- **Proper names:** 美奈子さんは来ないの？ Isn't Minako coming?
- **Identifiable names:** 空は曇っています The sky is cloudy.
- **Generic names:** イルカは頭がいいです Dolphins (generally) are intelligent.

In the first example above, the first time the word 亀 (turtle) appears, we introduce it with the subject particle が, and the second time, being information the person we are speaking to already knows (since it has become the "topic" of the conversation), we introduce it with the topic particle は. We could say that in English が = "a" and は = "the."

In the second example the person we are speaking to knows Minako. In the third, there's only one sky, so there's no possible confusion. In the fourth, we are talking about dolphins in general. Therefore, all three sentences use は.

🎧 Contrast and emphasis with は:

The topic particle は can also be used to indicate contrast between two objects or ideas, both of which are marked by は:

- イワンは日本酒は飲めるけど、ウオッカは飲めない
  Ivan can drink sake, but not vodka.
- 夏子さんは優しいけど、麗子さんは冷たいです
  Natsuko is kind, but Reiko is cold.

The particle は is also used as an emphatic marker. Let's see an example:

- 私はグッチは嫌いだ I hate Gucci.

In this sentence, the meaning implicit in は goes beyond a simple assertion of the kind "I hate Gucci (and that's it)." With は, the speaker is implying that the brand Gucci <u>in particular</u> is what he doesn't like. This might make it clearer:

- 私はグッチは嫌いだ（けどプラダは好きだ） I hate Gucci (but I like Prada).

Let's look at another group of sentences to clarify this usage of は.

- 私(わたし)は昨日(きのう)、日本語(にほんご)を勉強(べんきょう)しなかった
  I didn't study Japanese yesterday. (No emphasis)
- 私は昨日は日本語を勉強しなかった
  I didn't study Japanese yesterday. (Emphasis on "yesterday")
- 私は昨日、日本語は勉強しなかった
  I didn't study Japanese yesterday. (Emphasis on "Japanese")
- 私は昨日、日本語を勉強はしなかった
  I didn't study Japanese yesterday. (Emphasis on "study")

The second sentence implies "yesterday" I didn't study (but I did on another day). The third implies I didn't study "Japanese" (I studied something else). The fourth implies I didn't "study" Japanese (but I did something else with the language, such as speak it, write it, etc.).

The particle が

We have said that は is not a subject particle, but a "topic" one. The particle that indicates the subject in a sentence is が. It is used to mark a subject being introduced for the first time, as in the sentence こちらが三穂です ***kochira ga Miho desu*** (This is Miho), or in the sentence we saw earlier 池に亀がいます ***ike ni kame ga imasu*** (There is a turtle in the pond), i.e., when the subject is new information.

Generally, verbs of existence, such as ある or いる (Lesson 18), always require が to indicate the subject, as is the case in the sentence 池に亀がいます, except when we want to emphasize something, or the information is already known, in which case we will use は.

- **Normal:** 机(つくえ)に手紙(てがみ)がありません There isn't a letter on the table.
- **Emphasis:** 机に手紙はありません There isn't a letter on the table (but something else).
- **Known information:** 手紙は机にありません The letter (we know which one) isn't on the table.

Further usages of が

Let's look briefly at other usages of が:

a) Interrogatives like 何 (what?), 誰 (who?) or どこ (where) (Lesson 34) always go with が. This is logical, since we are always asking about new information.

- 誰(だれ)が来(き)たの？
  Who came?

  何(なに)がおもしろい？
  What is interesting?

b) The subject in subordinate clauses is always introduced with が.

• ジョンが来た時、私は買い物に出かけていた When John came, I'd gone shopping.

c) The particle が is always used with certain verbs and adjectives, shown in the table below. The exception is when we want to emphasize something, when we use は.

• 牛乳が好きだ I like milk | 牛乳は好きだ I like milk (*but not cheese, for example*).

🎧 **Usages of *ga* with certain verbs and adjectives**		
Verbs and adjectives of ability		
出来る	to be able to (Lesson 32)	英語が出来る
分かる	to understand	英語が分かる
上手な	skilled	英語が上手だ
下手な	unskilled	英語が下手だ
～られる	potential form (Lesson 32)	英語が話せる
Verbs of sense		
見える	to see (involuntary)	海が見える
聞こえる	to hear (involuntary)	海が聞こえる
Verbs and adjectives of need		
要る	to be necessary	お金が要る
必要な	necessary	お金が必要だ
Adjectives of desire		
欲しい	to want (Lesson 31)	お金が欲しい
～たい	to want (Lesson 31)	英語が話したい *
Verbs and adjectives of emotion		
好きな	like	海が好きだ
嫌いな	dislike	海が嫌いだ
怖い	frightening, scary	海が怖い
悲しい	sad	海が悲しい
* Often with を (Lesson 31) 英語: English | 話す: to speak | 海: sea | お金: money		

🎧 But

The particle が has another usage, meaning "but," to link two clauses (see Lesson 49):

- 私は本を読んだが、彼氏は読まなかった I read the book, but my boyfriend didn't.
- 河野君は金持ちだが、不幸です Kawano is rich but unhappy.

This が is also used to connect clauses without meaning "but":

- 今日は外食するが、一緒に行く？ I'm going out for lunch, will you join me?

Also が is used at the end of a spoken sentence as a softener, especially for requests:

- 先生の本を借りたいんですが I'd like to borrow your (the teacher's) book.

は vs. が

As we have seen, the particles は and が are closely related and often even appear together in the same sentence, as in the construction "X はY が Z."

- 象は鼻が長い The elephant's (X) trunk (Y) is long (Z).
- サムは背が低い Sam's (X) height (Y) is short (Z). (Sam is short.)

Likewise, many of the sentences formed with verbs or adjectives in the table on page 21 also have the structure "X は Y が Z."

- 彼はサッカーが下手だ He (X) at soccer (Y) is unskilled (Z). (He isn't good at soccer.)
- 田中さんは猫が怖い Tanaka (X) cats (Y) are scary (Z). (Tanaka is afraid of cats.)

🎧 The particle も

Let's leave は and が aside for a moment, and look at も, meaning "also," "too," "as well," or "neither," if it is a negative sentence. も can totally substitute particles は, が and を.

- 池に亀がいる。魚もいる There are turtles in the pond. There are fish too.
- 彼は先生ではない。私も先生ではない He's not a teacher. Neither am I.
- 靴を買ったが、シャツも買った I bought a pair of shoes and I also bought a shirt.

The particle も is also used to indicate "very much," "very many" or "no less than . . ." In negative situations, the meaning of this last kind of sentence is "not even."

- 私は彼女を何時間も待っていました I waited for her for many hours.
- 彼は本を2万冊も持っている He has no less than 20,000 books.
- 彼女は本を5冊も持っていない She doesn't even have 5 books.

The words 何も (nothing), 誰も (nobody), as well as the expression "not one," which is formed by "一 + counter + も"(Lesson 25), for example: 一枚も (not one page); 一人も (not one person), always go with negative sentences.

- 映画館には誰もいない There is nobody in the cinema.
- あの人はテレビを一台も持っていない That person has not even one TV set.

The words いつも (always / never) and どこも (everywhere / nowhere) can go with affirmative or negative sentences, as we will see in the manga examples.

🎧 漫画例 Manga Examples

You are probably able to understand by now the differences and similarities between particles は and が. Native-English speakers always have trouble learning to use them properly, because in our language the "topic" and the "subject" in a sentence are usually the same. Let's study some examples.

Manga Example 1: The most basic usage of *wa*

As we have already said, は is the particle that marks the topic of a sentence. Until now we have identified it in the manga examples as SP (Subject Particle), to simplify matters. However, now that we know exactly how it works, we will call it the TOP (Topic Particle). In this lesson we have studied the general guidelines for the usage of particles は and が, which will help us use these particles with relative confidence, knowing most times we won't be wrong.

Anyhow, don't despair if you can't fully understand some of their usages or if you do make a mistake every now and then. It's quite normal, and only time and practice will help. We will now show some specific examples that will give you a better understanding of the "real" usage of these particles.

This first example is a simple sentence where we find the most basic usage of は: its function as the topic particle. In this sentence, the topic Yamazaki is talking about is fear (恐怖), which is, moreover, an identifiable concept (there is only one concept called "fear" and we all know it). It is natural, then, that the particle は goes with 恐怖, because it indicates that this word is the "topic" and that it is an identifiable or generic concept as well.

J.M. Ken Niimura

Yamazaki: 恐怖は人間を壊す
きょうふ にんげん こわ

fear TOP people DOP destroy

Fear destroys people.

Manga Example 2: Emphatic usage of *wa*

Another much more subtle usage of the topic particle is its function as an emphatic marker. は can replace the particles が and を or combine with the particles に and へ (Lesson 38) to emphasize the word it is identifying.

Gabriel Luque

If this example was a neutral sentence, with no implicit or special meaning, it would be 解放をしてやる **kaihō o shite yaru** (I will release you). However, by replacing the direct object particle を with は we emphasize the word 解放. Thus, the implicit meaning of our sentence is something like "I am going to release you, but I can't guarantee anything else," or, as we suggest in the translation, "I will release you (but) ..."

Yaguro: 解放はしてやる

release TOP *do (give)*

I will release you (but) ...

Manga Example 3: A typical *wa - ga* sentence

You probably realize by now that the distinction between は and が can fill pages and pages of books and doctoral theses on Japanese linguistics. One of the clearest usages is the combination of both particles in sentences that we call "**wa-ga** sentences," where the topic is introduced first with は and then a characteristic or feeling related to this topic is developed using が. In this manga example sentence, the topic is "I" and the feeling described is liking something. Besides, we know the noun modified by the adjective 好きな **suki-na** (in this case the word 女 **onna** "woman") always requires が. It is, then, a very clear example. **Note:** One of the usages of the (rather colloquial) suffix っぽい, which is added to nouns and adjectives, is to convey the meaning "liable to" or "seems," for example, 怒りっぽい **okorippoi** (he is liable to get angry): しめっぽい (dampish) (Lesson 44).

Studio Kōsen

Hide: オレは大人っぽい女が好きなんだよな

I TOP *adult (seem) woman* SP *like be* EP EP

I like more mature girls.

Manga Example 4: A subordinate clause

We mentioned earlier that in a subordinate clause (a secondary clause within a sentence that is dependent on the main clause) the subject is indicated with the particle が. It is quite logical, then, that since the "topic" (the thing we are talking about) will always be in the main sentence, there can't be any possible confusion as to what the "subject" of the sentence is. In our example, the main sentence is あんたは怖くてしょうがないんだ *anta wa*

kowakute shōganai n da (You are terribly afraid). The topic is obviously あんた. The subordinate clause is ボクが生き延びる *boku ga ikinobiru* (I survive).

The particle の functions here as a nominalizer, turning the whole sentence preceding it into a noun phrase (see Lessons 40 and 57). The particle が follows this nominalized sentence (ボクが生き延びるの) because the adjective 怖い always takes this particle, as we saw in the table on page 21.

Finally, we have an example of a very useful construction: 〜てしょうがない, meaning "it can't be helped that . . ."

J.M. Ken Niimura

Nakajima: あんたはボクが生き延びるのが怖くてしょうがないんだ
you TOP I SP survive (nom.) SP fear (cannot be helped)
It's only natural that you are terribly afraid that I might survive.

Manga Example 5: Usage of *ga* with the meaning of "but"

One case where が cannot be confused with は is when the former comes at the end of a clause to indicate "but" or "however." In this manga example we have two sentences, いい手だった *ii te datta* (clause A) and 甘かったな *amakatta na* (clause B), linked by が in a "clause A が clause B" structure, that is, "clause A, but clause B." Words with the same meaning ("but," "however") and usage are けど, けれど and けれども (Lesson 49).

Notes: 手 usually means "hand," but here it has the connotation of "try." Regarding 甘い, we already saw in Manga Example 1 in Lesson 35 its main meaning is "sweet," but it can sometimes mean "naive" or "indulgent," like here.

Xian Nu Studio

Kuro: いい手だったが甘かったな
good hand be (but) indulgent EP
Nice try, but you have been naive.

Manga Example 6: The word "always"

Xian Nu Studio

Ako: いつものママじゃな〜い！！

always POP *mommy not be!!*

This is not my usual mommy!!

In his lesson we studied the most common usages of も, and we also mentioned that sometimes も is combined with interrogative pronouns like 誰 *dare* (who?) or 何 *nani* (what?) to form words with a new meaning, such as 誰も (nobody) or 何も (nothing), which are always used in negative sentences. The case of いつも which, as you can guess, derives from いつ (when?), is somewhat special, because it can function in both affirmative and negative sentences, meaning "always": いつも陽気です *itsumo yōki desu* (He is always happy).

Manga Example 7: A new usage of *mo*

Here も is used to express lack of definition or, as in this example, to evade a question one doesn't want to answer: we are talking about the A も B も ない structure, which can be translated as "neither A nor B." This construction is used in a somewhat special way:

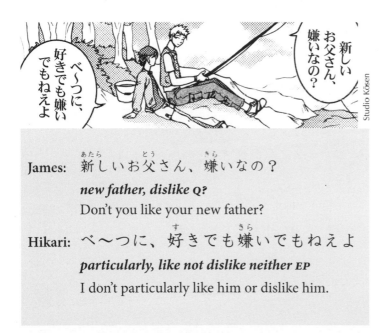

Studio Kōsen

James: 新しいお父さん、嫌いなの？

new father, dislike Q?

Don't you like your new father?

Hikari: べ〜つに、好きでも嫌いでもねえよ

particularly, like not dislike neither EP

I don't particularly like him or dislike him.

-*i* adjectives. Replace the last い with く:
小さくも大きくもない
chiisaku mo ookiku mo nai
Neither big nor small.
-*na* adjectives. Replace な with で:
安全でも危険でもない
anzen demo kiken demo nai
Neither safe nor dangerous.
Nouns. Add で:
先生でも学生でもありません
sensei demo gakusei demo arimasen
Neither teacher nor student.

In this example the structure is used with two **-*na*** adjectives: 好きでも嫌いでもない

Notes: James does without the particle が in his sentence (it should be 新しいお父さんが嫌い). This is quite common in spoken and colloquial language. The ねえ Hikari uses is a contraction of ない. In this context, べ〜つに (別に) means "specially," "particularly."

Exercises 練習

(1) In the sentence "The bread, I'll eat right away," which word is the topic and which the subject?

(2) Translate the previous sentence into Japanese.
(bread パン ; to eat 食べる ; right away すぐ)

(3) Translate the sentence "Turtles are slow."
(turtle 亀 ; slow のろい)

(4) Translate: 私 はチーズは食べられるが、トマトは食べられない。(チーズ cheese; トマト tomato)

(5) What meaning does 彼 は明日、 車 を運転したがっている acquire if we place は after 運転 ?
(車 car; 運転 する to drive)

(6) Use は to emphasise different words in this sentence: 彼 は明日、 車 を運転したがっている . How many sentences can you make?

(7) Translate: "You need 10,000 yen."
(10,000 一万 ; yen 円)

(8) Translate: "I have time but I don't have money."
(time 時間 ; money お金)

(9) Translate: "I don't want to go to Japan either."
(to go 行く ; Japan 日本)

(10) Translate: 私 はいつも派手でも地味でもない 服 を着ている 彼女 が好きです。(派手 flashy; 地味 discreet; 服 clothes; 着る to wear)

— **Answers to all the exercises can be found online by following the link on page 7.** —

Particles (2) ni / de / e

Following on from the previous lesson, we will keep the tone of an in-depth study for our next batch of particles: に, で and へ.

🎧 The particle に

The particle に has several usages. Perhaps the clearest is to indicate the place where something is. This category covers existence and permanence.

Existence: The verbs いる and ある, both mean "to be" (Lesson 18), always the thing that exists to be marked with に.

- 池に亀がいる There is a turtle in the pond.
- 姫路に白い城がある There is a white castle in Himeji.

Permanence: Verbs indicating a long stay in a place, such as いる and ある (i.e., when they indicate permanence instead of existence), 住む **sumu** (to live in), or 残る **nokoru** (to remain), among others, also take に.

- 直美ちゃんはそのぼろいアパートに住んでいる Naomi lives in that rundown apartment.
- 僕は居酒屋に残りたい I want to stay in the pub.

Be careful with this usage, because に indicates "existence" or "a relatively long stay" in a certain place, never something which "happens" or "is done" in that place. In this second case, we use the particle で, which we will study shortly.

🎧 Direction, contact and time

Direction: に is used to mean going "to/toward" a place. This usage is identical and interchangeable with that of the particle へ, which we will also see in this lesson.

- 来週、沖縄に行きます Next week, I'll go to Okinawa.
- 武文くんは家に帰りたがっている It seems Takefumi wants to go home.

Direct contact: We need に to mark the "surface over which something happens or an action is performed." It is also used with verbs of direction, such as 乗る *noru* (to ride/get on a vehicle), 入る *hairu* (to enter), 上がる *agaru* (to go up), etc.

- いたずらっ子は壁に落書きをした The naughty boy drew graffiti on the wall.
- 社長は新幹線に乗りました The president got on the shinkansen bullet train.

Specific time: We use に to indicate a specific point in time, such as a date or time.

- ６時半に待ち合わせをしている I have an appointment at half past six.
- アメリカは １ ４ ９ ２ 年に発見された America was discovered in 1492.

However, に is never used when the act cannot be determined with a specific date or time. The words 今日 *kyō* (today), 昨日 *kino* (yesterday), 明日 *ashita* (tomorrow), 来年 *rainen* (next year), and 最近 *saikin* (lately) go either on their own or with は (Lesson 37). The days of the week are an exception to this rule and can be used with に.

🎧 Indirect object, change, and grammatical constructions

Indirect object: に is used to mean "whom."

- 依津江ちゃんは友達にアドバイスした Itsue gave his friend some advice.
- 先生は生徒たちに数学を教えます The teacher teaches mathematics to his pupils.
- 国王は科学者にノーベル賞を与えた The king gave the scientist the Nobel Prize.

Change: The verbs of change, such as なる (to become), 変わる (to change), or 変化する (to vary), require the word being referred to to be marked by に . In Lesson 28 we saw how なる functions, so we recommend that you review that lesson before going on.

- 将来、サッカー選手になりたい In the future, I want to be a soccer player.
- 信号が赤に変わった The traffic light turned red.

Grammatical constructions: に is used in many other grammatical constructions:

⇒ Constructions of the "to go to" or "to come to" sort (Lesson 28). 買いに行く   *kai ni iku* (to go to buy).

⇒ Conversion of *-na* adjectives into adverbs (Lesson 22). 上手に書く *jōzu ni kaku* (to write skillfully).

⇒ Constructions with あげる (to give), もらう (to receive), and くれる (to receive) (Lessons 28 and 49). 本は父にもらった *hon wa chichi ni moratta* (I received the book from my father).

⇒ Passive and causative sentences (Lesson 60).

友達に料理をさせた
I made my friend cook.

🎧 The particle で

The particle で can sometimes be confused with に. We will first examine this more "problematic" usage, and then we will go over its other usages.

Japanese has a distinction between the "place where one exists or remains" and the "place where one performs an action." The first (existence/permanence) requires に, as seen on the previous pages. The second requires で.

🎧 Usages of *ni*	
Existence	母は京都にいる My mother is in Kyoto
Permanence	母は京都に住んでいる My mother lives in Kyoto
Direction	母は京都に行く My mother goes to Kyoto
Direct contact	母はキャンバスに絵を描く My mother paints on canvas
Specific time	母は6時に来る My mother will come at 6 o'clock
Indirect object	母は父に絵をあげる My mother gives my father a drawing
Change	母は変になった My mother has become strange
Grammatical construction	母は私に絵を描かせた My mother made me paint

母 *haha* (my) mother; 京都 *Kyōto* Kyoto; 住む *sumu* to live; 行く *iku* to go; 絵 *e* drawing; 描く *egaku* to draw; 来る *kuru*: to come; 変な *hen-na*: strange

- 彼は日本でテレビ出演している He is on TV in Japan.
- 千鶴さんはいつも家で勉強しなければならない Chizuru must always study at home.
- 私は横浜のオフィスで働いていました I worked at an office in Yokohama.

The verb ある doesn't always indicate "existence." It can also indicate the place where something happens, such as a public event, for example, in which case, the particle で is used.

- 明日、バルセロナで弁論大会がある There's a speech contest in Barcelona tomorrow.

🎧 Time and manner

Time: The particle で is used after an act which indicates "end of the action."

- 宿題は今週で終わりたい I want to finish my homework this week.
- あの人は6月で刑務所を出られる That person can leave prison in June. (に can also be used here. The differences are mainly connotative.)
- 契約は3月3日で / に終わる The contract expires on March 3.

In the final example on the previous page, if we use に, we are simply indicating the exact expiry date of the contract. With で, however, the sentence has the nuance "the contract is valid until March 3, and then it expires."

Required time: This usage is closely related to the previous one in that it indicates the time spent doing something. However, で cannot be replaced with に here.

- 彼は一年半で本を書いた He wrote a book in a year and a half.
- ６時間で仕事を終わらなければならない I must finish this job in 6 hours.

Manner / instrument / material: The particle で is also used to indicate "how," "with what," and "from/of what":

- 僕は船で韓国に行きたい I want to go to Korea by boat.
- 泥棒は人をナイフで襲った The thief attacked someone with a knife.
- 日本の家は木で作ってあります Houses in Japan are made of wood.

Cause/reason: で also marks the word indicating cause or reason, although it's rather weak—we are not placing much emphasis on the cause or reason.

- 理絵ちゃんは病気で仕事を休んだ Rie didn't go to work because she was sick.
- 竜くんは趣味でホームページを作る Ryu makes websites as a hobby.

Quantity: The last usage of で is with "how much / many."

- あのプラモデルは３０００円で買える You can buy that toy for 3,000 yen.
- 車は１０人で持ち上げることができた We managed to lift the car between the ten of us.

🎧 The particle へ

The particle へ (pronounced *e* and not *he* when it functions as a grammatical particle) is one of the easiest to learn, because it only has one function, to indicate "where to."

- 日本へ行きたがっている人が大勢います There are many people who want to go to Japan.
- 空港へ妹を迎えに行った I went to the airport to welcome (to meet) my sister.

Note: へ and に (when they mean "direction") can be used interchangeably.

- 彼はドイツへ / に勉強しに行く He is going to Germany to study.

🎧 Usage of two particles at once

A peculiarity of particles is that two of them can sometimes be combined and appear together. For example, the topic particle は can be combined with に, で and へ to indicate "topic / emphasis + something" (Lesson 37).

- 池には亀がいる Talking about the pond, there is a turtle in it.
- 中国へは行きたいが、ちょっと怖い I do want to go to China, but it scares me a little.

Note: は can never be combined with が and を because it directly replaces them.

🎧 Usages of *de*	
Place	学生は寮でケーキをつくる The student makes a cake in the dorm
Time	学生は一日でケーキをつくる The student makes a cake in one day
Required time	学生は3時間でケーキをつくる The student makes a cake in three hours
Manner / Instrument	学生はオーブンでケーキをつくる The student makes a cake in the oven
Material	学生はいちごでケーキをつくる The student makes a cake with strawberries
Cause	学生は義務でケーキをつくる The student makes a cake as an obligation
Quantity	学生は一人でケーキをつくる The student makes a cake alone

学生 *gakusei* student; 寮 *ryō* dorm; 一日 *ichi nichi* one day; オーブン oven; いちご strawberry; 義務 *gimu* obligation; 一人で *hitori de* alone

Other possible particle combinations are での (広島での仕事はおもしろくない *Hiroshima de no shigoto wa omoshirokunai* The job in Hiroshima is not interesting), への (日本への飛行機は少ない *Nihon e no hikōki wa sukunai* There are few planes flying to Japan), にも (家にも犬がいる *ie ni mo inu ga iru* There is a dog at home too), へも and でも.

🎧 Usage of でも

The combination でも can have two completely different meanings. The first is a mere combination of both particles:

- 電車の中でも勉強できる You can study in the train too.

The second でも has nothing to do with particle combinations, and means "even":

- 子どもでもこの文章が分かる Even a child can understand this sentence.

Note: The words 誰でも (anybody), 何でも (anything), いつでも (any time), and どこでも (anywhere) also use the combination でも.

🎧 漫画例 **Manga Examples**

Let's look at some manga-example panels that will help us clarify the different usages of particles, に, で, and へ. There's nothing better than a few situations showing real Japanese usage to help clarify the concepts we have been studying.

Manga Example 1: *ni* as place particle (existence)

Here is an example of the usage of the particle に in its "existence" mode. It's the first usage of に we studied in this lesson. Christine says the person she was looking for "was not" or, in other words, "did not exist" (いなかった) at the party. いなかった is the simple past-negative form of the verb いる ("to be," with animate objects, Lesson 18). Indeed, both verbs of existence in Japanese, いる and ある, take the particle に.

Also notice the simultaneous usage of two particles: に to indicate place, and the topic particle は. When adding は after に, the word the particles are attached to is stressed, and becomes the "topic" (Lesson 37). Here, exaggerating the example, the sentence can be literally translated as: "Talking about this party, (he/she) wasn't there." It's common to use は after に or で when the word or phrase marked by them becomes the topic of the sentence.

このパーティーにはいなかったわ。仕事は終わりよ。

Studio Kōsen

Christine: このパーティーにはいなかったわ。仕事は終わりよ。

this party PP TOP not be EP. Work TOP finish EP

He wasn't at this party. Work is over.

Manga Example 2: *ni* as place particle (direct contact)

Here is a new example of the usage of the particle に, this time to express direct contact. The action of "writing" must obviously be done "on" some surface. In this example, we are not told the kind of surface, we are just told where it is with the word ここ ("here," see Lesson 34), which must be marked with the particle に. Another clearer example would be: 紙に書いてある *kami ni kaite aru* (It is written on the paper). **Note:** The construction 〜てある (Lesson 35) indicates "a finished action that continues unchanged."

Gabriel Luque

Kenji: ここに書いてある

here PP *written is*

It is written here.

Manga Example 3: *ni* as indirect object particle

Here we have a good example of the usage of に marking the indirect object, that is, "for whom" the action is performed. In this case, it is the ball (ボール) that goes over to Oshima. To identify the indirect object we must ask "whom." Thus: "Whom did the ball go to?" Answer: "Oshima." Therefore Oshima must be marked by the particle に. **Note:** In this example we also find は (Lesson 37) used as the topic particle (here, "the ball"), and この a word of the *kosoado* kind (*this*, Lesson 34).

Xian Nu Studio

Speaker: サァ このボールは M・F 大島くんにわたった！

oh this ball TOP *midfield player Ōshima* SUF DP *gone over*

Well (now), the ball has gone over to midfielder Oshima!

Manga Example 4: *de* as a cause particle

Here we have an example of で used to express "why" but in a rather weak manner. In other words, these are cause-and-effect sentences which could almost be considered a pure "link of two sentences," since their causal relationship is hardly stressed. In this case, the effect is "I'm busy" and its cause (marked with で) is "I'm studying for the exams."

Xian Nu Studio

Yumiko: あたしは受験勉強で忙しいんだからねっ。

I TOP exam study busy be because EP

Let me tell you I'm busy studying for the exams.

Manga Example 5: Two combined particles

The particle は is used to indicate the "topic" of the sentence. The で is used to indicate the "place where the action is performed." In this example, the "action" is the fact of "being monsters" (it isn't existence or permanence, therefore で is used).

J.M. Ken Niimura

Mayeen: 地球の美人がここでは化け物…

Earth POP beauty SP here PP TOP monster . . .

Beautiful women of Earth are monsters here . . .

Manga Example 6: The particle *e*

The particle へ is only used with verbs of movement such as 行く *iku* (to go), 来る *kuru* (to come), 移動する *idō suru* (to move), and other similar verbs. In this sentence, the verb is 行く and the place the subject is going to is ブラジル, which is marked with へ. The particle に (see page 29) could also be used here. **Note:** This example shows the *-te* form connection between the two sentences "win" and "go to Brazil." (Lesson 35).

Studio Kōsen

Hiyama: 優勝^{ゆうしょう}してブラジルへ行^いくんだ！

win do Brazil DP *go be!*

I'll win and I'll go to Brazil!

Manga Example 7: A different usage of *de + mo*

でも has many usages. We have seen that でも can mean "even," or, if added to an adverb or an interrogative pronoun, can mean "any." In Lesson 49 we will see that でも can also mean "but." The でも in this example does not fall into any of these categories; it is used to indicate an undefined possibility. Tokuro doesn't specifically say "the toilet is out of order" (where the subject particle が would be used), but he ventures that the "the toilet or something" may be out of order. This is similar to the Japanese way of making an invitation: お茶でも飲みにいこうか *Ocha demo nomini ikō ka?* (Why don't we go have tea or something?) This でも might encompass tea, coffee, a soft drink, an ice-cream, et cetera.

Xian Nu Studio

Tokuro: トイレでもこわれたのかな？

toilet or something broken Q?

Is the toilet or something out of order?

Exercises 練習

1 Translate: "In the university there is a bookstore."
(university 大学(だいがく) ; bookstore 本屋(ほんや))

Translate: "I go into the shop." (shop 店(みせ)) **2**

3 Is the sentence 来年(らいねん) に 経済(けいざい) を 勉強(べんきょう) する つ もりだ correct? Why? (来年 next year; 経済 economics; 勉強する to study)

Translate: "Taro gives Hanako a flower." (Taro 太郎(たろう) ; to give あげる ; flower 花(はな) ; Hanako 花子(はなこ)) **4**

5 What is the difference between 道(みち) に 絵(え) を 描(えが)く , and 道(みち) で 絵(え) を 描(えが)く , and why? (道 road; 絵 drawing; 描く to draw)

Translate: "Naoko cut a cake with a knife." (Naoko 直子(なおこ) ; to cut 切(き)る ; cake ケーキ ; knife ナイフ) **6**

7 Translate: "I want to go back to LA." Which particle will you use, and why? (to go back 帰(かえ)る)

Look at sentence 1 again. Now imagine you want to emphasize that the bookstore is "in the university" (not elsewhere), making that part the sentence topic. How would you do it? **8**

9 Translate: 誰(だれ)でもこの 文章(ぶんしょう) を 読(よ)める。
(文章 sentence; 読む to read)

What different usages can でも have? List them and give an example for each of them. **10**

— **Answers to all the exercises can be found online by following the link on page 7.** —

Lesson 39 ● 第39課

Transport in Japan

Here we have another lesson that will help you develop your conversation skills, with lots of useful vocabulary, and the opportunity to practice and make the best use of the grammar points we have learned up to now. We will focus on the means of transport we will probably be using when we go to Japan: train, subway, taxi and bus.

🎧 Taxi

Let's start the lesson by having a look at a few sentences we can use when taking a taxi. It is worth mentioning that Japanese taxis are very expensive and, therefore, we probably won't be using them too often. A curiosity about Japanese taxis is that they all have automatic doors: that is, they open by themselves right in front of the passenger. Don't try to open one or you'll get a surprise!

- タクシー乗り場はどこですか？ Where is the taxi stop? (Lesson 34)
- 浅草ホテルまでお願いします To Asakusa Hotel, please. (Lesson 33)
- この住所に行ってください Go to this address, please. (Lessons 24 and 35)
- 次の角を左に曲がってください Turn left on the next corner.
- ここで止めてください Stop here, please. (Lesson 34)
- いくらですか？ How much is it? (Lesson 34)

🎧 Transport		🎧 Taxi and bus			
bicycle	自転車	basic fare	基本料金	stop button	降車ボタン
bus	バス	bus stop	バス乗り場	straight ahead	まっすぐ
car	自動車｜車	(loose) change	両替	taxi meter	メーター
motorcycle	バイク	change	お釣り	taxi stop	タクシー乗り場
ship	船	corner	角	(to the) left	左（へ）
subway	地下鉄	crossing	交差点	(to the) right	右（へ）
taxi	タクシー	door	扉｜ドア	traffic light	信号
train	電車	driver	運転手	vacant	空車

🎧 Bus

Let's see some sentences that can be helpful when we are touring the country by bus.

- 金閣寺行きのバス乗り場はどこですか？ Where is the bus stop for buses heading to Kinkakuji?
- このバスは鎌倉大仏へ行きますか？ Does this bus go to the Great Buddha in Kamakura?
- 大阪駅までいくらですか？ How much is it to Osaka Station? (Lesson 34)
- 空港行きのバスは何時に出ますか？ What time does the bus to the airport leave?
- 次のバスは何時に出ますか？ At what time does the next bus leave? (Lesson 34)
- 宮島までどれくらい時間がかかりますか？ How long does it take to Miyajima?
- 日光東照宮に着いたら教えてください Please tell me when we arrive at the Toshogu in Nikko.
- 次で降ります I'll get off at the next (stop).

Note: There are two words for "change" in the vocabulary table on page 39. The first, 両替 *ryōgae*, is the "loose change" we are given when exchanging a note for coins. The second one, お釣り *otsuri*, is the "change" we are given when paying for something.

🎧 Subway and local trains

In Japan, trains rule, especially in large cities, both underground and overground. Tokyo's most famous railway line, the ***Yamanote sen*** (山手線), is a JR (Japan Railways) circular line with stops at most key centers in Tokyo, such as 東京 ***Tōkyō***, 池袋 ***Ikebukuro***, 新宿 ***Shinjuku***, 原宿 ***Harajuku***, 渋谷 ***Shibuya***, 恵比寿 ***Ebisu*** and 品川 ***Shinagawa***.

You can buy tickets for underground and overground trains at vending machines. A fare chart above the machines gives ticket prices, which vary depending on the distance.

- ここから一番近い地下鉄の駅はどこですか？ Where's the closest subway station?
- 切符はどこで買えますか？ Where do you buy tickets? (Lessons 32 and 34)
- 渋谷までいくらですか？ How much is it to Shibuya? (Lesson 34)
- 切符の自販機の使い方を教えてください Could you please show me how the ticket vending machine works?

🎧 More situations

We will now see more possible situations on our trip by local train, subway or tram.

- 地下鉄路線図を一枚ください Can I have a subway map, please?

- 時刻表をください Can I have a timetable, please?
- 一日乗車券はいくらですか？ How much is a one-day pass? (Lesson 34)
- 梅田行きのホームはどれですか？ Which is the platform for Umeda? (Lesson 34)
- この列車は秋田に止まりますか？ Does this train stop at Akita?
- 中央線に乗り換えたいんですが、何番線ですか？ I'd like to change to the Chuo line, what is the platform number? (Lessons 31, 34 and 37)

Beware of the ticket gates in stations! Almost all stations in large cities have automatic ticket gates at entrances and exits to the station. The machine automatically calculates if we have paid the right fare for our journey and, if we haven't . . . the gates slam shut! Not to worry though, if this happens, all we need to do is go to a machine called 精算機 *seisanki* (fare adjustment machine), put our ticket in, and pay the remainder. Only then will we be able to leave the station.

- 南改札口はどこですか？ Where are the south exit gates? (Lesson 34)
- 精算機はどこですか？ Where is the fare adjustment machine? (Lesson 34)
- 精算機の使い方を教えてください Please show me how the fare adjustment machine works.
- 歌舞伎町の出口はどこですか？ Which is the Kabukicho exit?
- １１番出口です It's exit number 11.

🎧 Long-distance trains and the shinkansen

Finally, we will take a look at some situations you might encounter on long-distance trains and on the famous and extremely fast bullet train, the shinkansen.

- 切符売り場はどこですか？ Where is the ticket office? (Lesson 34)
- 広島までの片道切符を一枚ください A one way ticket to Hiroshima, please.
- 仙台行きの新幹線を予約したいんですが I'd like to reserve a seat on the shinkansen to Sendai.
- 次の京都行きの新幹線は何時発ですか？ What time does the next shinkansen to Kyoto leave?
- 札幌行きの特急列車は何番線から発車しますか？ From what platform does the express to Sapporo leave?
- ここに座ってもいいですか？ May I sit here? (Lesson 32)

🎧 Train vocabulary

bullet train	新幹線 しんかんせん	going to x	〜行き ゆ	station	駅 えき
change / transfer	乗り換え の か	last train	終電 しゅうでん	subway map	路線図 ろせんず
coin locker	コイン ロッカー	nonsmoking car	禁煙車 きんえんしゃ	super-express train	特急列車 とっきゅうれっしゃ
conductor	車掌 しゃしょう	one-day pass	一日乗車券 いちにちじょうしゃけん	terminal	終点 しゅうてん
entrance	入口 いりぐち	ordinary train	普通列車 ふつう れっしゃ	ticket	切符 きっぷ
exit	出口 でぐち	platform	ホーム	ticket gate	改札 かいさつ
express train	急行列車 きゅうこうれっしゃ	platform x	〜番線 ばんせん	ticket office	切符売り場 きっぷ う ば
fare	運賃 うんちん	reserved seat	指定席 していせき	ticket vending machine	切符自販機 きっぷ じはんき
first class	グリーン車 しゃ	seat for senior citizens	シルバー シート	timetable	時刻表 じこく ひょう
first train	始発 しはつ	smoking car	喫煙車 きつえんしゃ	unreserved seat	自由席 じゆうせき

🎧 Problems of various kinds

The sentences below will help you deal with some common problems.

- 切符をなくしてしまいました I have lost my ticket. (Lesson 35)
  きっぷ
- どこから乗りましたか？ Where did you get on the train? | 姫路です In Himeji.
  の　　　　　　　　　　　　　　　　　　　　　　　　　　　ひめじ
- 乗り越ししてしまいました I've completely passed my stop. (Lesson 35)
  の こ
- 列車を間違えました I've got on the wrong train.
  れっしゃ　まちが
- 乗り遅れてしまいました I've completely missed my train. (Lesson 35)
  の おく
- 予約を変更したいのですが I'd like to change my reservation. (Lessons 32 and 37)
  よやく へんこう
- 払い戻ししたいのですが I'd like to get a refund (for my ticket).
  はら もど

Cultural Note: The Shinkansen

The word 新幹線 *shinkansen* literally means "*new* (新)" "*trunk* (幹)" "*line* (線),*" although it is really the name given to the modern Japanese network of bullet trains. The first 新幹線 line—the famous 東海道線 *Tōkaidō sen* which links the capital, 東京 *Tōkyō*, with the second most influential city in the country, 大阪 *Ōsaka*—was opened on October 1, 1964, on the occasion of the Olympic Games that were held in Tokyo that same year.

But long before that, in 1939, there were already plans to build a network of high-speed trains. The then militarist Japanese empire intended to link 東京 with 下関 *Shimonoseki*, in the south of the main island, 本州 *Honshu*, with a railway network that would go all the way to Europe, via Korea and northern China, which were Japanese possessions at the time!

Obviously, this plan was never completed, but the future builders of the new line would inherit a few half-finished tunnels, which sped up the execution of the project.

Nowadays, there are several 新幹線 lines which cover the country, from the city of 函館 *Hakodate* in the south of the northern island of 北海道 *Hokkaidō*, to 鹿児島 *Kagoshima*, the southernmost city on the southern island of 九州 *Kyūshū*. There are also plans to make bullet trains go as far as 札幌 *Sapporo*, the capital of 北海道.

Since its opening in 1964, the 新幹線 has never had a serious accident—except for a derailment with no victims in 2004, due to a strong earthquake—and has been amazingly successful, probably due to the strict application of the "3 S" and the "3 C" slogans during its construction: *Securely*, *Speedily*, *Surely* and *Cheaply*, *Comfortably* and *Carefully*.

The aerodynamic 新幹線, which can reach 300 km/h (with an average speed of 200 km/h), transports a daily average of 700,000 people through thousands of kilometers of railroad tracks. If you are a tourist in Japan, it is highly recommended that you buy a Japan Rail Pass, a pass allowing you to get on all JR trains, including most of the 新幹線, for one, two, or three weeks. You can find more information online at japanrailpass.net.

The stylish and aerodynamic Nagano shinkansen (Photo: M. Bernabé)

🎧 漫画例 **Manga Examples**

The manga examples in this chapter will allow us to see some transport-related vocabulary and phrases in action. The star of the lesson is, undoubtedly, the train—the true king of Japanese transport!

Manga Example 1: Announcements at stations

The first word in this example is a station name: せんげん台 *Sengendai*. All stations are called 〜駅 *eki*, for example 東京駅 *Tōkyō eki*. Then we have the word 準急 *junkyū* (local express). Generally, there are three kinds of trains, from the slowest to the fastest: 普通 *futsū* or 各駅停車 *kakuekiteisha* (normal), 急行 *kyūkō* (express), and 特急 *tokkyū* (super-express), although the names may vary depending on the railway company. The 準急 *junkyū* in the example is probably equivalent to a 急行 express train.

Xian Nu Studio

The announcement in the manga is of the type you will hear at a Japanese station. These announcements are always accompanied by music, and the tune varies depending on the railway company. The complete version could be: 間もなく、X番線に準急浅草行きがまいります。危ないですから白線の内側までお下がりください *Mamonaku, X ban sen ni junkyū Asakusa yuki ga mairimasu. Abunai desu kara hakusen no uchigawa made osagari kudasai.* (The local express to Asakusa will shortly arrive at platform X. Because it is dangerous, please stay inside the white line.) **Notes:** 〜行き means bound for. まいる is the humble version of 来る (to come) (Lesson 52).

Sign:	せんげん台駅
	Sengendai station
	Sengendai station.
Announcement:	準急浅草行きがまいります。
	local express Asakusa direction SP *come*
	The local express to Asakusa is entering the station.

Manga Example 2: In the taxi

Here is an example of how to tell a taxi driver where to go. It would be better to add お願いします *onegai shimasu* (please) at the end, of course. 川口 **Kawaguchi** is a city in the prefecture of 埼玉 **Saitama** and 町 **cho** is a suffix that indicates a district. Here, the author has used two circles instead of specifying the name of the district. The Japanese use these circles, which they call まるまる in the same way we would use X: ○○さん **maru**

Gabriel Luque

maru san Mr. X. ○○市 **maru maru shi** (X city). Usually each circle replaces one kanji. The driver answers へい, a colloquial way of saying はい.

Rie:	川口の○○町まで
	Kawaguchi POP *xx suburb to*
	To the suburb of xx in Kawaguchi.

Manga Example 3: I'm sorry

Here is a sentence we can use to apologize for lateness. Notice how Emi only says あなた ("you," Lesson 7) and は (topic particle, Lesson 37). Although the sentence has been shortened by the speaker, it obviously means ("Who are) you?" Leaving out parts of a sentence

Studio Kōsen

and assuming it is understood in the context is frequent in spoken Japanese. すいません is a spoken distortion of the word すみません (I'm sorry). Now take a look at the 〜がわからなくて… As you know, the verb わかる (to know) takes the particle が (Lesson 37). Here it is in the negative *-te* form, indicating the sentence is incomplete.

Emi:	あなたは？
	you TOP?
	You?
Miho:	すいません、バス乗り場がわからなくて…
	I'm sorry, bus stop SP *not know . . .*
	I'm sorry, I couldn't find the bus stop and . . .

Manga Example 4: Ticket gates at train stations

In this example we see how the wickets at train stations work: you put in your 切符 *kippu* (ticket) or your 定期券 *teiki ken* (monthly pass)—used by almost all Japanese サラリーマン (office workers) to go to work—and the ticket gates open. If the pass has expired, as in this case, or if the fare we've paid is not enough, the gates will slam shut. This is exact-

ly what happens to the guy in this example. **Note:** The man says 入れちゃった, which is the colloquial form of 入れてしまった. The verb 入れる means "to put in" and the form ～てしまう, as seen in Lesson 35, has the meaning of "doing something one regrets" or "doing something by mistake."

J.M. Ken Niimura

Man: ありゃ期限切れの定期入れちゃったよ。

(exclamation) period finished POP pass put in EP

Damn! I've put in my expired pass.

Manga Example 5: The shinkansen

The 新幹線 *shinkansen* bullet train is a popular means of long-distance transport in Japan. Fast, safe and comfortable, its network stretches to most major cities. In this example

Gabriel Luque

we have a lot of vocabulary: ～発 *hatsu* (departing from), ～行き *yuki* (bound for), ～番線ホーム *X ban sen hōmu* (platform X), 発車する *hassha suru* (to depart, of a vehicle).

All 新幹線 have names. In this case, it is the あさひ (morning sun), going from 東京 *Tōkyō* to 新潟 *Niigata* on the 上越 *Jōetsu* line. On the famous 東海道・山陽 *Tōkaidō-Sanyō* line (from 東京 to 博多 *Hakata*), the trains are called, from the slowest to the fastest, こだま (Echo), ひかり (Light), and のぞみ (Wish).

Announcement: 東京発新潟行きあさひ３３３号、２１番線ホームから発車します

Tokyo departure Niigata going to Asahi 333 number, 21 number platform from depart

The Asahi 333 from Tokyo to Niigata will depart from platform 21.

Manga Example 6: Ticket prices

This panel shows station ticket vending machines and the fare chart. The chart represents the 東京 モノレール which goes from 羽田 **Haneda** airport to 浜松町 **Hamama-tsuchō** station, where you can change to the JR 山手 **Yamanote** line that circles 東京.

To check the price, find the words 当駅(this station) on the chart. Then look for the station you are going to and check the price it shows. Imagine we are going to 大井競馬場前 **Ooikeibajōmae**. In this case, from our station, 整備場 **Seibijō**, the 大人 **otona** (adult) fare is 260 yen and the 小児 **shōni** (child) fare 130.

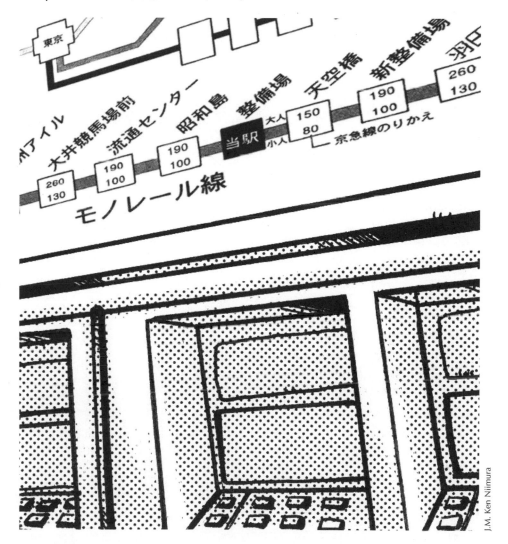

J.M. Ken Niimura

Exercises 練習

1 Translate the words "ship," "bus stop," "ticket," "ordinary express train" and "crossing."

2 Translate the words 空車 <ruby>くうしゃ</ruby>, 自動車 <ruby>じどうしゃ</ruby>, 指定席 <ruby>していせき</ruby>, 禁煙席 <ruby>きんえんせき</ruby>, 両替 <ruby>りょうがえ</ruby> and ホーム.

3 Translate: "To the Kamakura Ryokan, please." (ryokan 旅館 <ruby>りょかん</ruby>; Kamakura 鎌倉 <ruby>かまくら</ruby>)

4 Translate: このバスは 広島 原爆 ドーム へ行きますか？（原爆 atomic bomb)

5 Give the names of at least five means of transport in Japanese.

6 You are in the street and you want to ask someone where the closest JR station is. What do you say?

7 You want to go to 新宿, but you are not sure that the platform you are on is the right one. Make sure by asking someone.

8 You have just lost your ticket and you can't get out of the station. Try to explain the situation to the person in charge.

9 You hear this on the PA system: 間もなく、 2 番線 に 大阪 行きの 電車 がまいります。 What does it mean? (間もなく shortly)

10 According to Manga Example 6 on page 47, how much is a ticket to 流通 センター station?

— **Answers to all the exercises can be found online by following the link on page 7.** —

Particles (3) no / o

After the "rest" we took in the previous lesson, let's return to our grammar lessons, where we'll study two more particles in depth. Once you've completed the next two lessons, you will have covered most usages of the Japanese grammatical particles.

The particle の

We mentioned in Lesson 16 that the particle の marks the possessive. Now that our knowledge is greater than 24 lessons ago, this is a good time to look at various other usages of の.

First, let's define the term "noun modifier." A noun (Lesson 11) can be on its own or it can come with other words that describe it or complement it. These words are called "modifiers." In the sentence "Akira's red house" the words "red," and "Akira" modify the noun.

🎧 The particle の as a noun modifier

The particle の is the way to mark the noun modifier when the modifier is either another noun or a noun phrase. In short, we use の to connect two or more <u>nouns</u>.

We can distinguish up to five kinds of modifiers in Japanese: possessive, descriptive, positional, that of a creator, and appositional.

Possessive: This is the usage of の we already know. It obviously indicates possession.

- 私の家は広いです The house of I (my house) is roomy
- 筒井さんの車は小さくて赤いです Mr. Tsutsui's car is small and red.

Descriptive: It simply describes the noun, giving more information about it.

- これは鉄のパイプです This is a steel pipe.
- これは果物の店です This is a fruit store.

Positional: It describes the place where the modified noun is located.

- 木の下で休みたい I want to rest under a tree.
- 明はフランスの大学で勉強している Akira is studying at a French university.

Of a creator: It indicates the creator of something.

- 夏目漱石の小説を読んでください Read Soseki Natsume's novels, please.
- アイヌの文化は興味深いです The Ainu culture is interesting.

Appositional: An apposition, in English, is a construction which isn't explicitly connected to any word—it is usually separated by comas—but which refers or explains something relative to a noun. In Japanese, however, it is connected to the noun it modifies.

- はじめまして。部長の田辺です How do you do. I'm Tanabe, head of department.
- 友達の広美ちゃんは結婚しました My friend Hiromi got married.

🎧 Indefinite pronoun and nominalizer

Let's look at two new usages of の .

Indefinite pronoun: の replaces a noun when both speakers know what is being talked about.

- どんな映画が好きですか？
  What kind of films do you like?

- アクションのが好きです
  I like action ones.

We clearly see here how the の in the second sentence replaces the word 映画.

- どんなおかしにする？ Which bun will you choose? (Lesson 34)

- 甘いのが食べたい I want to eat a sweet one.

Nominalizer: To "nominalize" a sentence is to turn it into a noun phrase so that it works like a noun. For example, in the sentence "*riding a motorcycle* is difficult," the part in italics functions like a noun.

🎧 Usages of *no*	
Possession	これは先生の本です This is the teacher's book
Description	これは経済の本です This is a book on economics
Positional	机の上に本があります On the desk there is a book
Creator	ゲーテの本を読みたい I want to read a book by Goethe
Appositional	私は教師の岡本です I'm Okamoto, the teacher
Indefinite pronoun	これは私のです This is mine
Nominalizer	本を書くのは難しいです Writing a book is difficult
Question (colloquial)	本を書くのは難しいの？ Is it difficult to write a book?
Soft statement (feminine)	ゲーテの本を読みたいの I'd like to read a book by Goethe
Explanation	本を書いているのです I'm writing a book

教師 *kyōshi* teacher (humble form); 本 *hon* book; 経済 *keizai* economics; 机 *tsukue* desk; 上 *ue* on top of; 読む *yomu* to read; 書く *kaku* to write; 難しい *muzukashii* difficult

Notice how this part can be replaced with a noun, for example, "*chemistry* is difficult." This hint will help you identify a verb or a sentence which has been nominalized.

In Japanese, then, の is used to nominalize sentences. We can also use the word こと, which we will study in depth in Lesson 57.

- バイクを運転_{うんてん}するのは難_{むずか}しいです Riding a motorcycle is difficult.
- 水泳_{すいえい}をしに行_いくのは楽_{たの}しいです Going swimming is fun.
- 私_{わたし}は広子_{ひろこ}がどんな音楽_{おんがく}が好_すきなのか知_しらない I don't know what kind of music Hiroko likes.

🎧 At the end of a sentence

We saw in Lesson 17 how の can function as an end-of-sentence particle as either an informal question, a softened statement, or a soft command.

Question: In the informal register, の replaces か (Lesson 34) to indicate a question. It is worth mentioning that な must be placed between の and *-na* adjectives (as well as nouns).

- 明日_{あした}、何時_{なんじ}に京都_{きょうと}へ行_いくの？ What time are you going to Kyoto tomorrow?
- あの人_{ひと}は本当_{ほんとう}に先生_{せんせい}なの？ Is that person really a teacher?

Statement / soft command: This is used basically by women and children.

- 私_{わたし}はね、パリに何度_{なんど}も行_いったの As for me, I've been to Paris many times.
- しんちゃん、それに触_ふれないの！ Shin, don't touch that!

🎧 The particle を

The particle を, which is always pronounced *o* and never *wo*, is used to indicate the direct object, in other words "what" receives the verb's action. However, it has other usages as well.

Direct object:

- 太郎_{たろう}はパンを食_たべます
  Taro eats bread.

🎧 Usages of *o*	
Direct Object	私はりんごを食べます I eat an apple
Place of passage	私は橋を渡る I cross a bridge
Place from which one parts	私は電車を降りる I get off the train
Time passed	冬をハワイで過ごしたい I want to spend winter in Hawaii
りんご apple; 食べる *taberu* to eat; 橋 *hashi* bridge; 渡る *wataru* to cross; 冬 *fuyu* winter; ハワイ Hawaii; 過ごす *sugosu* to spend; 電車 *densha* train; 降りる *oriru* to get off	

• 哲治くんはスペイン語を勉強しています Tetsuharu is studying Spanish.

Note: There are certain constructions which contain a direct object that is not marked with を, as is the case with certain verbs that take が (Lesson 37).

• 私は日本語が [not を] 分かりません I don't understand Japanese.

🎧 Other usages of を

Place of passage: を can be used to indicate the space where a movement is carried out. This usage of を requires that the verb be one of movement, such as 歩く *aruku* (to walk), 走る *hashiru* (to run), 飛ぶ *tobu* (to fly), 通る *tooru* (to pass), 渡る *wataru* (to cross), etc.

• 鳥は空を飛びます Birds fly through the sky.
• 彼はいつも街を歩きます He always walks around town.

Place where a movement starts: を also marks the origin of a movement "outward" (be careful though, the "movement" may be abstract). It is usually used with the verbs 出る *deru* (to go out), 降りる *oriru* (to get off a vehicle), 離れる *hanareru* (to part from), etc.

• 里奈さんは6時に家を出た Rina left home at 6.
• 電車を降りる時、注意してください When you get off the train, be careful.
• 社長は大学を卒業していないよ The director has not graduated from university.

Time period: Finally, を is occasionally used to indicate the passing of periods of time.

• 私は夏を沖縄で過ごした I spent all summer in Okinawa.
• 彼は3ヶ月間を無駄にした He wasted three months.

A few adverbs

We hope you have mastered the different uses of the particles の and を. You have already seen in these few last lessons that particles can have many different uses and may seem tricky. However, they are indispensable to making grammatically sound sentences in Japanese, and it's important to get used to dealing with them. Don't worry if you get confused right now: with time and practice you'll get there!

🎧 The adverbs もう and まだ

The adverbs of time も う (which has nothing to do with the particle も, and is pronounced with a long *ō*) and ま だ are usually studied together. Their relationship is obvious, since も う can be translated as "already" and ま だ as "still." も う indicates something is not in the same state as it was before.

- 山田さんはもう昼ご飯を食べた Mr. Yamada has already eaten his lunch.
- 利香はもう宿題をしました Rika has already finished her homework.
- リックはもう中国語を勉強していない Rick doesn't study Chinese any more.

ま だ expresses the opposite idea of も う: it indicates something is still in the same state as it was before.

- カレーはまだ残っていますか？ Is there still some curry left?
- まだ何も食べていないよ I still haven't eaten anything.
- 私はまだ日本人のことを理解できない I still can't understand the Japanese.

🎧 The adverbs くらい and ごろ

The adverbs く ら い and ご ろ are usually both translated as "approximately" or "more or less." However, their usage is very different, so we must be careful not to confuse them.

く ら い and ぐ ら い are used to indicate an approximate quantity, be it either of volume, money, time, or any other thing. When having this nuance of "approximate something," く ら いand ぐ ら い have almost no difference of usage or meaning.

- そのバイクは２００万円くらいです That motorcycle costs about 2 million yen.
- この間、梨を２キロぐらい買ったよ The other day I bought more or less 2 kilos of pears.

Be careful, as く ら い is sometimes used in contemptuous tone, meaning "at least."
- 一点ぐらい入れろよ、お前！ At least put one point in, kid!

Whereas ご ろ refers to an approximate period of time:
- １０時ごろに家を出ますよ We will leave home at about ten.
- 日本は６月ごろに梅雨があります In Japan the rainy season is sometime in June.

Last of all, look at these differences between ご ろ and く ら い：
- 私は５時間ぐらい働きました I worked for about five hours.
- 私は５時ごろに働きに行った I went to work at about five.

🎧 漫画例 **Manga Examples**

Now let's go on to analyze some of the usages we have studied in the previous pages. Generally speaking の and を are among the least difficult particles to master and the manga examples in this section should help you consolidate what you've learned so far.

Manga Example 1: more uses of *o* and *no*

Let's start the manga examples with a double example, since we have both an を and a の in the same panel. Notice, too, a で of place (Lesson 38), and the omnipresent topic particle は, which turns the whole sentence into the topic of the conversation (Lesson 37).

The part of the sentence ending in は functions just like a noun, in other words, it has been nominalized. And what part of speech is responsible for this? The の, which, as we have seen, can function as a nominalizer. In the example, the clause この星でぜいたくなたべものをたべている preceding the の, becomes a noun like any other, with the same characteristics.

Studio Kōsen

As for the を, it functions as a direct object particle (DOP) in the sub clause たべものをたべている. To identify the direct object in a sentence, ask "what" to the verb. If we ask 何を食べているか *Nani o tabete iru ka*? (What is she eating?), the answer is 食べ物 *Tabemono* (Food). Thus, it is clear that the direct object is 食べ物 and that is must be marked with the particle を. If you always do it this way, you won't go wrong.

Gerne:　この星でぜいたくなたべものをたべているのは旅行者だけ...

this star PP *luxurious food* DOP *eat* (nom.) TOP *traveler only*...

On this planet, only travelers can eat sumptuous food...

Manga Example 2: Possessive and descriptive *no*

かすみ
の血の
におい！

J.M. Ken Niimura

This manga example has two similar but slightly different usages of the particle の. The first の links the words かすみ (Kasumi, a girl's name) and 血 ***chi*** (blood). In this case, it is the possessive (see Lesson 40, page 49). The first noun, かすみ, possesses the second one, 血, so we have "Kasumi's blood." The second の is descriptive, linking two nouns, 血 (blood) and におい ***nioi*** (smell), (see Lesson 40, page 49). The first noun, 血, describes the second one, 匂い, giving the meaning "smell of blood."

Note: For purely practical and simplifying reasons, we will keep on calling の a possessive particle (POP) every time it appears as a noun modifier.

Takeshi: かすみの血のにおい！

Kasumi POP blood POP smell!

It's the smell of (I smell) Kasumi's blood!

Manga Example 3: *no* as an end-of-sentence particle

In Lesson 17 we saw how の was used at the end of a sentence. We have just studied that の acquires different meanings depending on the context when it appears at the end of a sentence. In Lesson 17 we gave a quick explanation and we even saw a manga example

二〇一五年で西
暦が終わってし
まうの

Gabriel Luque

where の is used as an end-of-sentence particle to form questions in a colloquial register. However, の in this example, is used to soften a statement (in a feminine or childlike way). Generally, only women and children use の with this inflection.

Nami: 二〇一五年で西暦が終わってしまうの

2015 year TP Christian era SP finish EP

The Christian era will finish in the year 2015.

Manga Example 4: A new usage of *no*

Many manga example sentences in this book end with the construction "verb in simple form + のだ." Also possible are のです, んです or んだ (the ん in these last two is a spoken contraction of の). In fact, the の in Example 3 would also belong to this group. This

construction is used to state something in a soft way: it's a sort of tag many Japanese use so they don't have to finish a sentence categorically. のだ also gives a sentence some "emotion," so that the speaker can convey the interest he has in the conversation topic. **Note:** This example also shows the usage of the direct object particle を and of the possessive の.

Toshio: テル坊くん、きみのおかみさんをつれてきたのだ！
Terubō SUF *you* POP *woman* SUF DOP *bring come* EP*!*
Terubo, I've brought your wife!

Manga Example 5: Two consecutive *o*

We see here three clauses linked by *-te* form verbs (Lesson 35). The sentence ends with the 〜てください form (meaning "please"), also studied in Lesson 35.

Going back to what concerns us in this lesson, notice there are two direct objects (頭 and 腰), both marked with を.

Finally, you can see the particle に in the last sentence, which we studied in Lesson 38.

Attendant: 頭を下げて腰をかがめて席におつきください
head DOP *lower hip* DOP *bend seat* PP *occupy please*
Lower your head, bend forward, and take your seats, please.

Manga Example 6: The usage of *mō*

This panel has a good example of the adverb もう (already). Usually, もう indicates "change" and まだ "lack of change." However, both もう and まだ are relatively simple; all you need to know is that the first one means "already" or "now," and the second one "still."

Notice also that the phrase もう + 一*ichi* + counter means "one more X," for example: もう一度 *mō ichido* "one more time," もう一杯 *mō ippai* "one more drink," もう一日 *mō ichinichi* "one more day," etc.

Maki: もう行くね。お仕事。

already go EP. work

I'm going now . . . To work.

Manga Example 7: The usage of *goro*

Let's finish the lesson with a funny and absurd example showing the adverb ごろ at work. As we have seen, ごろ indicates "about" or "more or less," but is only used when it refers to an approximate time. In most cases it's used with clock time, as in this example. 何時ごろ means "At about what time?" The answer might be 五時 *go ji goro* (about five) or 一時半ごろ *ichi ji han goro* (about half past one). **Notes:** In this example we find the construction 〜後 *go* (in X time) which we saw in Lesson 34. The use of の to connect 十年後 to 何時 is the appositional usage described in Lesson 40, page 50.

Man: 十年後にきてくれっ

ten years in TP come

Come back in ten years' time.

Girl: 十年後の何時ごろ？

ten years in POP what time approximately?

At about what time in ten years?

Exercises 練習

1 Translate: "The JAL plane is big." (plane 飛行機(ひこうき) ; big 大(おお)きい)

2 Translate: "Wait in front of the library, please." (to wait 待(ま)つ ; in front of 前(まえ)で ; library 図書館(としょかん))

3 In 暖(あたた)かいセーターを着(き)てください, replace セーター with a pronoun. (暖(あたた)かい warm; セーター sweater; 着(き)る to wear)

4 Translate: 本当(ほんとう)に安土(あづち)の町(まち)に住(す)んでいるの？ (本当(ほんとう)に really; 安土 Azuchi; 町 town; 住(す)む to live)

5 Translate: "What is Mari reading?" "She is reading a book by Mishima." (Mari 真理(まり) ; to read 読(よ)む ; book 本(ほん) ; Mishima 三島(みしま))

6 Translate: "Yukio's dog got off the bus." (Yukio 由紀夫(ゆきお) ; dog 犬(いぬ) ; to get off 降(お)りる ; bus バス)

7 Translate: 修(おさむ)さんはまだ仕事(しごと)が終(お)わっていないの . (修 Osamu; 仕事 work; 終(お)わる to finish)

8 Translate: "She walked in the park for about two hours." (she 彼女(かのじょ) ; to walk 歩(ある)く ; park 公園(こうえん) ; two hours 二時間(にじかん))

9 Translate: どうしてコーヒーを飲(の)まないんですか？ What do you use んです for? (飲(の)む to drink)

10 Translate: "Bring another book, please." (to bring 持(も)ってくる ; book 本(ほん))

— **Answers to all the exercises can be found online by following the link on page 7.** —

影 The Kage Story

The manga Kage that runs through Volume 2 is an exciting story that will help you reinforce and consolidate all the language you learn in the lessons. Episode 1 of **Kage** was at the end of Volume 1 of this series. If you don't have Volume 1, you can find Episode 1 online at **www.tuttlepublishing.com/learn-japanese-with-manga-volume-2**. With art by J. M. Ken Niimura and story text by J. M. Ken Niimura and Marc Bernabé, **Kage** takes place in present-day Japan. Nuria, the main character, is a Spanish journalist and photographer, who has been sent to Tokyo by the newspaper where she works to write a feature on contemporary Japan. Once there, she meets Mina Tanimura, who works for a local newspaper, and who helps Nuria make the most of her stay in Japan, and carry out her work in the best possible conditions.

Characters

Nuria: Young Spanish photographer and journalist. She works for a newspaper in Madrid, and her boss sends her to Japan to write a feature story about the country.

Mina Tanimura: Young Japanese girl who works for a newspaper in Tokyo. She has been given the task of helping Nuria so that she can write her feature.

The Beggar: Mysterious Japanese vagrant who will be a key character in the story.

The Shadow: Nuria sees this shadow now and then during her stay in Japan. What could this shadow be, and why does it appear when it is least expected?

Nuria

Mina

The Beggar

The Shadow

Watch out: When the sides of the panel are painted black, what is narrated in these panels takes place in a different time period to that of the story being told, either in the past or in the future.

KAGE
影

二日目

首都を歩く

はい、こちらフロントの山田です。

ピーピー

部屋番号408で、ちょっと困っているんです。部屋のシャワーに問題があります。

シャワーが壊れていますか？

ガガガ ガタ・ガタ

はい、お水は出ますが、お湯は出ません。

わかりました。すぐ直します。

あたしは朝にシャワーを浴びたいから。お風呂が好きじゃない。

そうですか…

おはようございます。お元気ですか？

おはよう。あまり元気じゃないよ。シャワーが壊れていて、シャワーを浴びられなかった。結局、お風呂にした。困ったね。

え？どうしてですか？

はい、行きましょう。

ま、仕事をしに行こうか？

ね、私の荷物はもう届いたの？

いいえ、まだ届いていませんが…

行けます。今は三田にいますが、地下鉄に乗って、新橋で電車の山手線に乗り換えて、東京駅と秋葉原駅を通って、上野駅まで行けます。

上野までいくらなの？

330円です。お金をここに入れてください。

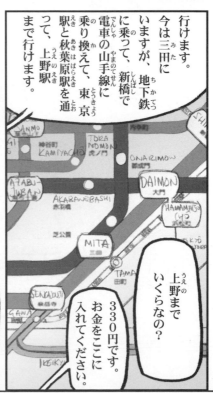

今日はどこに写真をとりにいこうか？

どこでもいいですが、上野公園でどうですか？

上野公園？いいよ。ここから電車で上野に行けるの？

あ！間違った!!
150円の切符を
買っちゃったよ！

上野駅で精算機が
使えますよ。

心配しないで
ください。

そう？
便利だね、
それは。

あ、路線図が
ほしい…

二番
ホームです。
あの角を右に
曲がって、
階段を上がって
ください。

はい、
どうぞ。
日本語が
お上手
ですね。

いいえ、
ありがとう。
上野行きのホームは
どれですか？

ありがとう
ございます。

すみませんが、
路線図を
お願いします。

間もなく、
2番線に上野
行きがまいります。
危ないですから、
白線の内側まで
お下がりく
ださい。

Review for Lessons 36–40

Answers to all the review exercises can be found online by following the link on page 7.

🎧 *KAGE* – New vocabulary 新しい単語

すぐ	at once	結局	after all
直す	to fix	心配	worry
浴びる	to pour water over oneself	顔色が悪い	to look unwell, to look pale

1. According to what you have read in the second episode of **Kage**, in the beginning, what is Nuria's problem at the hotel?

2. According to what you can deduce from the conversation between Nuria and Mina, has the hotel staff solved the problem?

3. Where does Mina suggest that Nuria could go to take photos today?

4. At which station do Mina and Nuria start their journey? Which way do they go to reach their destination (where do they change trains, and which stations do they go past)?

5. What happens to Nuria when she buys the ticket? What suggestion does Mina give to solve the problem?

6. At the end of the episode, what time does Nuria ask to be woken up in the morning?

7. What does the receptionist ask Nuria at the end of the episode? What do you think the expression used by Nuria in her answer, なんでもないです, means?

8. In Nuria's sentence あたしは朝にシャワーは浴びたいから , what is the connotation of the second particle は ?

9. Indicate the function の has in the following sentences:

a) フロントの山田です。 _____

b) 部屋のシャワーに問題があります。 _____

c) 私の荷物がもう届いたの？　＿＿＿＿＿＿＿＿＿＿＿＿＿＿＿＿＿＿＿＿

d) １５０円の切符を買っちゃったよ！＿＿＿＿＿＿＿＿＿＿＿＿＿＿＿＿＿＿

10. Indicate the function に has in the following sentences:

a) 部屋のシャワーに問題があります。　＿＿＿＿＿＿＿＿＿＿＿＿＿＿＿＿

b) 朝にシャワーを浴びたいから。　＿＿＿＿＿＿＿＿＿＿＿＿＿＿＿＿＿

c) 今は三田にいる。　＿＿＿＿＿＿＿＿＿＿＿＿＿＿＿＿＿

d) ここから電車で上野に行けるの？　＿＿＿＿＿＿＿＿＿＿＿＿＿＿＿

11. Find the sentences with the adverbs もう and まだ in the second episode of **Kage**, and translate them into English. Why is the verb in the sentence with まだ conjugated in the negative?

12. Give the meaning of the word どこでも in the sentence どこでもいいです.

13. Give the meaning of the word ごろ in the sentence 五時ごろにホテルに帰ってくださいね.

14. Fill in the blanks with the appropriate word from the box overleaf.

a) 東京からソウルまで飛行機で行けるが、＿＿＿＿＿＿＿＿＿でも行けます。

b) ホテルではベッドで寝るが、旅館では＿＿＿＿＿＿＿＿＿で寝ますね。

c) 渋谷から新宿まで＿＿＿＿＿＿＿＿＿＿＿＿＿＿＿＿＿＿で行けるが、
電車でも行けます。

d) 今日はとても暑いから、＿＿＿＿＿＿＿＿＿＿＿＿＿＿をつけましょう。

e) 私の部屋に＿＿＿＿＿＿がないから、共用風呂へ行かなければならない。

f) すみませんが、広島＿＿＿＿＿＿＿＿＿のバスはどこにありますか？

g) 広島までの＿＿＿＿＿＿＿＿＿＿＿＿＿＿＿＿は２３４０円です。

h) 私の部屋に＿＿＿＿＿がないから、共用トイレへ行かなければならない。

i) 私と妻と子ども一人だから、＿＿＿＿＿＿＿＿＿＿＿＿がほしい。

j) この建物には＿＿＿＿＿がないから、階段をのぼっていってくださいね。

冷房（れいぼう）	バス	運賃（うんちん）	行（ゆ）き	エレベータ
トイレ	地下鉄（ちかてつ）	三人部屋（さんにんべや）	船（ふね）	ふとん

15. Choose the sentence with the closest meaning to the original one.

a) 私は露天風呂（ろてんぶろ）がある旅館（りょかん）が大好きです。

   1. 私はお風呂（ふろ）がない旅館（りょかん）が大好きです。

   2. 私は外にお風呂（ふろ）がある旅館（りょかん）が大好きです。

   3. 私は朝にお風呂（ふろ）に入れる旅館（りょかん）が大好きです。

   4. 私は中にお風呂（ふろ）がある旅館（りょかん）が大好きです。

b) マキコさんは禁煙席（きんえんせき）の切符を買いました。

   1. マキコさんは食べてはだめな席（せき）の切符（きっぷ）を買いました。

   2. マキコさんはたばこをすってもいい席（せき）の切符（きっぷ）を買いました。

   3. マキコさんは食べてもいい席（せき）の切符（きっぷ）を買いました。

   4. マキコさんはたばこをすってはだめな席（せき）の切符（きっぷ）を買いました。

c) あのホテルには和室（わしつ）の部屋（へや）が一つありましたよ。

   1. あのホテルには畳（たたみ）とふすまがある部屋（へや）が一つありませんでした。

   2. あのホテルには畳（たたみ）とふすまがある部屋（へや）が一つありました。

   3. あのホテルには畳（たたみ）とふすまがない部屋（へや）が一つありましたよ。

   4. あのホテルには畳（たたみ）とふすまが一つもない部屋（へや）がありませんでした。

16. Choose the most suitable answer for each sentence.

a) ドアを開（あ）けられないよ。＿＿＿＿＿＿＿＿＿＿＿でもかかっているの？

   1. メーター　2. 庭（にわ）　3. 鍵（かぎ）　4. 窓（まど）

b) A：１５６０円です｜B：はい、２０００円、どうぞ。｜A：＿＿＿＿＿＿＿は
４４０円ですね。

   1. お釣（つ）り　2. 両替（りょうがえ）　3. 運賃（うんちん）　4. お金

c) このホテルの ＿＿＿＿＿＿＿＿＿＿＿＿＿＿＿＿ は一泊４０００円です。
　　1. 運賃　2. 現金　3. 予約　4. 宿泊 料

d) 大阪から神戸まで電車で行けます。＿＿＿＿＿＿ は４００円ぐらいです。
　　1. 運賃　2. 現金　3. 予約　4. 宿泊 料

e) すみません、＿＿＿＿＿＿ を忘れたんです。明日７時に ＿＿＿＿＿＿
　　をお願いします。
　　1. 電車　2. 目覚まし時計　3. モーニングコール　4. コンセント
　　1. 電車　2. 目覚まし時計　3. モーニングコール　4. コンセント

f) A: 運転手にバスをとめてもらいたいが... | B: じゃ、＿＿＿＿＿＿＿
　　を使ってください。
　　1. 出口　2. 押しボタン　3. フロント　4. 信号

g) ＿＿＿＿＿＿＿＿＿＿＿＿＿＿＿＿＿＿＿＿ は朝５時ごろです。
　　1. 始発　2. 終点　3. 終電　4. 始終

h) どこでも座れるのは「＿＿＿＿＿＿＿＿＿＿＿」と言います。
　　1. 指定席　2. 禁煙席　3. 喫煙席　4. 自由席

i) ＿＿＿＿＿＿＿＿＿＿＿＿＿＿＿＿＿＿ を金庫に入れてください。
　　1. 貴重品　2. コインロッカー　3. スリッパ　4. 冷蔵庫

17. Fill in the blanks in the following sentences with the most suitable expression formed by an adverb or interrogative pronoun followed by でも, as in the example.

a) たばこと酒は ＿どこでも＿ 買えないよ。

b) このカメラで＿＿＿＿＿＿＿＿＿＿＿＿いい写真をとれるぞ。

c) オレは仕事がないから、＿＿＿＿＿＿＿＿＿＿＿遊びにいけるよ。

d) ミキオさんは嫌いな食べ物がありません。＿＿＿＿＿＿食べますよ。

e) 英語が分かる人は＿＿＿＿＿＿＿＿＿＿＿＿＿＿＿＿いる。

f) この映画は＿＿＿＿＿＿＿＿＿＿＿＿＿＿＿＿＿好きだね。

18. In each case, complete with a suitable question or answer, forming full sentences. For indirect questions, use the underlined part as the object of the question.

a) 「共用トイレ」は誰でも使えますか？

_____。

b) _____ ？

お風呂は７時から１１時までです。

c) シルバーシートに誰でも座ってもいいですか？

_____。

d) _____ ？

新宿から乗りました。

19. This telephone conversation is out of order. Rewrite it in the correct order.

1) どんな部屋にしたいですか？

2) いいですよ。じゃ、その部屋にします。ありがとう。

3) あ、こんにちは。今夜、部屋を予約したいんですが... 空室ありますか？

4) もしもし？東京ビッグホテルですが...

5) 宿泊料は８０００円ですが...

6) 一泊、いくらですか？

7) はい、あります。

8) トイレつき、朝食なしの一人部屋にしたいが、大丈夫ですか？

フロントの人： _____

お客さん： _____

フロントの人： _____

お客さん： _____

フロントの人： _____

お<ruby>客<rt>きゃく</rt></ruby>さん：　_____

フロントの人：　_____

お<ruby>客<rt>きゃく</rt></ruby>さん：　_____

20. Complete this dialogue held at the train station with the most suitable words.

Clerk:　いらっしゃいませ。

Client:　<ruby>大阪<rt>おおさか</rt></ruby> (1)_____ の (2)_____ を買いたいが...

Clerk:　はい。<ruby>特急列車<rt>とっきゅうれっしゃ</rt></ruby>と (3)_____ があります。どれにしますか？

Client:　どれが<ruby>早<rt>はや</rt></ruby>いですか？

Clerk:　(4)_____ です。しかし、<ruby>特急列車<rt>とっきゅうれっしゃ</rt></ruby>はもっと安いですよ。

Client:　うーん... やっぱり、<ruby>新幹線<rt>しんかんせん</rt></ruby>にします。

Clerk:　分かりました。(5)_____ でいいですか？

Client:　どんな<ruby>席<rt>せき</rt></ruby>ですか、それは？

Clerk:　<ruby>誰<rt>だれ</rt></ruby>でも<ruby>座<rt>すわ</rt></ruby>れない<ruby>席<rt>せき</rt></ruby>で、<ruby>お客様<rt>きゃくさま</rt></ruby>だけが<ruby>座<rt>すわ</rt></ruby>れる<ruby>席<rt>せき</rt></ruby>です。

Client:　あ、じゃ、<ruby>お願<rt>ねが</rt></ruby>いします。

Clerk:　「のぞみ」、「こだま」と「ひかり」があります。どれにしますか？

Client:　「のぞみ」？それは何ですか？

Clerk:　「のぞみ」は<ruby>一番<rt>いちばん</rt></ruby> (6)_____ <ruby>新幹線<rt>しんかんせん</rt></ruby>です。

Client: じゃ、「のぞみ」の ⁽⁷⁾＿＿＿＿＿＿＿＿＿＿＿＿＿ をお願いします。

Clerk: はい、どうぞ。

Client: この電車は ⁽⁸⁾＿＿＿＿＿＿＿＿＿＿＿＿＿＿ から発車しますか？

Clerk: 5番線です。あの角を右に曲がって、階段をのぼってください。

21. Complete the following sentences with the particles は or が as appropriate.

a) 私の名前（ ）ジョナサンです。

b) ここで写真をとって（ ）いけないよ。

c) 新幹線は速い（ ）、とても高いですね。

d) アメリカとヨーロッパで、「アニメ」（ ）「日本アニメーション」です。

e) 「は」と「が」を上手に使うこと（ ）できますか？

f) 昨日、パーティに行きました。パーティ（ ）おもしろかった。

g) 昨日、パーティ（ ）あったよ。どうして来なかったの？

h) 昨日のパーティに誰（ ）来たの？

i) あそこに猫（ ）います。あの猫（ ）タチバナさんのですよ。

j) 私は日本語（ ）読めるが、漢字（ ）書けない。

k) トムさん（ ）日本語（ ）下手だね。

l) お金（ ）ほしい！

m) あなたと結婚したいんです（ ）...

n) 日本人（ ）髪の毛（ ）黒いです。

o) 家の近くに猿（ ）一匹います。あの猿（ ）お尻が赤いです。

p) 父（ ）魚（ ）とてもきらいです。

q) あの人（ ）寿司屋さんです。

r) 飛行機の窓からシベリア（ ）見えましたよ。

22. Answer the following questions, as in the example.

a) 先生の奥さんはもう来ていますか？

いいえ、<u>先生の奥さんはまだ来ていません</u>。

b) 彼女はもうケーキを作りましたか？

はい、＿＿＿＿＿＿＿＿＿＿＿＿＿＿＿＿＿＿＿＿＿＿＿＿＿。

c) 日本へもう行けるか？

いいえ、＿＿＿＿＿＿＿＿＿＿＿＿＿＿＿＿＿＿＿＿＿＿＿＿＿。

d) もう絵をかきましたか？

はい、＿＿＿＿＿＿＿＿＿＿＿＿＿＿＿＿＿＿＿＿＿＿＿＿＿。

e) 彼女はもう日本語が話せますか？

いいえ、＿＿＿＿＿＿＿＿＿＿＿＿＿＿＿＿＿＿＿＿＿＿＿＿＿。

23. Complete the following sentences with the particles に or で, as appropriate.

a) 私の家の庭（　）馬がいました。

b) あの人は赤いペン（　）絵をかいていた。

c) 山田さんのコンピュータは一週間（　）壊れていましたよ。

d) 8時（　）渋谷（　）買い物をしなければならない。

e) 月曜日（　）東京（　）行かなければならない。

f) オレは電車（　）あんな雑誌を読みたくないぞ。

g) どうしてあんな雑誌がお前の家（　）あったの？

h) こんな雑誌をどこ（　）買うことができますか？

i) 私の母はロンドン（　）住んでいると思います。

j) ここ（　）待ってください。私はすぐ来ます。

k) 山本さんは会社の前（　）川田さん（　）書類をあげました。

l) 私の家は遠いから、バス（　）来てください。

m) あそこ（　）バス（　）乗ってください。

n) 将来、日本語の先生（　）なりたくないよ。

o) この本を２０００円（　）私（　）売ってくれますか？

p) 彼は白い紙（　）えんぴつ（　）絵をかいていた。

24. Unscramble the following sentences.

a) 赤い | 尻 | は | 猿 | が | です

  猿は尻が赤いです＿＿＿＿＿＿＿＿＿＿。

b) 買えない | が | 車 | は | ほしい | 私 | が

  ＿＿＿＿＿＿＿＿＿＿＿＿＿＿＿＿＿＿＿＿＿。

c) 家 | を | マリちゃん | は | テレビ | 見ています | で

  ＿＿＿＿＿＿＿＿＿＿＿＿＿＿＿＿＿＿＿＿＿。

d) 弟 | は | で | 帰りました | 飛行機 | に | オランダ

  ＿＿＿＿＿＿＿＿＿＿＿＿＿＿＿＿＿＿＿＿＿。

e) あった | は | ここ | 花 | その人 | が | あげたの | に | に | 誰

  ＿＿＿＿＿＿＿＿＿＿＿＿＿＿＿＿＿＿＿＿＿？

f) で | の | 書いた | ナイフ | を | 学生 | 公園 | は | に | 木 | 名前

  ＿＿＿＿＿＿＿＿＿＿＿＿＿＿＿＿＿＿＿＿＿。

25. Complete the following sentences with the particle you consider most suitable, choosing from は, が, も, に, で, へ, の, を and か.

a) サンディー（　）娘さんはとてもきれいです。

b) 来年、アメリカ（　）行くつもりです。

c) 私は明日の３時（　）銀行へ行きたいです。

d) ジョンさんはどこ（　）国（　）人ですか？

e) 日本の冬（　）寒いです。

f)　私は彼女(かのじょ)に手紙(てがみ)（　）もらった。

g)　彼(かれ)は家（　）勉強(べんきょう)する（　）（　）好きです。

h)　この店（　）は安いケーキ（　）あるよ。

i)　このケーキ（　）食べて（　）いいですか？

j)　このケーキ（　）食べて（　）だめです。

k)　家（　）前（　）犬(いぬ)（　）いました。

l)　今、バス（　）降(お)りたが、次(つぎ)は電車(でんしゃ)（　）乗(の)らなければならない。

m)　あそこ（　）何（　）し（　）行く（　）ですか？

n)　はじめまして。社長(しゃちょう)（　）国山(くにむら)です。

o)　彼(かれ)はフォーク（　）人（　）殺(ころ)したよ。

p)　A: 私は妹(いもうと)（　）いる。|B: そうですか？私（　）妹(いもうと)（　）いますよ。

q)　9月（　）私（　）国（　）帰るつもりです

r)　鳥(とり)（　）空（　）飛(と)びます。

s)　日本語（　）上手（　）話したい。

t)　どれ（　）あなた（　）車ですか？

u)　庭(にわ)（　）（　）犬(いぬ)（　）いる。家（　）中（　）（　）犬(いぬ)（　）いる。

v)　A: どんなセーター（　）買いたい（　）？|B: 青い（　）（　）買いたい。

w)　カゴメさん（　）10時（　）家（　）出た。

x)　私は1999年（　）はじめて日本（　）行った（　）です。

y)　石橋(いしばし)（　）駅(えき)（　）前（　）とてもおいしいピザ（　）レストラン（　）ある。

z)　オレはバイク（　）北海道(ほっかいどう)（　）行きたいぞ！

i)　あのレストラン（　）ピザはとてもおいしい（　）、高いですね。

ii)　A: これ（　）誰(だれ)（　）写真ですか？|B: 私（　）ですよ！

iii)　新しいカメラ（　）買い（　）行きたい。

26. Choose the most suitable answer for each sentence.

a) 昨日、学校を休みました。今日_____休むつもりです。

  1. は   2. が   3. も   4. の

b) パーティーは５時_____に始まります。

  1. ぐらい   2. ごろ   3. くらい   4. まだ

c) A: 彼_{かれ}はまだ来ていませんか？| B: はい、_____ です。

  1. ごろ   2. もう   3. くらい   4. まだ

d) 私はタイへ行きたいが、インド_____行きたいよ。

  1. も   2. へ   3. に   4. へも

e) お腹_{なか}がすいたんですか？ケーキ_____食べますか？

  1. が   2. の   3. でも   4. にも

f) 昨日、５時間_____寝ました。

  1. ごろ   2. ぐらい   3. まだ   4. もう

g) A: 彼_{かれ}は _____ 来ていますか？| B: いいえ、まだ来ていませんよ。

  1. もう   2. まだ   3. くらい   4. のは

h) この漢字_{かんじ}はとてもやさしくて、子ども_____読めるよ！

  1. もう   2. でも   3. にも   4. のも

27. Correct the mistakes in the following sentences, as in the example.

a) 私の名前<del>が</del>ソフィーです。 〔は〕

b) 先生はもう来ていません。

c) 私は京都_{きょうと}で住_すみたいと思います。

d) 象_{ぞう}が鼻_{はな}は長_{なが}いですね。

e) ５時間ごろ働_{はたら}きましたか？

f) 庭_{にわ}で鳥_{とり}が一羽_{いちわ}います。あの鳥_{とり}が飛_とんでいます。

Kanji

開	閉	発	動	作	教	習	知	地	図	所
(120)	(119)	(247)	(95)	(133)	(134)	(135)	(137)	(143)	(184)	(144)
太	若	悪	重	館	駅	室	洋	漢	字	電
(85)	(110)	(112)	(113)	(175)	(178)	(179)	(164)	(196)	(156)	(158)

28. Practice writing the kanji below. Find the stroke order in the online Kanji Compilation by following the link on page 7.

動									
開									
悪									
地									
教									

29. Link each kanji with its most common reading (usually, the **kun'yomi**).

字	つくる	若い	おもい
作る	しる	室	わかい
知る	じ	電	でん
図	えき	悪い	しつ
所	ところ	重い	わるい
駅	ず	地	ち

30. Choose the correct kanji or kanji combination for each reading.

a) うごく

   1. 動く　2. 重く　3. 車く　4. 働く

b). ならう

   1. 教う　2. 習う　3. 便う　4. 知う

c) わるい

   1. 重い　2. 良い　3. 弟い　4. 悪い

d). しる

   1. 教る　2. 習る　3. 便る　4. 知る

e) でんしゃ

   1. 電話　2. 電車　3. 電気　4. 電語

f). しゅっぱつ

   1. 出登　2. 登出　3. 出発　4. 発出

31. Choose the correct reading for each kanji combination.

a) 駅前の図書館は何時に開きますか？

   駅前：1. えきぜん　2. えぎまえ　3. えきまえ　4. えぎぜん

   図書館：1. ずしょかん　2. ずどくかん　3. とどくかん　4. としょかん

   開きます：1. あきます　2. しきます　3. いきます　4. ききます

b) 日本語の文字を習うのはむずかしいです。

   文字：1. もじ　2. ぶんじ　3. ぶんし　4. ぶし

   習う：1. あきなう　2. からう　3. ならう　4. まなう

c) 先生は自動車の中で電話で話していました。

   自動車：1. じてんしゃ　2. してんじゃ　3. しどうじゃ　4. じどうしゃ

   電話：1. でんしゃ　2. でんわ　3. でんき　4. でんご

32. Give the *furigana* reading of the underlined kanji.

a) 閉店は８時だから、早く電車で出発しましょうね。

b) あの動物の心電図を見てください。

c) 教室で漢字がたくさん出てくる作文を作っている。

d) 西洋には悪習が多いですね。

e) 近所のおばさんは太っている知人に悪口を言った。

33. Write the following words in kanji, and give their meanings.

しめる _____ _____   おもい _____ _____

えき _____ _____   がくしゅう _____ _____

でんき _____ _____   わるい _____ _____

34. There are some mistakes in these words, either in the kanji or in the matching hiragana. Can you correct them?

池図	ちず	問ける	あける	発読	はつばい
漢字	かんし	電軍	でんしゃ	開会	へいかい
右い	わかい	犬字	ふとじ	東羊	とうよう

Lesson 41 • 第41課
Particles (4) to / kara / made

By the end of this lesson we will have studied in depth all the particles in Japanese grammar: は, が, も (Lesson 37), に, で and へ (Lesson 38), の and を (Lesson 40), and, here, と, から and まで. We will also study the usages of や and か.

🎧 The particle と

と, like most particles, has several different usages which we will have to study carefully and individually.

Listing things: と is used to link nouns or noun phrases (Lesson 40 and 57,) and to give an exhaustive and complete listing of two or more things.

- 私は映画と音楽とマンガが好きです I like movies, music and comic-books.
- 寿司と刺身と味噌汁を食べた I have eaten sushi, sashimi and miso soup.
- 彼は英語と中国語とチェコ語とロシア語が出来る He can speak English, Chinese, Czech and Russian.

Together with / with: と is also used to indicate "with" somebody or something.

- 原さんは大塚さんと囲碁を打っている Mr. Hara plays go with Mr. Otsuka.
- 彼女はジョンと（一緒に）観光をした She went sightseeing (together) with John.

The phrase と（一緒に）*tō (issho ni)* is frequently used, and means "together with." However, 一緒に is often omitted from the sentence because it's understood or implied, hence the brackets here. These kinds of sentence are called "reciprocal sentences," because the action indicated by the verb is the same for the two or more "subjects" who perform it. For example, the first sentence could mean both Mr. Hara plays go with Mr. Ōtsuka and Mr. Ōtsuka plays with Mr. Hara. They both have the same role.

There are several kinds of reciprocal sentences in Japanese, and this one indicating "together with" is just one of them. Other verbs, such as 話す *hanasu* (to talk); 結婚する *kekkon suru* (to marry); 似ている *nite iru* (to look like); 違う *chigau* (to be different); and adjectives such as 同じ *onaji* (the same), also use the particle と to make reciprocal sentences:

• 秋成くんはホステスと話している Akinari is talking with the bar hostess.

• りんごはなしと違います Apples and pears are different.

Quotes: To quote somebody's words, we use と. There are two kinds of quotation: indirect (reporting what was said), and direct (explicitly quoting what was said, between quotation marks).

• 博信は君がバカだと言ったよ Hironobu said you were stupid.

• サンドラは「休暇が欲しいなぁ!」と叫んだ Sandra yelled: "I want holidays!"

🎧 Usages of *to*	
List	太郎とジョンとマリアが来た Taro, John and Maria came
(Together) with	ジョンはマリアと映画を見る John watches a movie with Maria
Reciprocity	太郎はマリアと結婚する Taro marries Maria
Direct quote	彼は私に「好きだ」と言った He said to me "I like you"
Indirect quote	彼は私が好きだと言った He told me he liked me
Definition	愛とは何でしょう？ What is love?
With *gitaigo/ giongo*	彼はへなへなと座った He sat down, exhausted
Conditional	映画を見ると分かるよ If you see the film, you'll understand

来る *kuru* to come; 映画 *eiga* film; 見る *miru* to see; 結婚する *kekkon suru* to marry; 好き *suki* (to) like; 言う *iu* to say; 愛 *ai* love; へなへな weak; 座る *suwaru* to sit; 分かる *wakaru* to understand

These sentences use verbs such as 言う *iu* (to say), 叫ぶ *sakebu* (to yell), ささやく (to whisper), etc. Verbs such as 思う *omou* (to believe), 考える *kangaeru* (to think), 書く *kaku* (to write), also use と.

• 大阪は本当に楽しいと思っているよ I think Osaka is really fun.
• 「さくら」は漢字で「桜」と書く The word "sakura" is written " 桜 " in kanji.

Note: If we have a *-na* adjective or a noun before と, we will need the verb to be in its simple form (だ). The *-i* adjective, however, requires no conjugation.

Definition: Using the combination とは, or its complete form というのは, we can express a "definition."

• 「能験」とは「能力試験」の略です *"Nōken"* is short for *nōryoku shiken*.
• 「民主主義」というのは何ですか？ What is (that thing we call) "democracy"?

The expression という is useful when clarifying a concept or giving more information about something. For this usage, we don't write the verb 言う in kanji.

- 「Monster」というマンガは超面白〜い！ The manga "Monster" is reaaally good!
- 「アゲハ」という女を知ってる？ Do you know the woman called Ageha?

With *gitaigo* / *giongo*: と is often used with onomatopoeic words (see Lesson 29).

- 彼女はしくしくと泣いている She is sobbing silently.
- 飛行機がびゅーんと飛んでいた The plane flew (going *byuuun*).

Conditional: In Japanese there are four ways of expressing the conditional which we will study in Lesson 56. For now we will only say for reference that と is used in one of them:

- にんじんを食べると目がよくなります If you eat carrots, your sight will improve.

🎧 The particle から

Origin (from): から indicates origin or point of departure, be it spatial or temporal.

- パーティは6時からです The party is from six o'clock.
- どこから来たんですか？ Where have you come from? | Where are you from?
- 学校から家へ歩いていける I can walk home from school.
- パンは小麦から作る Bread is made from wheat.*

  *This is similar to the **Manner / instrument / material** usage of で in Lesson 38 (page 32). Both particles are almost interchangeable in this context: the only difference is that we use から when the original material is not obvious just by looking at it. You can't physically "see" that bread is made from wheat and so we use から. When we can determine by sight what the material used is, we use で.

Cause/reason: As seen in Lesson 34, から is used to answer a question with どうして (why?), like our "because." It can also be used independently, meaning "as" or "since."

- 銀座は高いからよそへ行きましょう As Ginza's expensive, let's go elsewhere else.
- 私は大丈夫だから、心配しないで I'm alright, so don't worry.
- 魚は嫌いだから肉にしますよ As I don't like fish, I'll have meat.

Note: As mentioned at the end of the **Quotes** section on page 81, after a *-na* adjective or a noun, the verb is in its simple form (だ). Again, this is not necessary with *-i* adjectives.

After doing: In Lesson 35 we saw how から is combined with the *-te* form to indicate "after doing . . ." Here's an example as a reminder.

- 日本へ行ってから台湾へ行きたい After going to Japan, I want to go to Taiwan.

🎧 The particle まで

This particle is easy to use, especially if we learn it together with から, because they have opposite meanings. If から is "from," then まで is "until" or "to." The third example below shows the common combination of から and まで together.

- 駅まで１０キロぐらいあると思う I think it's about 10 km to the station.
- いつまで韓国に残りたいの？ Until when do you want to stay in Korea?
- 授業は３時から４時半までだよ The class goes from three to half past four.

🎧 Usages of や

か and や are not considered "true" particles but they have similar functions to と (page 80). We use や to make lists, like と. But と is used to make exhaustive lists and や is used to make non-exhaustive lists of nouns or noun phrases (it can't be used with verbs or adjectives), to give feeling "and so on."

- 寿司や刺身を食べた I have eaten sushi and sashimi (among other things).
- 彼は英語や中国語やチェコ語が出来る He can speak English, Chinese, Czech (and others).
- 東京や岐阜や名古屋に友達がいる I have friends in Tokyo, Gifu, Nagoya . . .

The expression とか has practically the same meaning and usage as や. However, や is mainly used in written Japanese, whereas とか is used in colloquial contexts.

- 私は映画とか音楽とかが好きです I like movies and music (and other things).

🎧 Usages of か

Although か is used to list things in a similar way to と (page 80), and や, it has a very different meaning, as it indicates a choice between one or several things and something else.
Note: か can be used not only with nouns, but also with verbs and adjectives.

- 寿司か刺身を食べてください Eat the sushi or the sashimi, please.
- 電車で行くか歩いていくか決めよう Let's decide whether to go by train or walk.
- 東京か岐阜か名古屋に友達がいる He has a friend in Tokyo, Gifu, or Nagoya.

🎧 More usages of か

Another usage of か is 〜かどうか, used to make questions of the "yes or no" kind. The basic sentence is similar to the ones in the previous point but the second part of the sentence is replaced by 〜かどうか, similar to "or not" in English.

- 刺身が好きか嫌いか言ってね Tell me if you like or dislike sashimi, OK?
- 刺身が好きかどうか言ってね Tell me if you like sashimi or not, OK?
- 彼がサラリーマンかどうか知らない I don't know if he is an office worker or not.
- 夏美が元気かどうか聞いてもいい？ Can I ask if Natsumi is all right (or not)?
- 大会に出たかどうか分からないな I don't know if he took part in the event or not.

🎧 Something, someday . . .

Add か to interrogative pronouns/adverbs to create words like 何か **nanika** (something, some), いつか (sometime/ someday), どこか (somewhere), 誰か **dareka** (someone), etc.

- 誰か助けてください！ Someone help me, please!
- 何か問題がありますか Do you have any problems?
- どこかで彼女に会いたいな I'd like to meet her somewhere.

🎧 Usages of *kara*	
From	子どもはパリからくる The children come from Paris
Origin	豆腐は大豆から作る Tofu is made from soybeans
Cause/reason	宿題は難しいからやらない Since homework is difficult, I won't do it
After doing	宿題が終わってからテレビを見よう After finishing my homework, I'll watch TV
Usage of *made*	
To/until	仙台まで新幹線で行ける You can go as far as Sendai by shinkansen
Usage of *ya*	
Non-exhaustive list	オレンジやレモンを買った I bought oranges, lemons (and others)

Usages of *ka*	
List	オレンジかレモンを食べてください Eat an orange or a lemon, please
Yes or no? (かどうか)	食べたいかどうか言ってね Tell me if you want to eat or not, OK?
Something (何か)	何か食べたいんですか？ Do you feel like eating something?

子供 *kodomo* child; 豆腐 *tōfu* tofu;
大豆 *daizu* soybeans; 作る *tsukuru* to make;
宿題 *shukudai* homework;
難しい *muzukashii* difficult;
やる to do (col.); 終わる *owaru* to finish;
テレビ TV; 新幹線 *shinkansen* shinkansen;
行く *iku* to go; オレンジ orange;
レモン lemon; 買う *kau* to buy;
食べる *taberu* to eat

🎧 漫画例 **Manga Examples**

We will complete the lesson with a few examples taken from manga, as usual. This time we'll start with a focus on some of the many uses of the particle と that we have looked at in this chapter.

Manga Example 1: Several usages of *to*

Here are three different usages of と in one sentence! The first と gives a list" of only two elements, the nouns 15日 and 20日 (note the special pronunciation).

The second と goes with the **_gitaigo_** ピン (see Lesson 29 to review **_gitaigo_**). The word ピ ン indicates something like a thought that suddenly strikes you and is generally used as part of the expression ピンとくる, as in this example.

And now you'll be asking yourself where the third と is. Well, in fact, it's "hidden": the と seen when discussing quotes on page 81, is usually contracted into って in spoken Japanese. Pay careful attention to this, because it happens often. In this sentence, the contracted と is in 出かけると聞いて (I heard he went out). と connects the main sentence 聞く (to hear) and the subordinate clause 出かける (to go out).

15日と20日に出かけるって聞いてピンときたんだ

J.M. Ken Niimura

Kōsaka: 15日と20日に出かけるって聞いてピンときたんだ

day 15 CP day 20 TP go out SBP hear "flash" come

When I heard he went out on the 15th and the 20th, I suddenly understood.

Manga Example 2: Together with

Here is a good example of the second usage of と , studied on page 80: "together with/with." We said the 一緒 part of the expression 〜と一緒に *to issho ni* (together with) is often

left out, as is the case in this sentence, which could easily be ナオヤ先輩と一緒に行きたい. **Notes:** The word 先輩 (Lesson 15), indicates "someone with more experience, who does the same work or study as the speaker, but who started earlier." It is widely used. Also notice the tag んです at the end, explained in Manga Example 4, Lesson 40.

Gabriel Luque

> Mayumi: あたし、ナオヤ先輩と行きたい所があるんですけど…
> *I Naoya* SUF CP *go place* SP *there is but . . .*
> I . . . There is a certain place I'd like to go with Naoya . . .

Manga Example 3: Spoken contraction of *to iu*

In Manga Example 1, we saw how と is contracted to って in spoken Japanese. The same happens with the expression という and とは. Here we have an example of an indirect quote as described on page 81. Sachie quotes twice what they've told her using と plus the verb 言う *iu* (to say), which gives us という (says that), contracted into a simple って. Let's see, now, a usage of this って as a definition: 「民主主義」って何？ *Minshushugi tte nani?* (What is democracy?) This って as you know, is the equivalent of とは. **Note:** って can be the contraction of と , as in Manga Example 1, or of the full expression という (says that) or even the defining expression とは.

Studio Kōsen

> Sachie: ＯＫだって！街の近くまでのせてくれるって！！
> *OK says that! Village* POP *near to take (receive) says that!*
> He says OK! He's taking us somewhere near the village!

Manga Example 4: Usage of *made* and an idiomatic usage of *kara*

The particle まで is the equivalent of "until." In this example まで indicates a point in time: 迎えに来るまで. In the previous example, まで indicates a point in space: 街の近くまで (somewhere near the village). **Note:** The から at the end of the sentence indicating cause/reason is discussed on page 82. This usage is very common in spoken language, especially when the speaker is angry or in a bad mood. In such cases, rather than translating it as "because," it's better to use "huh!" or a similar interjection.

Mihoko: 迎えに来るまで帰ってやらないから。

fetch until go back (give) because

I won't go back until he comes to fetch me, huh!

Manga Example 5: Cause or reason

Here is a good example of the use of から: cause/reason (see page 82), linking the two sentences お前には聞かせられない (reason) and 息子の秀樹をよべ (consequence). In the sentence we also see the appositional usage of の (Lesson 40, page 50) in 息子の秀樹, as well as the imperative よべ (from the verb 呼ぶ *yobu*, to call), studied in Lesson 30. The inflection 聞かせられない is a combination of the causative form (Lesson 60), and the negative potential form (Lesson 32): it literally means "I can't let you hear," in other words, "I can't tell you."

Kūkai: お前には聞かせられないから息子の秀樹をよべ…

you IOP TOP hear (passive-reflexive) because son POP Hideki DOP call . . .

I can't tell you, so call my son Hideki.

Manga Example 6: *Ka dō ka*

In the second sentence of this manga example notice the construction 〜かどうかwhich is used to form questions of the "yes or no" type. The construction〜かどうか is used to

avoid repeating the verb and to simplify: the "extended version" of the sentence would be: お前の知ってる男か知らない男か確かめてみろ (Check if you know those men or if you don't know them). **Note:** In this sentence, we can also see 〜てみる, (Lesson 35), meaning "try to do something." Notice how 〜てみる is conjugated in the imperative: 確かめてみろ, literally "try to check," or "check and see."

Soldier: な…何を言ってるのかよくわからないが…

w . . . what DOP say SBP Q? well know but . . .

Wha . . . ? I don't understand very well what you are saying, but . . .
とにかくお前の知ってる男かどうか、確かめてみろ！！

anyhow you POP know man "yes or no," check (try)!!

Whatever it is, go and check if you know those men or not!!

Manga Example 7: Something

This example shows the combination of an interrogative adverb or pronoun plus か, to mean "something." In this case we have なんか, but other variants such as どれか (which one), いつか (sometime), どこか (somewhere) are also possible. **Note:** We also see here the use of the *-te* form for a request, without ください, characteristic of spoken language, as we saw in Lesson 35.

Emika: なんか言って徳永君ッ

something say Tokunaga SUF

Say something, Tokunaga!

Exercises 練習

(1) Translate: "I want to buy potatoes, tomatoes and onions." (to buy 買う; potatoes じゃがいも; tomatoes トマト; onions 玉ねぎ)

(2) Translate: "I want to buy potatoes, tomatoes, onions, etc."

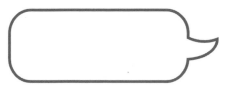

(3) Translate: "I want to buy potatoes, tomatoes, or onions."

(4) Translate: "I think you are very beautiful." (to think 思う; you 君; very とても; beautiful きれい)

(5) Translate: 恵比寿から新宿まで電車で１０分かかる。(恵比寿 Ebisu; 新宿 Shinjuku; 電車 train; 分 minutes; かかる to take)

(6) Translate: "Since I'm tired, I'm going to rest." (to be tired 疲れている; to rest 休む)

(7) Translate: "I don't know if Naoki can speak Spanish or not." (to know 知る; Naoki 直樹; to speak 話す; Spanish スペイン語)

(8) Translate: どうか手を貸してください。(手を貸す to give a hand)

(9) Translate:「七人の侍」って映画は古いね。(七人 seven people; 侍 samurai; 映画 movie; 古い old)

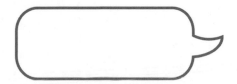

(10) What is the equivalent of って in the previous question? Besides this one, what other constructions are equivalent to って?

— Answers to all the exercises can be found online by following the link on page 7. —

Shopping

After the hard battle fought against particles in the last four lessons, let's relax a little in this chapter while learning a lot of new vocabulary.

🎧 Let's go shopping!

Let's revise some sentences which can be helpful whenever we go shopping.

- 何か探しているんですか？ Are you looking for something? (Lesson 41)
- はい、Xはありますか？ Yes, do you have x?
- いいえ、見ているだけです No, I'm just looking.
- あれを見せてください Could you please show me that?
- これはいくらですか？ How much is this? (Lesson 34)
- お支払いは現金ですか、カードですか？ Will you pay by cash or credit card? (Lesson 41)
- カードでお願いします Credit card. | 現金でお願いします Cash.
- これをお願いします Could I have this, please?

🎧 Buying clothes

Most Japanese words for clothes come from English, because it wasn't until the Meiji Era (1868) that the Japanese began dressing in Western style.

In addition to the traditional clothing words in the table on the facing page you may also come across 帯 *obi* (kimono sash), はかま (a sort of skirt nowadays used almost exclusively in martial arts), 下駄 *geta* (Japanese clogs), 足袋 *tabi* (socks with the big toe separated).

- 自分用の浴衣を探しているんですが
  I'm looking for a yukata for myself. (Lesson 40)
- 女性用のTシャツはありますか？
  Do you have T-shirts for women?
- 日本のサイズがわかりません
  I don't know how sizes in Japan work.

🎧 Shopping	
bag	袋
to bargain	値切る
bill	領収書
cash register	レジ
discount	割引
price tag	値札
bargain	バーゲン
to pay	払う
bargain sale	特売
tax	税
to wrap	包む

- このサイズはいくつですか？ What size is this?
- もう少し安いものがありますか？ Do you have something a little bit cheaper?
- 試着してもいいですか？ Can I try it on? (Lesson 32)

			🎧 Clothes		
belt	ベルト	kimono	着物	suit	スーツ
blouse	ブラウス	pajamas	パジャマ	sweater	セーター
boots	ブーツ	panties	パンティ	swimming costume	水着
bra	ブラジャー	scarf	マフラー	tie	ネクタイ
coat	コート	shirt	シャツ	trousers	ズボン
dress	ドレス	shoes	靴	T-shirt	Tシャツ
gloves	手袋	skirt	スカート	underpants	パンツ
jacket	ジャケット	socks	靴下	underwear	下着
jeans	ジーンズ	stockings	ストッキング	yukata	浴衣

🎧 Buying manga and books

Visiting Japan is an ideal opportunity for manga fans to stock up!

- 「ＧＴＯ」というマンガを探しています I'm looking for a manga called "GTO." (Lesson 41)
- 作者か出版社はわかりますか？ Do you know the author or the publishing company? (Lesson 41)
- このマンガをください I'll take this manga. (Lesson 41)

🎧 Buying souvenirs

To conclude, we will learn how to buy the unavoidable souvenirs and presents.

- この人形は伝統的ですか？ Is this doll a traditional one?
- その急須は壊れやすいから、気をつけてくださいね This teapot is fragile, so please be careful. (Lesson 41)
- プレゼントだから、包んでください It's a present, so could you wrap it up, please? (Lesson 41)
- あのせんべいの賞味期限はいつですか？ When do those rice crackers expire?
- 安いお土産を売っていませんか？ Do you sell cheap souvenirs? (Lesson 40)

Cultural Note: A Passion for Fashion

The term "fashion victim" seems to have been invented specifically to describe Japanese urban youth. Although that's not true, what is true is that if you walk around the 渋谷 **Shibuya** and 原宿 **Harajuku** districts in 東京 **Tōkyō**, or the 梅田 **Umeda** and 心斎橋 **Shinsaibashi** districts in 大阪 **Ōsaka**, you are likely to come across vast numbers of young people who might fit that description.

Japanese urban fashion is eclectic, colorful, sometimes extreme, and sometimes absolutely outlandish. There are times when you feel you really are at one of those flamboyant fashion shows in Paris or Milan: super-short skirts, conspicuous accessories, cowboy hats, spike-heel boots, pink angora sweaters, hair dyed platinum blonde, ridiculously expensive designer handbags, knee-high stockings with sneakers . . . All this and a lot more rules Japanese ファッション, which changes at a hectic pace.

Shinsaibashi: extreme-fashion addicts in their habitat
(Photo: M. Bernabé)

But not everybody can afford to change their wardrobe completely every two or three months. In fact, this represents one of the most urgent problems for urban youth (especially for girls): how to find money to "be fashionable." Not everybody in Japan is rich enough to be able to afford such frantic spending. Therefore, money is obtained via all kinds of scheming: from asking one's parents or simply having an アルバイト (part-time job) in a コンビニ (convenience store), to practically prostituting oneself with the so called 援助交際 **enjo kōsai** (literally, "relationship in exchange of help"), which entails teenage girls going out with middle-aged men (generally, forty or over) in exchange for money. The デート (date) can involve anything: from an innocent afternoon snack or coffee to ending up in bed.

The thing is fashion is like a religion, or rather, pure mimicry: if my neighbor has that Gucci or Cartier handbag, why shouldn't I have it? Thus, it is not in vain that the world's main luxury firms consider 日本 **Nihon** their most important market.

🎧 漫画例 **Manga Examples**

These manga examples illustrate some situations that you might find yourself in while shopping in Japan, along with some useful language.

Manga Example 1: Great bargains

This example gives useful language when looking for a bargain, such as the word 半額 (half price). Also take a look at the pamphlets, which say バーゲン半額 (half-price bargains) and 大安売り *ooyasuu-ri* (special bargain sale). 安売り is a native Japanese word and バーゲン is imported from English: they both mean "bargain." **Note:** ティッシュ are "tissues" and 箱 means "box," so 箱ティッシュ are "tissue boxes." These boxes are, according to Kazue, バカ安. If you remember Lesson 23, バカ is an insult meaning "silly, stupid." バカ安 is literally "foolishly cheap," in other words, "dirt cheap."

J.M. Ken Niimura

Kazue: おおっ箱ティッシュがバカ安！ブラウス半額！？

wow box tissues sp foolish cheap! Blouse half price!?

Wow! Tissues are dirt cheap! And blouses at half price?!

Manga Example 2: 2500 yen altogether

Here we see the clerk giving the customer the total price: the verb しめる (締める), is used here as an adverb (remember verbs in the -*te* form can sometimes function as adverbs, Lesson 22), meaning "altogether." 締める is used to give the final figure after adding up the

Gabriel Luque

total prices. A further example is 学費は締めて２００万円もかかったよ *gakuhi wa shimete 200 man en mo kakatta yo* (School expenses amounted to 2 million yen altogether). Notice the usage of the particle も to emphasize the number (Lesson 37).

Man: しめて２５００円ね

total 2500 yen EP

That's 2500 yen altogether.

Tezuka: に　にせんごひゃく円だー！？

t...two thousand five hundred yen be!?

T . . . two thousand five hundred yeeen?!

Manga Example 3: Brand fever

On page 92 we mentioned the Japanese obsession with luxury designer goods, and this example proves it. The speaker boasts to his friend about having a Louis Vuitton bag which

cost a whopping ２０万円. Since Kojima's second sentence is extremely distorted by his colloquial style of speech, we will transcribe it into "normal" Japanese to analyze it properly: いくらすると思っているの？ The expression いくらする is an alternative way of saying いくらです (How much is it?). It's also worth pointing out the use of the construction と思う (I think), which we studied in the section about quotes on page 81 of Lesson 41.

Kojima: ほら　このバッグなんかヴィトンよ？ヴィトン！
look this bag Vuitton EP? Vuitton!
Look at this handbag. It's a Vuitton, man, a Vuitton!
いくらすっと思ってんのよ　２０万よ？２０万！
how much SBP think Q? EP 20 man EP? 20 man!
How much do you think it costs? 200,000, man, 200,000!

Manga Example 4: To bargain

In Japan bargaining is not paramount, but sometimes, maybe in フリーマーケット (flea markets) or in some electronics stores, you might obtain a discount if you insist a little. The standard expression, which would be ちょっとまけてください (Give me a little discount, please), uses the verb まける (to reduce), which we see in this example in its imperative form, まけろ (Lesson 30). **Notes:** ちょっと means "a little." For obvious reasons,

安い and its opposite 高い *takai* (expensive) are key words when bargaining and when generally buying. Notice って in the sentence: it's a contraction of という (the "definition" usage of と, Lesson 41, page 81).

Kishida: 安くまけろってサインだそうですーっ！
cheap bargain SBP sign be seems be!
It looks like the sign for "give me a discount"!

Manga Example 5: A discount

Often, we will see offers marked with a number plus the word 割引 *waribiki* (discount) or, as in the example, just 割. These are, obviously, discounts—the number indicates the percentage. For example, this 2割 a 20% discount, and 5割 would be a 50% discount (notice how the number is multiplied by ten). You will frequently find labels or signs indicating discounts mainly in supermarkets and boutiques. Many use the formula **X** 割 which we have

just seen, and others use the word 半額 *hangaku*, which we saw in Manga Example 1 and which means "half price." **Note:** The shop assistant is talking about 鯛 *tai* (sea bream). Since the pronunciation of the word 鯛 is the same as the last part of the adjective おめでたい (joyous, happy), in Japan, sea bream is eaten on celebratory occasions.

Man: そいつはオメデタイから…
that TOP *"omedetai" because . . .*
Well, because it's a "joyous bream . . ."

Woman: 2割ほど定価から引いて！
20% approximately price from take out!
(You will) lower the price 20%!

Manga Example 6: The computer?

This example reveals how most computer terms have been introduced into Japanese through English, like almost all languages in the world. Such is the case for the words コンピュータ and インターネット.

The word "computer" curiously has two Japanese names: the "orthodox" コンピュータ and the more cryptic パソコン, a contraction of the word パーソナル・コンピュータ. **Note:** Notice the でも in the example. It's the same usage we saw in Manga Example 7 in Lesson 38.

Kei: ああ…コンピュータ？インターネットでもやる？
oh . . . computer? Internet or something do?
Oh, the computer? Do you want to connect to the Internet or something?

Exercises 練習

1 Translate into English the words 包む, 手袋, ベ
ルト, ソフト, 画集, 水着 and セーター.

2 Translate into Japanese the words "suit," "scarf,"
"discount," "doll," "electronic dictionary," and
"tie."

3 You go into a shop to browse around. What do
you reply if the clerk asks you if you want anything special?

4 You are looking for a book called "Kimono," and
the clerk asks you 何か探しているんですか？
What do you answer?

5 Translate into Japanese the sentence: "Do you
have a size 'small' in pants?"

6 Translate into English: あのマンガとそのビデオ
ゲームをください。

7 You want to buy a video game, but you don't
know whether you will be able to use it in your
country. Ask the clerk.

8 Translate into Japanese: "Since this pottery piece
is fragile, could you wrap it up, please?" (pottery
piece: 陶器)

9 You are at a flea market, and you are interested
in something. Try to start bargaining in Japanese.

10 Give the three ways of saying "at half price"
which we have studied in this lesson.

— **Answers to all the exercises can be found online by following the link on page 7.** —

Suppositions and Conjectures

We know that the Japanese tend to be ambiguous: they prefer hiding behind vagueness and imprecision, as opposed to risking categorical statements. In this lesson we will study the wide variety of expressions for supposition and conjecture.

Maybe, baby . . .

Ambiguity in the Japanese language often causes confusion and misunderstandings. A Japanese person will never say "no" directly; rather, they will let out a rhetorical alternative in the form of "hmm, it might be a little difficult," or "I'd have to say that's not quite possible," which will make a Western mind think "they say it's difficult, but they don't say no, so maybe it could be done," when what the Japanese person really means is no. Let's now look at the Japanese expressions which might be used in such cases.

🎧 I think that と思う

We already saw the this expression in Lesson 41.

- スピーチを始^{はじ}めたいと思^{おも}います (I think) I'd like to start my speech.
- 論文^{ろんぶん}をもう一度^{いちど}書^かいてもらいたいと思^{おも}う I think I'd like you to write the thesis again.

🎧 Perhaps / maybe / might かもしれない (かもしれません)

The phrase かもしれない is used after a verb in its simple form, an *-i* or *-na* adjective, or a noun.

- 彼^{かれ}はスペイン人^{じん}かもしれない He might be Spanish.
- 来年^{らいねん}、日本^{にほん}へ行^いくかもしれませんよ Maybe I'll go to Japan next year.
- このカメラは高^{たか}かったかもしれないな Perhaps this camera was expensive.

🎧 Apparently ようだ・みたいだ

Some of the expressions that follow are similar, and confusing them is easy. We will try to explain clearly, although more often than not the "borders" of their usage are a bit hazy!

The expression よ う だ means "apparently," and is used when the speaker has direct information (either visual or sensory) taken from the speaker's previous knowledge about the subject and his capacity to reason. It is a conjecture with a high degree of certainty. It goes after a verb in its simple form or an *-i* adjective, without adding anything. *-na* adjectives keep な. You must add の between a noun and よ う だ.

- 田中さんは気絶したようだ Apparently, Tanaka has fainted.
  (Because I can see that he is lying on the floor.)
- この店は花屋さんのようだ I'd say that shop is (seems like) a flower shop.
  (Because there are lots of flowers for sale inside.)
- この時計は高いようですね (I'd say) that watch is expensive, isn't it?
  (Because I'm familiar with the brand name.)

よ う だ is really a *-na* adjective (よ う な), so it can also go in the middle of a sentence functioning as "is like." The adverbial form よ う に is also possible. (See also Lesson 54.)

- 徹は F 1 のような車を運転しています Tetsu drives a car that looks like a F1.

よ う だ is usually used in written or formal Japanese. On informal occasions, み た い だ is preferred. This is, theoretically, an equivalent to よ う だ, that is, an expression based on direct information, with a high degree of certainty. However, み た い だ is used on occasions that don't always have a high degree of certainty. It goes after a verb in its simple form, an *-i* or *-na* adjective, or a noun.

- フラン君はひげを生やしたみたいだよ！ It looks like Fran has grown a beard!
- あの公園は静かみたいだ That park looks quiet.

み た い だ is also a *-na* adjective (み た い な) and it works just like よ う だ:

- 徹は F 1 みたいな車を運転しているぞ Tetsu drives a car that looks like a F1.

Probably だろう

だ ろ う is the verb "to be" (で す) in the -ō form (Lesson 34). It is slightly different to other verbs in the -ō form, because it doesn't have the meaning of "let's . . . ," but is used at the end of a sentence and has two different meanings. The first is expressing a pure conjecture (not necessarily based on previous information). It is added after a noun, an *-i* or *-na* adjective, or a verb in its simple form. **Note:** The formal version of だ ろ う is で し ょ う.

- あのパソコンは古いだろう That computer is probably old.
- 正子ちゃんは多分来ないだろうね I suppose Masako (probably) won't come.
- 木村さんの娘さんはきれいでしょう (I imagine) Kimura's daughter is probably beautiful.

The second meaning of だろう is that of a "tag" asking for a reply to the speaker's statement, similar to "isn't it?" or "right?" It's usage is very similar to ね (Lesson 17).

- おい、木村！あんたの娘、きれいだろう？ Hey, Kimura! Your daughter is beautiful, isn't she?

- このケーキはおいしいでしょう？ This cake is delicious, isn't it?

Note: It is worth learning these adverbs which are often used in expressions of supposition: 多分 *tabun* (perhaps), おそらく (probably), もしかすると/もしかして (possibly), どうやら (likely), ひょっとすると (by chance), and きっと (surely).

🎧 Apparently らしい

らしい expresses something the speaker knows because she has heard or read (it repeats information which is not firsthand). It's not as certain as ようだ, or as uncertain as だろう. Add らしい after a noun, an *-i* or *-na* adjective, or a verb in its simple form.

- ドイツ人は頑固らしいよ (From what I've read / heard) Germans are stubborn.
- スミスさんはアメリカに帰らないらしい (Apparently) Mr. Smith will not be going back to the USA.

らしい is also an *-i* adjective meaning "worthy of," "as is expected from," or "becoming," conjugated like any *-i* adjective: Negative: らしくない | Past: らしかった | Past negative: らしくなかった.

- 愛ちゃんは日本人らしいですね Ai is so Japanese-like.
  (Ai is just like how you'd expect a Japanese girl to be.)
- おい、お前！男らしく振る舞え！ Hey, you! Man up! (Act like a man would!)

🎧 From what I've heard そうだ (1)

There are two そうだ expressions. The first is similar to the other expressions we have seen: simply add そうだ to a verb, adjective or noun. But with the second one you must "conjugate" verbs and adjectives.

The first そうだ means exactly the same as らしい: we use it to pass on information the speaker has obtained directly from another source. The differences between そうだ (1)

and らしい are that そうだ (1) is completely based on hearsay, whereas らしい is based on what we've heard, seen, read or reasoned. It goes after a verb in its simple form or an -*i* adjective. だ must be added between そうだ and -*na* adjectives or nouns.

- 宮崎で電車事故があったそうだ (I've heard / read that) in Miyazaki there was a train accident.
- 学校の制服は高かったそうだ (From what I heard) the school uniform was expensive.
- ジムさんは先生だそうですね (From what I've been told) Jim is a teacher, isn't he?

🎧 Looks or seems そうだ(2)

The second そうだ has nothing to do with the first one. It expresses conjecture about the state of something, based on what the speaker sees or has seen. そうだ (2) isn't used in the past because it is only used when talking about things that are probably true in the present or might be true in a foreseeable future. Words conjugated with そうだ (2)

Inflections for そうだ (2)		
Verbs	〜ます + そう	倒れる ⇒ 倒れます ⇒ 倒れ ⇒ 倒れそうだ To fall ⇒ it looks like it's falling (it's about to fall)
-*i* adj.	〜い + そう	寒い ⇒ 寒 ⇒ 寒そうだ cold ⇒ it looks like it's cold
-*na* adj.	〜な + そう	元気な ⇒ 元気 ⇒ 元気そうだ cheerful ⇒ he looks cheerful

become -*na* adjectives and function as such. そうだ (2) is not used with nouns. Study the usages shown in the table above.

- あのバイクはとても古そうだ That motorcycle looks very old.
- この仕事は君に出来そうだと思う I think you can (probably) do that job.
- 今日は元気そうな顔をしているね You look cheerful today, don't you?

When used with verbs, そうだ (2) sometimes has the connotation of "to be about to":

- 雪が降りそうですね It looks like it's about to snow, doesn't it?
- 父は怒りそうになった My father looked like he was going to get angry.

🎧 Supposed to はずだ and にちがいない

はずだ is used to express that the speaker hopes that what he expects is real. It is equivalent to "supposed to . . ." it goes after a verb in its simple form or an -*i* adjective, without adding anything. -*na* adjectives keep な. You must add の between a noun and はずだ.

- ベロニカさんは家にいるはずだ (I imagine) Veronica is supposed to be home.
- 彼女は歌が上手なはずです (I'm almost sure) she is supposed to sing very well.

The expression にちがいない expresses something which is "without doubt." We add nothing but にちがいない after a noun, an *-i* or *-na* adjective, or verb in its simple form.

• ベロニカさんは家にいるにちがいない There is no doubt Veronica is home.
• 彼女は歌が上手にちがいありません She undoubtedly sings very well.

Finally, here is a summary table of the whole lesson, with the formal versions of each one of the expressions, in brackets.

🎧 Suppositions: General summary table		
かもしれない	Pure supposition	その男は日本人かもしれない （かもしれません） That man might be Japanese (but I'm not sure)
ようだ	Supposition based on something directly perceived and qualified by the speaker's reason or knowledge	その男は日本人のようだ （のようです） (Considering what I see now and what I knew before about the Japanese in general) that man seems to be Japanese
みたい	Informal version of ようだ	その男は日本人みたい （みたいです） (Considering what I see now and what I knew before about the Japanese in general) that man seems to be Japanese
だろう	Pure supposition (not necessarily based on something)	その男は日本人だろう （でしょう） That man is probably Japanese
らしい	Supposition based on something the speaker has heard, seen, or read	その男は日本人らしい （らしいです） (From what I've heard) that man might be Japanese
らしい (2)	Adjective indicating "worthy of" or "to be expected of"	その男は日本人らしくない （らしくありません） That man doesn't behave like a Japanese (although he probably is)
そうだ	Similar to らしい. Supposition based on something read or heard	その男は日本人だそうだ （だそうです） (From what I've heard) that man might be Japanese
そうだ (2)	Supposition based on what the speaker sees or feels, but with medium probability	その男は日本語を話しそうだ （話しそうです） That man (it looks to me) probably speaks Japanese
はずだ	Supposition the speaker almost considers fact	その男は日本人のはずだ （のはずです） That man is (supposed to be) Japanese
にちがいない	Very high probability, almost considered as a fact: "there is no doubt"	その男は日本人にちがいない （にちがいありません） That man is undoubtedly Japanese

男 *otoko* man; 日本人 *nihonjin* Japanese (person); 日本語 *nihongo* Japanese (language); 話す *hanasu* to speak

🎧 漫画例　Manga Examples

You might be feeling a little overwhelmed after being exposed to such a massive amount of suppositions and conjectures! Let's take a look now at some examples to help clarify the fine lines between the types of conjectures we have studied.

Manga Example 1: A typical greeting

Our first example uses そうだ (2) to make a conjecture based on visual information. The characteristic of そうだ (2) is that it inflects verbs and adjectives. Here the -*na* adjective 元気な (healthy, cheerful) becomes 元気そうな (look healthy or cheerful).

The expression in this example, is often used to greet someone you haven't seen for a long time. より means "more than" and we will have a better look at in Lesson 54. The literal translation of this expression is "You look well and there's nothing better than that."

Note: The -*sō* form of the negative ない is なさそう. The negative (of adjectives, not verbs) is formed replacing the い in "normal" negatives (Lessons 13 and 14) with 〜さそ:

- -*i* adj.: 青い *aoi* | neg: 青くない | *sō* neg: 青くなさそう (it doesn't look blue).
- -*na* adj.: 元気な | neg: 元気ではない | *sō* neg: 元気ではなさそう (it doesn't look cheerful).

There are a couple of exceptions: かわいそう and えらそう. They don't mean "it looks cute" (from かわいい, cute) or "it looks important" (from えらい, important), but "pitiful" and "self-important," respectively. Also note that the *sō* form of いい (good) is よさそう (looks good).

Yajirō:　お元気そうで何よりです先生。

(honorific) cheerful (look) what more be teacher

I'm glad to see you (look like you) are well, teacher.

Manga Example 2: A colloquial "perhaps"

Here we see the most colloquial usage of かもしれない (perhaps, maybe, might), shortened to a simple かも which is often used by young people. **Note:** 出ちゃう is the colloquial contraction of 出てしまう (Lesson 35), which literally means "something comes out (and then one might regret it)." The と is used to indicate the conditional.

Gabriel Luque

Sawada: 早くしないと死人が出ちゃうかもよ | クス

quickly do (conditional) dead SP come out perhaps EP? | (coy snicker)

If you don't hurry up, someone might end up dying. | He-he . . .

Manga Example 3: Usage of *yō da* for supposition

As we know, ようだ often appears at the end of a sentence. Here, since what comes before ようだ is いねぇ, a vulgar and rough contraction of いない (there isn't), we don't add anything between it and ようだ. The phrase ようだ means "apparently," and is used when the speaker makes a conjecture based on what they see and on what they already know

J.M. Ken Niimura

about the situation. Thus, there's a high probability that the conjecture is close to the truth. Here, the character could have used みたいだ instead, a more colloquial expression with a similar meaning. **Note:** As in Example 1, we have here a より (more than), which we will study in Lesson 54.

Matsuda: ここに オレより強い力をもった人間はいねぇようだ

here PP I more than strong strength DOP have human TOP no there is looks like

It appears that there's no one here stronger than me.

Manga Example 4: *Hazu* for almost-certain conjecture

We saw on page 100 that はずだ is almost a statement disguised as a conjecture. As we see in the example, the character uses はずだ to suppose something which is almost assumed as true. This expression is very common in Japanese. **Note:** There are two ways to express the negative of はずだ. The first, as here, is to conjugate the verb in the negative (そんな人間じゃないはずだ). For the second, you negate the だ ending: そんな人間のはずでは(じゃ)ない.

J.M. Ken Niimura

Takada: 田辺(たなべ)さん…あなたはそんな人間(にんげん)じゃないはずだ…

Tanabe SUF *. . . you* TOP *such human no be look like*

Mr. Tanabe . . . You're not supposed to be that type of person.

Manga Example 5: Expressing "-ish" with *ppoi*

Studio Kōsen

Generally, the expression っぽい after an adjective means "looks . . ." (赤っぽい *akappoi*, "reddish"; まじめっぽい "looks serious"), and after verbs like 怒る *okoru* (to get angry) or 忘れる *wasureru* (to forget) it's more or less like our "-ish" or "-ful" (怒りっぽい, "peevish"; 忘れっぽい, "forgetful"). Traditionally, っぽい has essentially negative connotations. However, there is a growing tendency among the young to use it with non-negative connotations, as in this example. Use the expression by adding っぽい to the verb/adj. root:

- 忘れる ⇒ 忘れ ⇒ 忘れっぽい (forgetful)
- *-i* adj.: remove い and add っぽい: 安い *yasui* ⇒ 安っぽい (cheap looking)
- *-na* adj.: remove な and add っぽい: 元気な *genki-na* ⇒ 元気っぽい (looks well).

Mayeen: 競争(きょうそう)でもしてるのかな？ Emi: なんかかーちゃんとアニキはマジっぽいな…

competition or do Q? EP?   *I don't know mom* CP *brother* TOP *seriously (look)* EP

They're competing?   I'd say mom and my brother are serious . . .

Manga Example 6: *Mitai-na* as a comparative

The expressions ような, みたいな and そうな meaning "to be like . . ." can not only go at the end of the sentence, but also in the middle, as they are really *-na* adjectives. We will study the comparative form in Lesson 54, but here we have a good example. Placing みたいな after あたし, we obtain あたしみたいな and then あたしみたいな女. Regarding verbs and adjectives inflected in the そうだ (2) form, they become normal *-na* adjectives which work like this: 元気な *genki-na* (cheerful) ⇒ 元気そうな (looks cheerful)

⇒ 元気そうな男 *genkisō-na otoko* (cheerful looking man) | 高い *takai* (expensive) ⇒高そうな (looks expensive) ⇒高そうな本 *takasō-na hon* (expensive looking book).

Ami: あたしみたいな女をなぜ守るの！？

I like woman DOP *why protect* Q*?!?*

Why are you protecting a woman like me?!

Manga Example 7: As is expected . . .

Finally, here is an example of らしい as an *-i* adjective. As we have seen, when らしい functions as an adjective it has the meaning of "as is expected" or "worthy of." Here, we

have 男らしい, but here らしい has been transformed into an adverb, 男らしく (manly). らしい can also go in the negative (男らしくない, not manly), in the past (男らしかった, was manly), and in the past negative (男らしくなかった, was not manly). **Note:** We already saw the imperative 〜たまえ in Lesson 30. It is used by someone who is or feels superior to the person they are talking to. It is quite authoritarian.

Nobuhito: マコトくん　もっと男らしく入りたまえ

Makoto SUF *more man like come in*

Makoto, you must come in more like a man.

Exercises 練習

1. Use かもしれない to give a connotation of doubt to the sentence: ジョンさんは 独身 です。(ジョン John; 独身 single)

2. What does the expression ようだ mean, and when do we use it? Give an example. Is there an equivalent for it?

3. Translate, using だろう: "I suppose it will rain tomorrow." (tomorrow 明日; to rain 雨が降る)

4. Translate: 斉藤さんはとても金持ちだろう？
（斉藤 Saito; とても very; 金持ち rich)

5. Translate: "(I've heard / read that) apparently, the director quit." (director 社長; to quit 辞める)

6. Is the sentence 美穂ちゃんは 学生 そうだ correct? Why? Which of the two usages of そうだ is it?
（美穂 Miho; 学生 student)

7. Translate: "There is no doubt that Akiko has a boyfriend." (Akiko 晶子; boyfriend 彼氏)

8. Translate: あの 女 の子はかわいそうですね。
（女の子 girl)

9. Translate: "This tempura doesn't look good."
(tempura 天ぷら; good おいしい)

10. Translate: 茂夫くんは黒っぽい服を着ている。
（茂夫 Shigeo; 黒い black; 服 clothes; 着る to wear)

— **Answers to all the exercises can be found online by following the link on page 7.** —

Transitive and Intransitive Verbs

Let's begin to fine-tune our Japanese by studying transitive and intransitive verbs. This lesson will help you learn a large number of verb pairs.

🎧 What are transitive and intransitive verbs?

A transitive verb takes a direct object, and an intransitive one doesn't. As a simple example, "to remove," "to put" or "to take out" are transitive, and "to arrive," "to swim" or "to run away" are intransitive: one can remove "something" but can't swim "something."

Japanese also has transitive and intransitive verbs, for example, 殺す **korosu** (to kill) is transitive, while 死ぬ **shinu** (to die) is intransitive. The peculiarity in Japanese are the "pairs" of transitive-intransitive verbs. Sometimes, there are two similar but essentially different verbs for one type of action, a transitive one (which needs a direct object), and an intransitive one (without a direct object). For example, take a look at the pair 始める **hajimeru** and 始まる **hajimaru**. Both mean "to begin" but the first is transitive and the second isn't. With the first, a subject needs to perform the action, whereas with the second, the action is performed "by itself." Look at the examples:

- 香里さんは試験を始めた Kaori began the exam.
- ６時に試験が始まる The exam begins at six.

Look at the basic structure, where Y performs the action and X receives the action:

Transitive verb: Y が X を V trans. 香里が試験を始める Kaori begins the exam.

Intransitive verb: X が V intrans. 試験が始まる The exam begins.

Some recommendations

There is no easy way to learn how to use the transitive-intransitive pairs of verbs except to learn them by heart, using the table on page 109 to help you. We have divided the verbs according to the changes they undergo when changing from intransitive into transitive (some change from -**aru** to -**eru**, others from -**reru** to -**su**, etc.)

You will see the kanji reading rarely varies: only the ending changes. Three exceptions are 消える **kieru** (to be put out, to disappear) and 消す **kesu** (to put out, to erase); 出る **deru** (to go out) and 出す **dasu** (to take out); 入る **hairu** (to go in) and 入れる **ireru** (to put in). Often, the meaning of each pair of verbs is identical, but when translating here we use the passive form ("the door is opened," "the child is found," "the fire is put out"). This is a trick to memorize and better understand how these verbs work.

🎧 聞こえる and 見える

In Lesson 32 in Volume 1, we saw that the verbs 聞こえる *kikoeru* (to hear) and 見える *mieru* (to see) are different to 聞く *kiku* (to hear) and 見る *miru* (to see): the former indicate seeing or hearing something unconsciously or passively, while the latter indicate seeing or hearing something because that is what one wants to do. Indeed, they are two pairs of transitive-intransitive verbs: 聞こえる and 見える are intransitive, whereas 聞く and 見る are transitive:

- 波の音が聞こえる You can hear the sound of the waves. (intransitive)
- 純子さんは波の音を聞いている Junko is listening to the sound of the waves. (transitive)
- ここからは富士山が見える You can see Mount Fuji from here. (intransitive)
- 私は富士山を見るのは初めてです This is the first time I've seen Mount Fuji. (transitive)

🎧 More examples

Let's study a few examples with some of the pairs of verbs from the table opposite:

- 人々が会場に集まった People gathered in the hall. (intransitive)
- 僕は書類を全部集めました I gathered all the documents. (transitive)
- 私の家が燃えました My house was burnt down. (intransitive)
- その葉っぱを燃やしてください Burn those leaves, please. (transitive)
- マイクはレストランに入りました Mike went into the restaurant. (intransitive)
- ママは卵を冷蔵庫に入れた Mom put the eggs in the fridge. (transitive)

Notice that often when we translate intransitive sentences, we use the passive form.

A final example is the pair 落ちる *ochiru* (to fall) and 落とす *otosu* (to drop). If you drop a vase and use 落ちる, you are saying the vase fell; if you use 落とす, you are saying you let the vase drop. This shows the difference between transitive and intransitive verbs.

🎧 Compound verbs

Compound verbs in Japanese are formed with the root of the verb (the -*masu* form without the final ます), plus the appropriate ending. The ending やすい means "easy to . . ."

分かる (to understand) ⇒ -*masu* form: 分かります ⇒ Root: 分かり ⇒ We add 〜やすい: 分かりやすい (easy to understand).

🎧 Pairs of transitive and intransitive verbs

Intransitive		Transitive		Intransitive		Transitive	
-aru		**-eru**		残る (のこる)	to be left	残す (のこす)	to leave
上がる (あがる)	to rise	上げる (あげる)	to raise	回る (まわる)	to turn round	回す (まわす)	to turn
集まる (あつまる)	to be gathered	集める (あつめる)	to gather	戻る (もどる)	to go back	戻す (もどす)	to give back
終わる (おわる)	to end	終える (おえる)	to finish	**-eru**		**-asu**	
変わる (かわる)	to change	変える (かえる)	to change	遅れる (おくれる)	to be late	遅らす (おくらす)	to make late
決まる (きまる)	to be decided	決める (きめる)	to decide	逃げる (にげる)	to escape	逃がす (にがす)	to let escape
下がる (さがる)	to go down	下げる (さげる)	to lower	冷える (ひえる)	to get cold	冷やす (ひやす)	to cool
閉まる (しまる)	to be closed	閉める (しめる)	to close	増える (ふえる)	to be increased	増やす (ふやす)	to increase
かかる	to be hung	かける	to hang	燃える (もえる)	to be on fire	燃やす (もやす)	to burn
静まる (しずまる)	to calm down	静める (しずめる)	to calm	**-u**		**-asu**	
高まる (たかまる)	to rise	高める (たかめる)	to raise	動く (うごく)	to move	動かす (うごかす)	to move
助かる (たすかる)	to be saved	助ける (たすける)	to save	飛ぶ (とぶ)	to fly	飛ばす (とばす)	to make fly
捕まる (つかまる)	to be caught	捕まえる (つかまえる)	to catch	泣く (なく)	to cry	泣かす (なかす)	to make cry
伝わる (つたわる)	to be transmitted	伝える (つたえる)	to convey	**-u**		**-eru**	
止まる (とまる)	to stop	止める (とめる)	to stop	開く (あく)	to be open	開ける (あける)	to open
始まる (はじまる)	to begin	始める (はじめる)	to begin	片付く (かたづく)	to be tidy	片付ける (かたづける)	to tidy up
曲がる (まがる)	to be bent	曲げる (まげる)	to bend	育つ (そだつ)	to grow up	育てる (そだてる)	to bring up
見つかる (みつかる)	to be found	見つける (みつける)	to find	立つ (たつ)	to stand	立てる (たてる)	to erect
-reru		**-su**		付く (つく)	to stick to	付ける (つける)	to attach
現れる (あらわれる)	to appear	現す (あらわす)	to show	続く (つづく)	to continue	続ける (つづける)	to continue
壊れる (こわれる)	to be broken	壊す (こわす)	to break	届く (とどく)	to arrive	届ける (とどける)	to deliver
離れる (はなれる)	to separate	離す (はなす)	to separate	**Other verbs**			
倒れる (たおれる)	to fall	倒す (たおす)	to throw down	生まれる (うまれる)	to be born	生む (うむ)	to give birth
汚れる (よごれる)	to be stained	汚す (よごす)	to stain	起きる (おきる)	to get up	起こす (おこす)	to raise
-reru		**-ru**		落ちる (おちる)	to fall	落とす (おとす)	to drop
売れる (うれる)	to sell	売る (うる)	to sell	降りる (おりる)	to get off	降ろす (おろす)	to drop off
折れる (おれる)	to be folded	折る (おる)	to fold	下りる (おりる)	to get down	下ろす (おろす)	to take down
割れる (われる)	to be broken	割る (わる)	to break	消える (きえる)	to be put out	消す (けす)	to put out
-ru		**-su**		聞こえる (きこえる)	to be heard	聞く (きく)	to hear
写る (うつる)	to be reflected	写す (うつす)	to reflect	出る (でる)	to go out	出す (だす)	to take out
返る (かえる)	to return	返す (かえす)	to give back	脱げる (ぬげる)	to come off	脱ぐ (ぬぐ)	to take off
帰る (かえる)	to go back	帰す (かえす)	to let go back	乗る (のる)	to ride in	乗せる (のせる)	to carry
通る (とおる)	to pass	通す (とおす)	to pass	入る (はいる)	to go in	入れる (いれる)	to put in
直る (なおる)	to be mended	直す (なおす)	to correct	見える (みえる)	to be seen	見る (みる)	to see
治る (なおる)	to recover	治す (なおす)	to cure	分かれる (わかれる)	to be divided	分ける (わける)	to divide

汚れる (to be stained) ⇒ *-masu* form: 汚れます ⇒ Root: 汚れ ⇒ We add 〜やすい: 汚れやすい (easily stained).

- 先生の授業は分かりやすいです The professor's classes are easy to understand.
- この服はとても汚れやすいね These clothes are very easily soiled, aren't they?

🎧 Easy to and hard to

The endings 〜やすい (easy to) and 〜にくい (hard to) work like *-i* adjectives.

- この音楽は聞きにくい This music is hard to listen to.
- あのマンガはとても読みやすかったです That manga was very easy to read.
- 日本は住みにくくない国だ Japan is a country where it isn't hard to live.

🎧 Start doing, finish doing and keep on doing

We can also add 〜始める *hajimeru* (start doing), 〜終わる *owaru* (finish doing), and 〜続く *tsuzuku* (keep on doing) to a verb root. The resultant verb works like any other verb: you can conjugate it in the *-te, -ō, -tai,* and many other forms.

- 先生は急に話し始めました The teacher suddenly started talking.
- レポートを書き終わってください Finish writing that report, please.
- 彼は来ないから、飲み続けよう！ Since he's not coming, let's keep on drinking!

Other auxiliary verbs for creating compounds

Other auxiliary verbs are 〜終わる and 〜続ける as shown in the table below.

🎧 Compound verbs with 食べる (*taberu*, to eat)		
〜やすい	easy to . . .	食べやすい easy to eat
〜にくい	hard to . . .	食べにくい hard to eat
〜始める	to start doing . . .	食べ始める to start eating
〜終わる	to finish doing . . .	食べ終わる to finish eating
〜続ける	to keep on doing . . .	食べ続ける to keep on eating
〜かける	nearly, half (intrans.)	食べかける to leave something half-eaten

🎧 漫画例 Manga Examples

Transitive and intransitive verbs can be difficult to master perfectly. If you make mistakes, keep on trying, and learn from your errors: this is the only way to improve.

Manga Example 1: A pair of transitive-intransitive verbs

Let's look at the verb pair 出る **deru** and 出す **dasu**. The transitive verb is 出す (to take out) and requires a subject to perform the action (in this case the subject is "the vegetables"), and a direct object, which receives the action (in this case, 甘味). The intransitive verb 出る only needs a subject, 風味, and there is no direct object. Notice another transitive verb, 入れる **ireru** (to put in). The subject is most likely "I," and the direct object is 砂糖. The intransitive version of 入れる is 入る **hairu** (to go in). 私が入る **Watashi ga hairu** means "I go in." You should study 出る and 出す and 入る and 入れる carefully.

Studio Kōsen

Yōichi: ただの砂糖を入れるんじゃ風味が出ない…

normal POP *sugar* DOP *put in then flavor* SP *go out . . .*

Adding normal sugar won't bring out the flavor . . .

野菜を使ってかくし味の甘味を出してやるんだ…！

vegetables DOP *use hidden flavor* POP *sweetness* DOP *take out do . . . !*

You must use vegetables to bring out the sweet hidden flavor!

Manga Example 2: "To decide," transitive version

The Japanese word for transitive verb is 他動詞 *tadōshi* (他, "other"; 動詞, "verb"), "verb whose action is performed by another subject." The transitive verb in this example, 決める, means "to decide." As a transitive verb, it requires "another" subject (it is omitted here, but it would be "I") to perform the action of the verb on a direct object

(in this case, 名前). Therefore, 私は名前を決める means "I decide the name." **Note:** In spoken Japanese, certain particles are sometimes left out, を in this case (名前を決める). Notice also the まだ, which we saw in Lesson 40.

Gabriel Luque

Jirō:　そういえば…名前まだ決めてなかったな…

that say . . . name still decide EP . . .

Speaking of which . . . I still haven't decided the name . . .

Manga Example 3: "To be decided," intransitive version

The Japanese for intransitive verb is 自動詞 *jidōshi* (自, "oneself"; 動詞, "verb"), "verb whose action is performed by oneself." We saw the transitive verb 決める in the previous example, and we will now study its intransitive partner, 決まる which means "to be decided." Here the action is performed by "oneself," there is no direct object. In the example, the subject (the one performing the action), is left out, but it could be 試合が決まる *shiai ga kimaru* (the match will be decided). In English we often use the passive form to translate intransitive verbs. **Note:** The counter used to count shots, 本, is usually used to count long and thin things, such as pencils, trees, toothpicks, etc. (Lesson 25).

Xian Nu Studio

Hideki:　あと一本のドライブシュートできまるんだ！

After one (counter)! POP drive shoot IP can be!

This will be decided with one more drive shoot!

Manga Example 4: Something "gets cold" (intransitive)

The verb 冷える is an intransitive verb whose action is performed by "itself." The wind (風) cools down (冷える) by itself, no one cools it down. If we wanted to say "God cools down the wind," we would use 冷やす the transitive verb: 神様は風を冷やす**kamisama wa kaze o hiyasu**, as it would be someone else (神様) doing the cooling down. **Note:** Take a moment to review the other grammatical structures in this sentence. We have a formal **-ō** form (帰りましょう, Lesson 34), a ～てくる construction (Lesson 35), and even a conjecture with ～ようだ (Lesson 43).

Xian Nu Studio

Yoneda: 帰りましょう…風が冷えてきたようだ

go back . . . wind SP cool down come looks like

Let's go back . . . It looks like the wind has cooled down.

Manga Example 5: Someone "conveys" something (transitive)

J.M. Ken Niimura

The verb 伝える in this sentence is transitive. Its intransitive counterpart is 伝わる. Here, the speaker asks someone to convey a message to another person. A summary of the sentence, would be something like あなたはメッセージを伝える (you convey the message). But if the message were to be conveyed by itself, we would use the intransitive form: メッセージが伝わる (the message is transmitted). **Notes:** ～てくれ is the imperative form of ～てくれる (somebody else does you a favor, Lesson 45). Notice the second と: it is the "quote" usage that we studied on page 81, Lesson 41).

Sano: 女房と娘に…「パパは最後までがんばった」と伝えてくれ

wife CP daughter IOP . . . "dad TOP end until hold out" SBP convey (imperative)

Tell my wife and my daughter . . . that, "dad held out till the end."

Manga Example 6: An intransitive compound verb

In this example we have another intransitive verb, 燃える. If there was a subject responsible for the fire (let's say a 泥棒 *dorobō*, "thief"), we would have to use 燃やす, its transitive counterpart: 泥棒が倉を燃やす.

Notice also how the compound verb 燃え出す *moedasu* has been formed. We have already seen that adding 〜出す to a verb means "begin to" or "burst into" (with the connotation of violence or speed). 燃え出す means "begin to burn (quickly, suddenly)."

Man: きてくれーっ 倉が燃えだしたぁっ
come (imperative) warehouse SP *burn (go out)*
Come! The warehouse is burning!

Manga Example 7: More compounds

Here the ending 〜がたい means something like 〜にくい (hard to . . .), but is more formal and stronger. Compound verbs with 〜がたい are formed in the same way as 〜にくい and 〜やすい: add 〜がたいto the root of the verb (*-masu* form without ます), for example: 許す *yurusu* (to forgive) ⇒ *-masu* form: 許します ⇒ remove ます ⇒ 許し ⇒ add 〜がたい: 許しがたい (hard to forgive). The resultant verb functions like an *-i* adjective. There are a few more endings or auxiliary verbs, such as 〜合う *au* (mutually) or 〜きる (to completely finish). However, for the moment, those we have studied will be sufficient.

Nishida: だから差別は無くしがたい
therefore discrimination TOP *lose (hard to)*
I'm telling you discrimination is hard to eradicate.

Exercises 練習

(1) Which of these verbs are transitive and which intransitive? 変える, 続く, 通す, 壊れる, 開く, 残る.

(2) Give the transitive or intransitive counterparts (depending on each case) of the verbs in the previous question.

(3) What are the intransitive counterparts of the transitive verbs 入れる, 出す, 助ける and 聞く?

(4) Translate: "Reiko turned the TV off." (Reiko 礼子 ; TV テレビ)

(5) Translate: "Suddenly, the light went off." (suddenly 突然 ; light 電気)

(6) Is this sentence correct? 窓が閉めました。 Why/why not? (窓 window)

(7) Translate: 鳥の声が庭から聞こえましたよ。 (鳥 bird; 声 voice; 庭 garden)

(8) Translate: "This lesson is hard to understand" using a compound verb. (lesson 課 ; to understand 分かる)

(9) Translate: 中国語を勉強し始めたいです。 (中国語 Chinese (language); 勉強する to study)

(10) Form two sentences, one using 決める and the other using 決まる.

— **Answers to all the exercises can be found online by following the link on page 7.** —

Lesson 45 • 第 45 課

To Give and to Receive

In Lesson 28 we looked at the verbs meaning to give and to receive: あげる, もらう and くれる. At that time we just skimmed through them, because these are essential verbs in Japanese and it was advisable for you to know about them at a relatively early stage in your learning. Now the time has come to study them in depth.

The concept of *uchi* and *soto*

We will start by explaining two characteristically Japanese concepts: 内 **uchi** (inside) and 外 **soto** (outside). The Japanese distinguish between what is "inside" their group (内) and what is "outside" it (外), and this distinction is present in all aspects of everyday life:

Everyday life:	内: me, my closest family.
	外: any other person (not-so-close family is closer to 内).
School:	内: me, my classmates, my course tutor, my club.
	外: any other teacher, people from other classes, clubs, and schools.
Work:	内: me, my workmates (including my bosses).
	外: anybody belonging to another company, a client or a supplier.

There are gradations: one can get closer to the 内 group of another person in a deep, lasting relationship: the deeper the relationship, the closer to 内. For example, a boy and a girl meet (a completely 外 relationship), become friends (still 外 to each other, but less so), fall in love and start dating (now they are more **uchi** than 外) and finally marry (100% 内).

The point of view is essential: which part of the sentence carries the most weight, who is speaking, and who performs a certain action. It is important that all these aspects are clear.

🎧 The verb あげる

Let's look at the usage of the three verbs expressing relationships of "giving" and "receiving," あげる, もらう and くれる.

In the diagram, right, the bottom arrow shows the 内 – 外 relationship. The more to the left, the more 内 the character is; the more to the right, the more

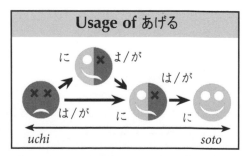

Usage of あげる

外. A smiling face shows the character "receives" something. A surly face means the character "gives" something (the half-half faces indicate they are both receiving and giving). Dark faces represent the main point of view (the character responsible for the action). The particles used by each character are also shown. The verb あげる is used to mean "give."

- 私は友達に薬をあげる I give my friend some medicine.
- 妻は井口さんにサーカスの切符をあげた My wife gave Mr. Iguchi a ticket for the circus.
- 警察官はおじいさんに新聞をあげた The policeman gave the old man a newspaper.
- 先生は来客にお土産をあげました The teacher gave the visitor a souvenir.

Note: The verb あげる is <u>never</u> used in sentences such as "Hanako gave me (me or someone in the 内 group) a flower." In this case, we use the verb くれる.

🎧 The verb もらう

もらう means "to receive," used to express: "I or someone in the 内 group receives something." **Note:** The giver can be marked by either に or から.

- 私は息子にケーキをもらう I receive a cake from my son.
- 僕は同僚にいいアドバイスをもらった I received a good piece of advice from a colleague.
- 娘は友達からプレゼントをもらいました My daughter received a present from a friend.
- 高い時計をもらって、とてもうれしい I received an expensive watch and I'm happy.

🎧 The verb くれる

The verb くれる is like a mixture of あげる and もらう, and is hard to master if we are not sure who is performing the action or of the 内 – 外 relationship. くれる is used when the "giver" is someone 外 (he can also be 内, but it is not common), and the "receiver" must be someone in the 内 group. The point of view is placed on the <u>giver</u>, never on the receiver. The sentence "Hanako gave me a flower" must, then, use く

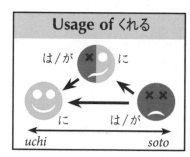

れる. Study the diagram to understand this better: "I" (内) am the smiling light gray face on the left, and "Hanako" (外) is the surly dark gray face on the right.

- 花子は私に花をくれた Hanako gave me a flower | I received a flower from Hanako.
- 友達は娘にアドバイスをくれた A friend gave my daughter some advice.
- ジョンは（私に）その本をくれると思うよ I think John will give me that book.
- 彼はいい人だから、お金をくれた As he is a good person, he gave me (or 内) some money.

🎧 The concept of *tate*

Japanese society is divided along a vertical axis called 縦 *tate*. There are those in superior positions to oneself, those in equivalent positions and those in inferior positions. This is also reflected in language. The verbs あげる, くれる and もらう have "families" of verbs whose usage depends on these distinctions (see diagrams, below). For example, we use あげる when we give something to somebody in the same position as us, but if their position is superior, we use さしあげる. If we are giving something to someone in an inferior position we use やる. The verbs もらう and くれる have no "inferior" versions, only neutral and superior: いただく and くださる, respectively. Let's look at some examples:

- 私は先生にプレゼントをさしあげたい I want to give the teacher a present.
- 僕は弟にお金をやった I gave my younger brother some money.
- 彼は犬におもちゃをやった He gave the dog a toy.
- 私は井上さんに１万円をいただいた I received 10,000 yen from Mr. Inoue.
- 井上さんは私に１万円をくださった Mr. Inoue gave me 10,000 yen.
- お客様は微笑みをくださいました The client gave (offered) me a smile.

Note: The Japanese don't usually show "superiority" to anybody, so the やる is limited to family (sentence 2), close friends, or animals (sentence 3). Don't use it; it sounds arrogant.

🎧 あげる, もらう and くれる as auxiliary verbs

These verbs can function as auxiliary verbs following verbs in the *-te* form. For example, 私は花子に花を買ってあげた *watashi wa Hanako ni hana o katte ageta* literally means "I bought a flower for Hanako" (and, doing so, I did her a favor). The usage of あげる, くれる and もらう (and their respective "families") as auxiliary verbs is identical to their usage as main verbs (so the previous explanatory diagrams are valid here), and they add the connotations of "doing/being done a favor" to sentences. These constructions are common so it is advisable to learn their usage well.

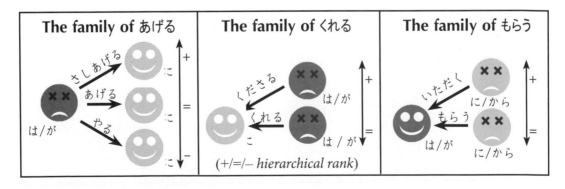

- 友達に英語を教えてあげたい I want to teach my friend English.
- 私は妹にケーキを焼いてやる I bake a cake for my younger sister.
- 先生に本を貸してさしあげました I lent my teacher a book.
- りんごをもらってきた I went (and came back) to receive some apples.
- 先生は娘に親切してくださっています The teacher is kind to my daughter.
- 友達は彼女にマンガを買ってくれた My friend bought my girlfriend a comic.
- 説明していただきたいんですけど I'd like you to explain this (to me)

🎧 Way of: 〜方

Let's look at how to form nouns from verbs meaning "way of . . . ing." Simply add 〜方 **kata** to the root of the verb (-*masu* form without the final ます). For example: 書く **kaku** (to write) ⇒ -*masu* form: 書きます ⇒ root: 書き ⇒ add 〜方: 書き方 (way of writing).

With suru verbs, place の between the noun and the する verb :洗濯のし方.

- 焼きそばの作り方は簡単です (The way of) making yakisoba is very simple.
- この漢字の書き方を忘れた I have forgotten how (the way) to write this kanji.
- 洗濯のし方を教えてください Please teach me (the way) to do the washing.

🎧 Not much: あまり

The adverb あまり means "not much," used with verbs and adjectives in the negative. Sometimes, あまり, when adding に, is used with non-negative verbs and adjectives, and it then means "so much" or "very much." See the last two examples directly below.

- サラは日本語があまり上手ではない Sarah is not very good at Japanese.
- 寿司はあまり好きじゃない I don't like sushi much.
- 今日はあまり歌いたくない Today, I don't feel very much like singing.
- あまりに眠かったので授業で寝てしまった I was so tired I fell asleep in class.
- あまりに失礼だったから殴ってしまった He was so rude, I hit (punched) him.

Let's also look here at the use of the adverb とても, meaning "very."

- ダンは日本語がとても上手です Dan is very good at Japanese.

Pay attention to the distinction between とても (very) and たくさん (a lot).

- 漢字はとても難しいです Kanji are very difficult.
- 漢字はたくさんあります There are a lot of kanji.

🎧 漫画例 Manga Examples

We hope this lesson has helped you start mastering the verbs of giving and receiving. Let's look at a few manga examples to help you remember these new concepts.

Manga Example 1: The verb *ageru*

As you know あげる is used to indicate "give." Be careful, because when someone gives something to somebody in the ***uchi*** group we must use くれる and not あげる. In all other cases, we use あげる.

Here, Kani is going to give Kudō a present. The point of view is of the speaker himself, who is also the performer of the action of giving: therefore, あげる is used. Notice how the verbs to give and to receive are normal verbs, and conjugated as such. Here, あげる is in the *-te* form with the ～しまう construction (Lesson 35), indicating "to finish doing something completely." ～しまう is conjugated in the *-ō* form (Lesson 34), which gives the whole sentence the sense of "I'm going to give you (completely)." **Notes:** ごくろうさん is the informal version of ご苦労様 (Lesson 27), literally "thank you for getting tired." じゃった is the version of だった used by older men.

Xian Nu Studio

Kani:	そうかそうか　ごくろうさんじゃったな	Kudō:	プレゼント？
	that Q? that Q? good job be EP		*present?*
	Well, well . . . You have done a good job.		A present?
Kani:	では　お礼にステキなプレゼントをあげてしまおう		
	well gratitude for nice present DOP give going to		
	Well then, I shall give you a nice present to thank you.		

Manga Example 2: *Kureru* as an auxiliary verb

くれる functions as an auxiliary verb in this example. The verbs of giving and receiving often appear combined with other verbs conjugated in the *-te* form. This sentence is very clear: we see あんた perform the action of giving, and あんた is also the point of view (marked with the particle は). Receiving the action is あたし, who is in the *uchi* group,

therefore くれる is the logical option. くれる as an auxiliary verb adds the nuance of "doing a favor." Thus, 助けてくれる would literally mean something like "someone does the favor of saving somebody in the *uchi* group."

Gabriel Luque

Phoebe: あんたはあたしを助^{たす}けてくれました

you TOP *I* DOP *save (favor)*

You saved me.

Manga Example 3: The usage of *yaru* and the imperative *-kure*

Here, there are two forms to highlight. First, 〜てやる, that is, やる as an auxiliary verb. Remember やる belongs to the family of あげる and is used when speaking to people in an "inferior" position. Walter uses やる to get the other person to understand his supposed superiority, or simply to act cool: this usage often appears in manga, but in real life is rarely used because it is too rude and arrogant.

The second form is 〜てくれ. The imperative くれ, (Lesson 30) is often used to give orders. In this case, we have 飲んでくれ, which literally means "do me (me or someone in the *uchi* group) a favor and drink." The pure imperative 飲め (Drink!) is much stronger. **Note:** Walter gives the other person a pill, and asks him to 飲んでくれ. (Curiously enough, in Japanese one doesn't "take" medicine, but "drinks" it.)

J.M. Ken Niimura

Walter: いいとも、会^あわせてやるぜ。そのまえにこれを飲^のんでくれ。

all right (emphasis), put together (allow to) EP. *that before this* DOP *drink (order)*

All right, I'll fix you up with her. But before that, take this (pill).

Manga Example 4: *Morau* as an auxiliary verb

Here もらう functions as an auxiliary verb. Ieyasu tells Hanako he "wants to receive" (もらいたい) something from her (in this case an action) for Hidetada. Remember もらう is used to say "I or someone in the **uchi** group receives something. Hidetada is Ieyasu's son and, therefore, belongs to his **uchi** group, which justifies the usage of もらう. The basic sentence would be 秀忠は花子に相手をしてもらう (Hidetada receives the fact of Hanako entertaining him). **Note:** 相手 means "addressee," "opponent," etc., but the expression 相手をする means to "keep company," "take care of," or "entertain." のじゃ is a distortion of のだ (Lesson 40), used by older men.

花子
今夜は
秀忠の相手をして
もらいたいのじゃ

Xian Nu Studio

Ieyasu: 花子　今夜は秀忠の相手をしてもらいたいのじゃ
はなこ　こんや　ひでただ　あいて

Hanako tonight TOP *Hidetada* POP *the other* DOP *do receive* POP *be*

Hanako, I want you to entertain Hidetada tonight.

Manga Example 5: Usage of *kudasaru*

Formality levels are important in Japan (see Lesson 52. Giving and receiving verbs have formal and informal versions depending on the occasion. Here we have 下さる, the formal version of くれる, as an auxiliary verb. It literally means "I or someone in the **uchi** group receives something from/is done a favor by someone I respect and treat with formality." The expression 〜てください (please) comes from 〜てくださる. **Notes:** 方 is the formal word for 人 **hito** (person), used to show respect (Lesson 52). The suffix たち denotes the plural: 子どもたち **kodomotachi** (children), 先生たち **senseitachi** (teachers), 洋一たち **Yōichitachi** (Yoichi and the others). わざわざ means "expressly" or "(somebody other than me) takes the trouble to do something."

この方たち
トオルの
お友達で
わざわざ東京
からたずねて
来て下さった
のよ

Studio Kōsen

Man: この方たちトオルのお友達でわざわざ東京からたずねて来て下さったのよ
かた　　　　　ともだち　　　　　とうきょう　　　　　　き　くだ

this people Tooru POP *friend expressly Tokyo from visit come (favor)* EP EP

These people are Tooru's friends and have taken the trouble to come from Tokyo to visit him.

Manga Example 6: Usage of *-kata*

Gabriel Luque

The suffix 〜方 means "way of doing something." In our manga example we have the word まわし方, which means "way of spinning" and obviously comes from the transitive verb 回す (to spin): *-masu* form ⇒ 回します, root ⇒ 回し, add 〜方 ⇒ 回し方 (way of spinning).

Takeo says, literally, (コマの)回し方を教えて "Teach me the way of spinning (the spinning top)," but we have chosen a more natural form, "Teach me how to make it spin." **Note:** There is an example of the usage of the "softening" or "assertive" tag んだ at the end of the first sentence. (Lesson 40, Manga Example 4).

Takeo: 父ちゃんコマ買ったんだよ　まわし方 教えてー

Dad spinning TOP buy be EP spin (way of) teach

I have bought a spinning top, Dad. Teach me how to make it spin!

Manga Example 7: Usage of *amari*

J.M. Ken Niimura

Here we see the word あんまり, a colloquial distortion of the word あまり meaning "not much." Notice that the verb that goes with あまり (when this means "not much") must be conjugated in the negative. If you say 肉をあまり食べた, with the verb 食べる in the affirmative, this would mean "I ate a lot of (too much) meat." **Notes:** Sometimes (mainly in women and children's speech) the honorific prefix お〜 is placed before some words: おトイレ, お肉, etc. Notice too, the usage of 〜し as a "softener" of sentences. We we will study this in Lesson 46.

Emi: ママ　おトイレ長いなァ…

Mom toilet DP go besides . . .

Mom has gone to the toilet . . .

お肉あんまり食べなかったしー

meat not much eat besides

And she hasn't eaten much meat . . .

Exercises 練習

1 Which of these people are **uchi** and which are **soto**? Me, the tailor, my mother, the cook, my sister, my brother-in-law.

Translate: "I give the girl a candy." (girl 女の子; candy あめ) **2**

3 In 友達は由美に本をくれた, who gives and who receives? Why is the verb くれる used? (友達 friend; 由美 Yumi)

What is the difference between the sentences **4**
私はジョンにビールをもらう and ジョンは私にビールをくれる？

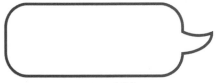

5 Translate: "I receive a bribe from the government." (bribe わいろ; government 政府) (The government is superior.)

Translate, using an auxiliary verb: "I want to buy **6**
the parrot a pencil." (to buy 買う; pencil えんぴつ; parrot オウム)

7 Translate: 足立さんはスピーチをしてくださった。(足立 Adachi; スピーチ speech). What does the usage of くださる imply?

Turn the following verbs into nouns with the **8**
meaning "way of": 食べる, 働く, 勝つ, 買う, 飲む and 破る.

9 Translate: "Since I didn't work much yesterday, I worked overtime." (yesterday 昨日; to work 働く; to work overtime 残業する)

Translate: 阪神タイガーズ、この試合に勝ってくれ。(阪神タイガーズ Hanshin Tigers; 試合 match; 勝つ to win) **10**

— **Answers to all the exercises can be found online by following the link on page 7.** —

ガシャッ

ガシャッ

ガシャッ

RI

お客さん！この店で写真をとってはいけませんよ！だめです！

そうですか？すみません、知らなかったんです。

今まで店の中でとった写真を消してほしいですが…

Review for Lessons 41–45

Answers to all the review exercises can be found online by following the link on page 7.

🎧 *KAGE* – New vocabulary 新しい単語

実は	the fact is, the truth is	盗む	to steal
影	shadow	ヨーロッパ	Europe
故障	damage, breakdown	監督	(film) director
何度も	over and over again	ゾーン	zone
ペンダント	pendant	禁止	prohibition

1. According to what you have read in the third episode of *Kage*, what is it that Nuria says appears in her photos? What does Mina suggest it could be?

2. What does Nuria buy at the clothes shop in Shibuya?

3. According to the salesclerk at the record and DVD store, can you play Japanese DVDs in Spanish DVD players? Why?

4. How does Nuria pay for the DVD she buys: cash or card?

5. In the end, does Nuria erase the photographs she has taken at the manga store?

6. What "falls" on the ground in Mina's sentence どこかで落としたんでしょうね？ And what fell in Nuria's sentence 昨日は上野駅の階段から落ちた？ Why are the two verbs in different forms?

7. Indicate with a circle the degree of certainty, high (H) or medium (M), in the following conjectures:

a) 指をレンズの前に出したのかもしれませんね。　　　H / M

b) カメラが故障しているに違いありません。　　　H / M

c) カメラは大丈夫そうだ。　　　H / M

d) どこかで落としたんでしょうね。　　　H / M

e) 誰かが盗んだみたいだ。   H / M

f) 荷物が見つけられないらしいです。   H / M

g) ちょっと高そうですね。   H / M

h) 彼女はそれを知らなかったはずだよ。   H / M

8. What do the two や indicate in the sentence ズボンやＴシャツやセーターはありますか

9. Turn the sentence この店で写真は禁止です into a conjecture, using the grammatical expressions given below.

a) _____。（かもしれません）

b) _____。（ようです）

c) _____。（そうです）

d) _____。（はずです）

10. What does the suffix ～にくい indicate in the sentence 日本のサイズは分かりにくいです?

11. Add the ～にくい and ～やすい suffixes to the following verbs that appear in the dialogue, and give the meaning they acquire.

	～にくい	Meaning	～やすい	Meaning
a) 写る	_____	_____	_____	_____
b) 盗む	_____	_____	_____	_____
c) 落とす	_____	_____	_____	_____
d) 見つける	_____	_____	_____	_____

12. Fill in the blanks with the most suitable word from the box at the end of the exercise.

a) 私は寝る前に、お風呂に入って、_____を着る。

b) この靴はヨーロッパで「４２」ですが、日本でいくつの_____ですか？

c) 京都の芸者さんはきれいな_____を着ています。

d) このセーターを買いたいが、その前に＿＿＿＿＿＿してもいいですか？

e) 今日は彼氏(かれし)とデートがあるから、セクシーな＿＿＿＿＿にしてみました。

f) ハワイは暑いから、＿＿＿＿＿＿＿＿＿をもって行かなくてもいいよ。

g) 日本のサラリーマンは皆黒い(みんなくろ)＿＿＿＿＿＿＿＿＿＿を着ている。

h) 結婚(けっこん)した姉は白くて、長い(なが)＿＿＿＿＿＿＿＿＿を着ていました。

i) 日本では、夏の夜、＿＿＿＿＿＿＿＿を着た女の子をよく見ます。

j) ケイコちゃんは胸(むね)が小さいから、＿＿＿＿＿＿＿＿要(い)らないね。

k) 仕事が決まった！だから、白いシャツと黒い(くろ)＿＿＿＿＿＿＿＿＿
を二本買いに行こう。

試着(しちゃく)	着物	浴衣(ゆかた)	サイズ	下着	スーツ
コート	パジャマ	ネクタイ	ドレス	ブラジャー	

13. Fill in the blanks with the most suitable verb from the box below.

a) ね、ね、お姉ちゃん。スパゲッティにチーズを＿＿＿＿＿＿の？

b) 来月＿＿＿＿子どもの名前を＿＿＿＿＿＿＿＿＿必要(ひつよう)がある。

c) 飛行機(ひこうき)で日本まで＿＿＿＿＿＿＿＿＿＿つもりです。

d) 日曜日の朝、子どもを八時(よう)に＿＿＿＿＿＿＿＿＿＿＿。

e) ケチャップに気をつけろ！Tシャツを＿＿＿＿＿＿＿＿なよ！

f) タオルを貸(か)してくれてありがとうね。＿＿＿＿＿＿＿＿わ！

g) 学校から家へ＿＿＿＿＿＿＿＿＿＿のは6時半です。

h) 映画(えいが)は4時半から＿＿＿＿＿らしい。あまり時間がないから、急ごう(いそ)！

i) マイコさんはヘビーメタルを＿＿＿＿＿＿＿のが好きみたいだ。

j) 先生、この病気(びょうき)は＿＿＿＿＿＿＿＿＿のですか？

k) どうして私が食べる前に、チョコレートが＿＿＿＿の？猫(ねこ)でもいるの？

汚す(よご)	入れる	飛ぶ	始まる(もど)	戻る(もど)	治る(なお)
聞く	起こす(お)	決める	生まれる(う)	助かる(たす)	消える

14. Choose the most suitable answer for each sentence.

a)　A: 日本の音楽はどこですか？ | B「＿＿＿＿＿＿＿＿＿＿　」と書いてあるところにあります。

　　1. ジャズ　2. 邦楽　3. クラシック　4. 洋楽

b)　日本語が分からないから、このパソコンの＿＿＿＿＿＿が英語でほしい。

　　1. 説明書　2. カメラ　3. シャツ　4. 時計

c)　この本を＿＿＿＿＿＿＿＿＿＿＿＿＿＿で払ってください。

　　1. バーゲン　2. 銀行　3. レジ　4. パンツ

d)　冬の夜は寒いから、＿＿＿＿＿＿＿＿＿＿＿をつけてくださいね。

　　1. ネクタイ　2. マフラー　3. 足袋　4. Tシャツ

e)　昨日は＿＿＿＿＿＿＿＿＿の映画を見に行きました。怖かったよ！

　　1. ホラー　2. アクション　3. ドラマ　4. コメディー

f)　このDVDはアメリカの＿＿＿＿＿＿＿＿＿で使えますか？

　　1. プレーヤー　2. ポスター　3. ポップス　4. テクノ

g)　女性用の下着を探しています。＿＿＿＿＿と＿＿＿＿＿をお願いします。

　　1. ブラウス　2. セーター　3. スーツ　4. パンツ

　　1. ブーツ　2. シャツ　3. ブラジャー　4. スカート

h)　この浴衣を１０％の＿＿＿＿＿＿＿＿＿で売っているよ。お得だよね！

　　1. 値札　2. 割引　3. 袋　4. 税

i)　昨日は＿＿＿＿＿＿＿の映画を見に行きました。たくさん笑ったよ！

　　1. ホラー　2. アクション　3. ドラマ　4. コメディー

15. Fill in the blanks in the following sentences with the most suitable expression formed by an adverb or an interrogative pronoun followed by か , as in the example.

a)　私は＿いつか＿金持ちになるつもりです。

b)　このおかしの中の＿＿＿＿＿＿＿＿＿＿一つだけを選んでください。

c)　A: あたしのパンツどこにあるの？ | B: この部屋の＿＿＿＿＿にあるはずよ。

d) 試験を始める前に、＿＿＿＿＿＿＿＿＿分からないことがありますか？

e) 泣かないでください。＿＿＿＿＿＿＿＿＿＿＿＿＿＿また会えるよ！

f) 泥棒だ！＿＿＿＿＿＿＿＿＿＿＿＿＿＿＿＿助けてください！

16. Fill in the blanks in the following sentences with the most suitable adverb from the box below.

a) 彼女の部屋には＿＿＿＿＿＿＿＿＿のアニメポスターがあるみたいよ。

b) ＿＿＿＿＿＿＿＿＿日本語を習いたので、日本へ留学しにきた。

c) ビールを＿＿＿＿＿＿飲まないでくださいよ。後が大変だから。

d) 彼は＿＿＿＿＿＿頭がいいです。東京大学で勉強しています。

e) マンガを＿＿＿＿＿＿読みたいから、日本語を習っている。

f) 日本映画は＿＿＿＿＿＿＿＿おもしろいと思いますよ。

あまり	とても	たくさん	あまりに	非常に	たくさん

17. This dialogue is out of order. Rewrite it in the correct order.

1) どんなビデオカメラですか？

2) はい。ビデオカメラを買いたいのです。助けてください。

3) 英語の説明書もついているんですか？

4) いらっしゃいませ！何かお探しですか？

5) はい、ついています。

6) これはどうですか？今よく売れている小さいカメラです。

7) じゃ、このカメラにしようと思います。お願いします。

8) 小さくて、使いやすいカメラがいいです。

店員さん：＿＿＿＿＿＿＿＿＿＿＿＿＿＿＿＿＿＿＿

お客さん：＿＿＿＿＿＿＿＿＿＿＿＿＿＿＿＿＿＿＿
＿＿＿＿＿＿＿＿＿＿＿＿＿＿＿＿＿＿＿

店員さん：＿＿＿＿＿＿＿＿＿＿＿＿＿＿＿＿＿＿＿

お客_{きゃく}さん ： ＿＿＿＿＿＿＿＿＿＿＿＿＿＿＿＿＿＿＿＿＿

店員_{てんいん}さん ： ＿＿＿＿＿＿＿＿＿＿＿＿＿＿＿＿＿＿＿＿＿

お客_{きゃく}さん ： ＿＿＿＿＿＿＿＿＿＿＿＿＿＿＿＿＿＿＿＿＿

店員_{てんいん}さん ： ＿＿＿＿＿＿＿＿＿＿＿＿＿＿＿＿＿＿＿＿＿

お客_{きゃく}さん ： ＿＿＿＿＿＿＿＿＿＿＿＿＿＿＿＿＿＿＿＿＿

18. Complete this dialogue held at a clothes shop.

Clerk: いらっしゃいませ。寒いですね！

Client: はい！東京_{とうきょう}はこんな寒い天気だと思いませんでした。暖かい服_{あたた　　ふく}が
必要_{ひつよう}です。

Clerk: 何を探_{さが}していますか？

Client: 首_{くび}が寒いから、⁽¹⁾＿＿＿＿＿＿＿＿＿＿＿ をお願_{ねが}いします。

Clerk: はい、分かりました。手はどうですか？

Client: そうですね。同じ色_{おな　　いろ}の⁽²⁾＿＿＿＿＿＿＿＿＿＿＿＿＿＿＿ もください。

Clerk: はい。これで大丈夫_{だいじょうぶ}ですか？

Client: いいえ、暖_{あたた}かいセーターもほしいです。

Clerk: ⁽³⁾＿＿＿＿＿＿＿＿＿＿＿＿＿＿＿＿ は「Ｓ」や「Ｍ」や「Ｌ」があります。

Client: 「Ｍ」で大丈夫_{だいじょうぶ}かもしれないが、⁽⁴⁾＿＿＿＿＿＿ してもいいですか？

Clerk: はい、あの部屋_{へや}を使ってください。

*** 十分後 ***

Client: ちょっと小さいから、「Ｌ」にします。

Clerk: 分かりました。支払_{しはら}いは⁽⁵⁾＿＿＿＿＿＿＿＿＿＿ でお願_{ねが}いします。

Client: すみません。⁽⁶⁾＿＿＿＿＿＿＿＿＿＿ に２万円と書いているが、
正_{ただ}しいですか？

Clerk: はい。しかし、今⁽⁷⁾＿＿＿＿＿＿＿＿＿＿＿ だから、５０％の
⁸⁾＿＿＿＿＿＿＿＿＿＿＿ があります。

Client: じゃ、１万円でいいですね？

Clerk: はい、そうです。お得ですよ！

Client: そうですね。⁽⁹⁾_____ で払えますか？

Clerk: いいえ。すみませんが、この店は現金だけです。申し訳ありません。

Client: 買ったものを着て帰るから、⁽¹⁰⁾_____ に入れなくてもいいですよ。

19. Complete the sentences choosing from the particles と or から , まで , や or か , as appropriate.

a) あの人は広美 (　　) 言います。

b) お金がほしい (　　)、働きたいよ。

c) いつ (　　) いつ (　　) 日本に住むつもりですか？

d) 彼はたくさんの国へ行ってきたよ。中国 (　　) 日本 (　　) 韓国など...

e) 肉 (　　) 魚、一つだけを選んでください。

f) 私は彼女 (　　) 一緒に映画を見に行った。

g) 私はあなた (　　) 結婚したくない。

h) 彼はアジアの一つの国へ行ったよ。中国 (　　) 韓国 (　　)、忘れたが ...

i) 「コーヒー」 (　　) いうのは豆 (　　) 作る飲み物です。

j) 僕はたくさんの漢字を知っている :「月」(　　)「火」(　　)「水」...

k) 彼は中国 (　　) 日本 (　　) 韓国へ行ったよ。この３つの国が好きだそうだ。

l) テレビを見て (　　)、寝ましょう！

m) 僕は３つの漢字を知っている :「月」(　　)「火」(　　)「水」です。

n) あしたの弁論大会は何時 (　　) ですか？

20. Choose the correct verb in each sentence.

a) 昨日、私は渋谷で財布を（落とした／落ちた）よ。

b) 弁論大会は六時ごろに（終わる／終える）と僕は思います。

c) ここから電車の音が（聞く／聞こえる）。

d) ボブさん、テレビを（消して／消えて）くださいよ！

e) テレビが（壊れた／壊した）から、サッカーを見られなかった。

f) アキコちゃん、家に（入って／入れて）くださいね。待っていますから！

g) あ、この建物も新しいよ！この街は（変わった／変えた）ね。

h) テルくんの趣味はコインを（集まる／集める）ことです。

i) 電車が（止まる／止める）まで待ってください。

j) あの猫を殺したいの！？あんた、車を（止まって／止めて）！

k) ボブさんはテレビを（壊れた／壊した）から、サッカーを見られない。

l) 暑いから、ドアを（開いて／開けて）ください。

m) 本田さんは住所を（変わった／変えた）らしいよ。

n) ドアが（開いて／開けて）いるよ。私がドアを（閉まろう／閉めよう）か？

21. Change the following sentences into conjectures using the expressions in brackets, as in the example. Then, indicate whether what is expressed in the sentence has a high (H) or medium (M) probability of taking place.

a) 今日は雨が降っています。（ようだ）(H / M)

　　<u>今日は雨が降っているようです　　　</u>。

b) タクさんの友達は警察官だよ。（そうだ）(H / M)

　　_____。

c) 彼女の買ったスカートは長かったです。（はずだ）(H / M)

　　_____。

d) 青木さんの娘はやさしい。（みたいだ）(H / M)

　　_____。

e) 来年、オーストラリアに留学します。（かもしれない）(H / M)

_____。

f) 見て！高田さんの家はとても広いです。（そうだ 2）(H / M)

_____。

g) あの人のお父さんは多分死にました。（だろう）(H / M)

_____。

h) 先生はマリコちゃんと結婚するつもりだ。（らしい）(H / M)

_____。

i) 山田さんはとても金持ちになりましたね。（ようだ）(H / M)

_____。

j) スミスさんは新しい着物を買った。（そうだ 1）(H / M)

_____。

k) ヨシオはハンサムだから、彼の妹さんもきれいだ。（かもしれない）
(H / M)

_____。

l) 社長は一億円ぐらい持っています。（にちがいない）(H / M)

_____。

m) マルタさんはまたアニメのＤＶＤを買うね。（そう 2）(H / M)

_____。

n) 部長の奥さんは親切です。（はずだ）(H / M)

_____。

22. Choose the most suitable answer for each sentence.

a) 彼は英語を_____にアメリカに行ったから、とても困ったそうだ。

　　1. 話して　2. 話せない　3. 話せないて　4. 話せず

b) エアコンを_____まま、眠ってしまったから病気になった。

　　1. つけて　2. つける　3. つけた　4. つけないで

c) 明日は雨＿＿＿＿＿＿＿＿＿＿＿＿＿＿＿＿＿＿＿、試合をしないでください。

　　1. の場合　2. だ場合　3. な場合　4. は場合

d) どうして電話＿＿＿＿＿＿＿来ちゃったの？ 今、あんたに会いたくないよ！

　　1. しない　2. せずに　3. しずに　4. する

e) きのうは手紙を書い＿＿＿＿＿＿＿、ゲームで遊ん＿＿＿＿＿＿＿しました。

　　1. だり／だり　2. たり／たり　3. たり／だり　4. だり／たり

f) アイコちゃんは＿＿＿＿＿＿＿＿＿＿まま死にたいといつも言っている。

　　1. きれいな　2. きれいに　3. きれいたっだ　4. きれいの

g) 彼女は先生では＿＿＿＿＿＿＿＿＿＿＿＿＿＿＿＿＿＿、学生ですよ！

　　1. しないで　2. せずに　3. しません　4. なくて

h) この車は＿＿＿＿＿＿＿＿＿＿＿＿＿＿＿＿＿＿＿＿し、速いです。

　　1. きれいだ　2. きれいな　3. きれい　4. きれいの

i) 電話で＿＿＿＿＿＿＿料理をした。そして、料理がおいしくなかった！

　　1. 話したながら　2. 話すながら　3. 話さながら　4. 話しながら

23. Correct the mistakes in the following sentences.

a) 彼は数学の先生だかもしれません。

b) 肉や魚を一つだけ選んでください。

c) A: どうして寝ているの？ | B: 疲れているまでだ。

d) シンちゃん、あの新聞を燃えてください！

e) あの人は東京に住んでいるから、日本語が上手なだろう。

f) 映画は五時に始めたらしい。

24. Choose the most suitable answer for each sentence.

a) 日本は＿＿＿＿＿＿＿＿＿＿＿＿＿＿＿＿＿やすい国だと思います。

　　1. 住む　2. 住み　3. 住んでいる　4. 住んだ

b) 彼女は「家に帰りたい」＿＿＿＿＿＿＿＿＿＿＿＿＿＿＿言った。

1. まで　2. や　3. に　4. と

c) 青山部長はスパゲッティが好き＿＿＿＿＿＿＿＿＿＿＿＿＿知らない。

1. はずだ　2. かもしれない　3. かどうか　4. や

d) 私はマドンナ＿＿＿＿＿＿＿＿＿＿＿＿女性があまり好きじゃない。

1. みたいな　2. みたいに　3. ようだ　4. ようで

e) ブッシュさんの英語はとても＿＿＿＿＿＿＿＿＿＿＿にくいそうです。

1. 分かる　2. 分かり　3. 分かって　4. 分かった

f) 私は冷蔵庫からたまごを二個＿＿＿＿＿＿＿＿＿＿＿＿＿＿＿＿。

1. 出た　2. 入れた　3. 出した　4. 入った

g) 母の生まれた街はとても安全＿＿＿＿＿＿＿＿＿＿＿＿らしいです。

1. な　2. に　3. ○　4. だ

h) 今日の試験はとても＿＿＿＿＿＿＿＿＿＿＿＿＿＿＿＿＿。

1. やさしくそうだ　2. やさしいそうだ　3. やさしいなそうだ　4. やさしのそうだ

i) アイコちゃんは渋谷＿＿＿＿＿、新宿 ＿＿＿＿＿へよく行っています。

1. とか／とか　2. と／と　3. に／に　4. まで／から

j) 山田さんはパソコンを作っている会社の社長 ＿＿＿＿＿＿＿そうだ。

1. な　2. に　3. ○　4. だ

k) 新宿 ＿＿＿＿＿渋谷＿＿＿＿＿、電車で１０分ぐらいかかります。

1. まだ／から　2. とか／とか　3. と／と　4. から／まで

l) 水着を着てから、川に飛び＿＿＿＿＿＿＿＿＿＿＿＿ください。

1. 込んで　2. にくくて　3. やすくて　4. 終わって

m) あの国はとても危険＿＿＿＿＿＿＿＿＿はずだよ。気をつけていってくださいね。

1. な　2. に　3. ○　4. だ

Kanji

花	犬	牛	魚	鳥	不	用	海	風	野	屋
(155)	(167)	(168)	(169)	(170)	(225)	(226)	(163)	(165)	(166)	(180)
歩	走	品	質	起	服	正	度	台	工	場
(250)	(251)	(227)	(228)	(252)	(260)	(203)	(204)	(205)	(176)	(177)

25. Link each kanji with its most common reading.

牛	や		鳥	だい
服	いぬ		海	かぜ
不	うし		花	さかな
犬	ふ		魚	はな
屋	ふく		風	うみ
度	ど		台	とり

26. Choose the correct kanji or kanji combination for each reading.

a) お<u>しょうがつ</u>に近所の<u>パンや</u>さんできれいな<u>いけばな</u>が見られる。
   しょうがつ：1. 正月　2. 正日　3. 王月　4. 王日
   パンや：1. パン野　2. パン屋　3. パン室　4. パン質
   いけばな：1. 生け化　2. 生け花　3. 先け花　1. 先け化
b) あの大きい<u>うし</u>は<u>きんぎょ</u>を食べた。
   うし：1. 午　2. 度　3. 犬　4. 牛
   きんぎょ：1. 全魚　2. 全漁　3. 金魚　4. 金漁
c) <u>おくじょう</u>で、きれいな<u>さくひん</u>を書いた。
   おくじょう：1. 屋場　2. 室場　3. 室上　4. 屋上
   さくひん：1. 作品　2. 下品　3. 上品　4. 手品
d) 皆^{みな}さん！<u>きりつ</u>してから、<u>ようじ</u>をしにいってください！
   きりつ：1. 野立　2. 歩立　3. 走立　4. 起立
   ようじ：1. 冊服　2. 用事　3. 用服　4. 冊事

27. Choose the correct reading for each kanji combination.

a) 北海道にはきれいな海や野があります。

北海道：1. ほくかいど　2. ほっかいど　3. ほくかいどう　4. ほっかいどう

海：1. うみ　2. あみ　3. そら　4. そる

野：1. やに　2. はら　3. け　4. の

b) 八百屋の前にある質屋はとても小さいです。

八百屋：1. はちひゃくや　2. はっぴゃくや　3. やおや　4. はちおや

質屋：1. しちや　2. しつや　3. しつじょう　4. しちじょう

c) 今、私が勉強しているのは「人工心臓」という分野です。

人工：1. じんこう　2. にんこう　3. じんこ　4. にんこ

分野：1. ふんの　2. ふんや　3. ぶんの　4. ぶんや

d) オランダの風車の品質はとてもいいと皆言っている

風車：1. かぜぐるま　2. かぜくるま　3. ふしゃ　4. ふうしゃ

品質：1. ひんしつ　2. ひんしち　3. しなしつ　4. しなしち

28. Write the kanji for the given *furigana*.

a) 私は＿＿＿＿＿＿と＿＿＿＿＿＿が大好きです。
   (はな)　　　　　(とり)

b) 父は＿＿＿＿＿＿の＿＿＿＿＿＿で働いています。
   (はな　び)　　(こう　じょう)　　(はたら)

c) ＿＿＿＿＿＿さんの前に小さい＿＿＿＿＿＿がいる。
   (さかなや)　　　　　　　　　(いぬ)

d) 友達はあの＿＿＿＿＿＿で＿＿＿＿＿＿な空手を習っている。
   (ともだち)　(どう　じょう)　　(じょうひん)　　(なら)

e) 彼女は＿＿＿＿＿＿の近くを＿＿＿＿＿＿くのがとても好きです。
   (かのじょ)　(うみ)　　　　　(ある)

f) あの人は私が買った＿＿＿＿＿＿を好きかどうか、＿＿＿＿＿＿ですよ。
   (ようふく)　　　　　　　　　　(ふあん)

Lesson 46 • 第46課

Compound Sentences (1)

In the next part of the book we'll see several ways of creating compound sentences in Japanese. In this chapter we will take a close look at expressions of continuity.

🎧 The easiest linking method

We saw in Lesson 35 that we can use the *-te* form to link sentences. This may be applied to verbs (寝て起きる **nete okiru** "to sleep and wake up"), *-i* adjectives (広くて明るい **hirokute akarui** "roomy and bright"), *-na* adjectives (丈夫で便利な **jōbu de benri-na** "robust and practical") and nouns (先生で

研究者 **sensei de kenkyūsha** "professor and researcher"). This method of linking sentences has up to five different usages: 1) combining elements, 2) sequencing actions, 3) mode, 4) simultaneous action or state, and 5)cause/reason:

1) 毎朝、牛乳を飲んでパンを食べる Every morning I drink milk and eat bread.
2) 早く起きて遠足に行きたい！ I want to wake up early and go on an excursion!
3) いちごを使ってケーキを作った I made a cake using strawberries.
4) 私は映画を見て、彼女は音楽を聞いた I was watching a movie, and my girlfriend was listening to music.
5) 博之が帰って広子が安心した Hiroyuki came back and (so) Hiroko was relieved.

To link negative sentences with the *-te* form, we use 〜ないで:

- 塩を使わないでハンバーガーを作った He made a hamburger without using salt.
- 勉強しないで試験に合格した I passed the exam without studying.

You can also link negative sentences by replacing the ないで of the negative *-te* form with ずに (寝ないで **nenai de** ⇒ 寝ずに **nezu ni**, "without sleeping"). The only exception is する: it isn't しずに but せずに. This ending is used in written and formal registers.

- 塩を使わずにハンバーガーを作った He made a hamburger without using salt.
- 勉強せずに試験に合格した I passed the exam without studying.

🎧 Another way of linking sentences in the negative

The negative forms 〜ないで and 〜ずに, can't be used with the five cases in the affirmative we saw in the first point. To be precise, 〜ないで can't be used to express cause/reason, and we don't use 〜ずに to express cause/reason or a simultaneous action or state.

To express cause/reason, we use the **-te** form of a verb conjugated in the negative, for example 使う *tsukau* (to use) ⇒ negative: 使わない ⇒ negative -**te** form: 使わなくて. We saw the negative conjugations for the -**te** form of verbs in the table in Lesson 35.

- 博之が帰らなくて広子が心配していた Hiroyuki didn't return home and (so) Hiroko was worried.
- 車を買わなくてよかった I didn't buy the car, (so) I'm happy.

To link two **-i** adjectives in the negative (not only cause/reason, but generally) we also use the -**te** form of the negative, for example 広い *hiroi* (broad) ⇒ negative: 広くない ⇒ -**te** form of the negative: 広くなくて. In the case of -**na** adjectives and nouns, we use ではなくて or, in colloquial register, じゃなくて (じゃ is the contraction of では).

- アパートは明るくなくて古いです The apartment is not bright and is old.
- 彼女は日本人では（じゃ）なくて、韓国人です She isn't Japanese, she's Korean.

🎧 Simultaneous actions: 〜ながら

To form sentences expressing simultaneous actions, we use verb root + 〜ながら. For example, 使う *tsukau* (to use) ⇒ root: 使い ⇒ add ながら: 使いながら (while I'm using). **Note:** 〜ながら is only used with verbs, and the subject (performing the action) must be the same for both verbs (that is, the performed actions) in the sentence.

- 音楽を聞きながら、本を書いている While listening to music, I write the book.
- ジョンは笑いながら映画を見ていた John laughed as he watched the movie.
- 辞書を引きながら翻訳する I translate, (while) consulting a dictionary.
- コーヒーを飲みながら話しましょう Let's talk, while we drink (have) a coffee.

In sentences with 〜ながら, there is usually is a central action and an incidental action. The verb of the latter takes 〜ながら. Compare these sentences:

- ご飯を食べながら新聞を読む While eating, I read the newspaper. (center: to eat)
- 新聞を読みながらご飯を食べる While reading the paper, I eat. (center: to read)

🎧 A situation remains unchanged: ～まま

The expression ～まま indicates that the action or situation described by the attached verb is unchanged. ～まま is used after verbs conjugated in the past tense, for example: 寝る **neru** (to sleep) ⇒ past: 寝た ⇒ add ～まま ⇒ 寝たまま (he is still asleep / there is no change to the state of his being asleep). This expression is also used with some *-i* adjectives (we don't change anything), *-na* adjectives (keep な), and nouns (add の).

- テレビをつけたまま仕事に行ってしまった I went to work, leaving the TV on.
- 百合子はドイツへ行ったまま戻らない Yuriko went to Germany and is not coming back.
- ずっと学生のままでいたいな I'd like to be a student for ever.

If the verb before ～まま is negative, we don't have to conjugate it in the past tense.

- 鍵をかけないまま家から走り出した I ran out of the house not locking the door.
- 彼は休まないままずっと働いている He works constantly, without a break.

🎧 Non-exhaustive list of actions: ～たり～たりする

This expression is a kind of や (Lesson 41) for verbs and adjectives. ～たり～たりする expresses a non-exhaustive list of actions or states. We indicate two or more actions or states, and whether there could be more is left up in the air. To form, add り to the past tense. The last element in the sentence is followed by する, for example 買う **kau** (to buy) ⇒ past: 買った ⇒ add り (and する if it is the last element): 買ったり(する) (to buy, etc.). *-i* adjectives also go in the past tense, like 高かったり(する) **takakattari (suru)** (expensive, etc.). *-na* adjectives and nouns need the verb "to be" in the *-tari* form (だったり), for example: 便利だったり(する) **benri dattari (suru)** (to be convenient, etc.) and 先生だったり(する) **sensei dattari (suru)** (to be a teacher, etc.).

- 仕事でインターネットをしたり、書類を作ったりするよ
  At work, I browse the Internet, write documents, etc.
- 毎朝、コーヒーを飲んだり新聞を読んだりします
  Every morning, I drink coffee, read the newspaper, etc.

～たり can be used with only one verb or adjective, with a similar connotation:

- 鍵をなくしたりしてはいけないね Don't lose the keys (or anything like that), OK?
- 恋に落ちたりするのは危ない！ Things like falling in love are dangerous!

🎧 In case of: 場合

The word 場合 (case, occasion, circumstance) means "in case of." It can follow verbs and
-i adjectives conjugated in any form. After *-na* adjectives and nouns it requires の .

- 戦争が起きた場合、逃げてください If war is declared, please run away.
- 雨の場合は体育館で練習しよう In case of rain, we will train in the gym.

🎧 Not only X, also Y: 〜し

〜し can follow any verb or *-i* adjective conjugated in any form. With *-na* adjectives and
nouns, it requires the verb "to be" (です/だ).

- 明日は試験があるし、塾にも行かなければならない
  Tomorrow I have an exam and, besides, I must go to cram school.
- この家は広いし、駅が近い Not only is this house roomy, the station is also close.

Sometimes we can find more than one 〜し in a sentence, as if forming a list:

- 彼女は頭がいいし、きれいだし、金持ちだし...完璧だな！
  She is intelligent, as well as beautiful, as well as rich . . . She's perfect!

Compound sentences (1): General summary table		
〜て	Linking sentences	景色を見て絵をかいてください Look at the landscape and draw a picture, please
〜ないで 〜ずに	Linking sentences. The first sentence is in the negative	景色を見ないで（見ずに）絵をかくのは難しいです Drawing a picture without looking at the landscape is difficult
〜なくて	Linking sentences. The first sentence is in the negative. Expresses cause/reason	彼と会わなくて残念だ It's a pity I won't meet him
〜ながら	"While I'm doing X, I do Y" (two simultaneous actions)	景色を見ながら絵をかいた While looking at the landscape, I drew a picture (Note: the drawing doesn't need to be of the landscape)
〜まま	A state or action already done which remains unchanged	私は疲れたままマラソンに参加した I took part in the marathon, tired as I was
〜たり 〜たりする	Non-exhaustive list of actions	マラソンに参加したり、絵をかいたりするのは楽しいです I enjoy taking part in marathons, drawing pictures . . . (and so on)
場合	"In the case of . . ."	雨の場合、マラソンに参加しません If it rains, I won't take part in the marathon
〜し	"Not only X, also Y"	マラソンに参加したし、絵もかいた I not only took part in the marathon, I also drew a picture

景色 *keshiki* landscape; 見る *miru* to look; 絵をかく *e o kaku* to draw a picture; 難しい *muzukashii*
difficult; 彼 *kare* he; 会う *au* to meet; 疲れる *tsukareru* to get tired; 残念だ *zannen da* it's a pity;
マラソン marathon; 参加する *sanka suru* to take part; 楽しい *tanoshii* enjoyable; 雨 *ame* rain

🎧 Conjunctions

Let's look at some expressions placed at the beginning of a clause to link two or more clauses or ideas. In the last lesson in the series (Lesson 49), we will give a summary table with all these conjunctions.

For example: 例えば

- 僕は日本料理が大好きです。例えば、寿司や天ぷらや親子丼が好きです
  I love Japanese cuisine. For example, I like sushi, tempura, oyakodon, etc.
- 多くの武道は、例えば空手とか柔道とかが日本から来ている
  Many martial arts, like for example karate or judo, come from Japan.

By the way: ところで

- 君は２５歳なの？ところで、俺は何歳だと思う？
  You're 25? By the way, how old do you think I am?
- 今日は天気がいいな ... ところで、何か飲みに行こうか？
  The weather is beautiful today, isn't it . . . By the way, shall we go out for a drink?

Besides: それに (This expression is almost equivalent to 〜し .)

- 明日は試験がある。それに塾にも行かなければならない
  Tomorrow I have an exam. And besides, (on top of that) I must go to cram school.
- 今日、彼女と別れた。それにバイクで事故にあった
  Today, I split up with my girlfriend. And besides, (to crown it all) I had a motorcycle accident.

🎧 Nominalizing adjectives

Let's look at the formation of nouns from *-i* and *-na* adjectives.

-i adjectives: We replace the last い with さ .

広い　wide　⇒ 広さ width　　　　黒い　black　⇒ 黒さ　blackness
太い　fat　⇒ 太さ plumpness　　　明るい bright ⇒ 明るさ　brightness

-na adjectives: We replace the last な with さ .

便利な convenient ⇒ 便利さ convenience 親切な　kind　⇒ 親切さ　kindness
丈夫な robust　　⇒ 丈夫さ robustness きれいな pretty ⇒ きれいさ prettiness

🎧 漫画例 **Manga Examples**

Let's relax now with a few manga examples where we will review the expressions we have studied in this chapter as well as a few interesting variations.

Manga Example 1: Usage of *zu ni*

Our first manga example will show us how to link two different sentences when the first one is negative. In this chapter we have seen that this is achieved with the negative -*te* form. In this case, the two ideas to be linked are 誰も傷つけない and 生きてきた人.

If we conjugate the first one in the negative -*te* form and we link both sentences, we get: 誰も傷つけないで生きてきた人 (person who has lived without hurting anybody). This kind of linking is the simultaneous action or state we saw on page 145. However, we have also said that there is a similar alternate construction, used in the formal register. This form, 〜ずに, is the one used in this panel. The speaker is in a tense situation, and he probably chooses 〜ずに to give more "weight" to his statement. The formation of 〜ずに is as simple as replacing the ないで ending in the negative -*te* form of any verb with ずに. Thus, the final sentence is as we see in the example: 誰も傷つけずに生きてきた人 (person who has lived without hurting anybody). **Notes:** There is another idea linked to this compound sentence: いない (there isn't). The word など (in kanji 等) could be translated as "et cetera." Also, notice the usage of 誰も ("nobody," Lesson 37) and of 〜てくる (Lesson 35), and take the opportunity to review these expressions.

誰も傷つけずに生きてきた人などいない

J.M. Ken Niimura

Hirose: 誰(だれ)も傷(きず)つけずに生(い)きてきた人(ひと)などいない

nobody wound put live come person or other not there is

No one has ever lived without hurting anybody.

Manga Example 2: Usage of *kono mama*

Here we have a small and very common variation of 〜まま: linking 〜まま to the demonstrative pronouns この (this), その (that), and あの(that over there) (Lesson 34). The resultant words could approximately be translated as "as it is."

A typical example (in the supermarket): 袋が要りますか？ *Fukuro ga irimasuka?* "Do you need a bag?" いいえ、このままでいいです "No, it's fine as it is." This sentence means you will take the product or products "as they are," without the necessity of a

bag to carry them. **Notes:** This sentence uses the contraction 〜ちゃう (Lesson 35); the non-contracted version would be 迷惑がかかってしまう (to cause trouble). いたら is the conditional (Lesson 56) of いる: if I stayed.

Kuroda: このままでいたら みんなに迷惑がかかっちゃうもんな…
this (no changes) be all IOP nuisance SP put (the fact is) EP . . .
The fact is that if I stay the way I'm now, I'll be a nuisance to you all . . .

Manga Example 3: Non-exhaustive list of actions

Here we have a good example of 〜たり〜たりする. Remember this is used to form a sort of non-exhaustive "list" of actions or states. Thus, in the sentence 楽しんだり笑っ

たりする, the main character indicates that he is "having fun and laughing," but he also suggests there are more actions which are not mentioned (that's why we have chosen translating "or anything"). Notice how the verb する usually closes the "list" (but be careful, as sometimes it is omitted). **Note:** 〜しちゃいけねえ is the contracted and vulgar version of 〜してはいけない (prohibition, Lesson 32). The んだ at the end is a very common softening tag (contraction of のだ), which we studied in Manga Example 4 in Lesson 40.

Calvin: おれは楽しんだり、笑ったりしちゃいけねえんだ。スーザンは…
I SP have fun (or something), laugh (or something) do must not. Susan . . .
I shouldn't have fun, or laugh, or anything. Susan . . .

Manga Example 4: A slightly different usage of *ba'ai*

We saw before that the word 場合 is used in constructions indicating "in the case of . . ." Here we have a different usage, where the negative inflection of 場合だ (to be the time to) is used: 場合では(じゃ)ない. This expression is often used in films or manga but you seldom hear it in real life. An example: 今は笑っている場合ではない！ *Ima wa waratte iru ba'ai de wa nai!* This is not the time to laugh! **Note:** There is a triple compound verb なすりつけあってる (-*te* form of なすりつけあう). The base is なする

Studio Kōsen

(lit. "to rub in"), followed by the suffix 〜つける, which adds the connotation of "pushing, pressing, throwing." なすりつける is translated as "placing the blame on somebody." Finally, 〜合う *au* makes it a little bit more complicated, adding a connotation of reciprocity, "mutually" (Lesson 44).

Fujita: 責任なすりつけあってる場合じゃないでしょうがあァ！！

responsibility recriminate mutually occasion not be true but!!

I don't think this is time to ask for responsibilities, is it?!

Manga Example 5: *Shi* to soften a sentence

A few pages ago we learned that 〜し is used to link sentences and give them a connotation of "not only x, also y." Here we have an example of this construction, although its usage is slightly different.

In spoken Japanese we often use 〜し at the end of a sentence to soften a statement or as a simple tag. Sentences like 今日は疲れたしな *Kyō wa tsukareta shi na* "Today I'm tired and (besides) . . ." or 台湾にも行ったしな *Taiwan ni mo itta shi na* "I also went to Taiwan and (besides) . . ." indicate the speaker wants to express more things in a veiled form, but doesn't, so as not to sound long-winded. Hence our tentative translation with "besides" at the end of each sentence. **Note:** The end-of-sentence particle な (Lesson 17) is used in these kinds of sentence. It's an informal usage, to soften a sentence or to express a wish.

Gabriel Luque

Man: ああ　スーツも銃も見つかったしな

yes suit also gun also find besides EP

Yes . . . And besides, I have found a suit and a gun.

Manga Example 6: Besides

それに is one of the three expressions used to link different sentences or ideas which we have studied in this lesson. それに is used in a similar way to our adverbs or adverbial constructions "besides," "apart from that," "to crown it all," "moreover," and so on.

In our example, Yuji is going to help someone whose car has broken down on the road. We don't know the previous sentence, but we can suppose, because of the それに, that Yuji had given another reason to offer his help to this person. **Note:** The *-i* adjective もったいない doesn't have a direct translation into English, but it mainly indicates that something is "a waste," "a pity," or "it's not worth . . .": it is generally used with money, time, or other things that can be "spent."

Yuji: それにレッカーはお金かかるからもったいないっすよ

besides wrecker **TOP** *money cost because waste be* **EP**

Besides, the tow truck costs money, and it would be a waste.

Manga Example 7: Formation of nouns from adjectives

We will conclude the lesson with an example of how to turn an *-i* adjective into a noun. The process is as simple as replacing the last い with さ. Thus, from the *-i* adjective 恐ろし (terrible, frightful) we obtain the noun 恐ろしさ (frightfulness). **Notes:** The literal translation of this sentence would be "that is the frightfulness of that guy as a warrior." Finally, あいつ is a vulgar term meaning "that guy."

Powell: それがあいつの戦士としての恐ろしさだ！

that **SP** *that guy* **POP** *warrior as* **POP** *frightfulness be!*

Such is his frightfulness as a warrior!

Exercises 練習

1 Link 浴衣を着る and 外に出ていきたい。
(浴衣 *yukata* summer kimono; 着る to put on, to wear; 外 outside; 出る to go out)

2 Do the same as in exercise 1, but this time the sentence 浴衣を着る must be conjugated in the negative (two possible negative forms).

3 Translate: "This book is not thick and it's light."
(book 本 ; thick 厚い ; light 軽い)

4 What is the difference between these sentences: ビールを飲みながら踊ろう and 踊りながら ビールを飲もう？(飲む to drink; 踊る to dance)

5 Translate: エアコンをつけたまま寝てしまった。
(エアコン air conditioning; つける to turn on; 寝る to sleep)

6 Translate using 〜たり : "This summer I swam, walked, rested . . ." (summer 夏 ; to swim 泳ぐ ; to walk 歩く ; to rest 休む)

7 Translate using 〜し : "This summer I swam and I walked as well."

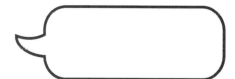

8 Translate: "By the way, shall we go out for a tea (or something)?" (to drink 飲む ; tea お茶).

9 Turn these adjectives into nouns: 辛い (spicy, hot), 大切な (important), 元気な (cheerful), and 白い (white).

10 Translate: "This is no time to dance the flamenco!"
(now 今 ; to dance 踊る ; flamenco フラメンコ)

— **Answers to all the exercises can be found online by following the link on page 7.** —

Lesson 47 ● 第 47 課

At a Restaurant

Are you ready to enjoy some Japanese food? You'd better prepare yourself, because we are going to see a lot of food vocabulary that will have you salivating and smacking your lips by the time you are done with this chapter!

Buying food

Before you start, we recommend that you review the section "Let's go shopping!" in Lesson 42 to refresh your memory on basic sentences to do with shopping.

   Now, we are ready to fill our pantry. Our first test will be an expedition to a supermarket.

At the store

Going to the supermarket doesn't involve much linguistic danger. Aside from what you already know (questions such as "Will you pay by cash or credit card?" and so forth, studied in Lesson 42 and in previous lessons), the cashier may ask you at most:

• スーパーマーケット X のカードを持っていますか？ Do you have the X supermarket card?

Many people have a supermarket card to earn points, and cashiers always ask if you have one. But the acid test entails buying food at the market or at the corner shop run by that little smiling old woman. Make sure to review the counters thoroughly (Lesson 25) because you will have to use them quite often.

🎧 いらっしゃいませ！

Ready to enter the jungle of いらっしゃいませ? This word, which we've touched on already, means something like "welcome," and in all shops throughout Japan (absolutely all of them, restaurants and パチンコ parlors included) you can hear rounds of いらっしゃいませ when a possible customer is spotted. Some vendors distort the expression to the utmost: things like らっしゃい！ are common. The right thing to do when greeted by one of these shouts is to ignore it. You don't need to answer, or even look at the shop clerk.

• これは何ですか？ What is this? (Lesson 34)
• 北海道特産の大根です They are daikon radishes, a speciality from Hokkaido.
• その大根を一本ください I'll have one of those daikon radishes, please. (Lesson 25)

- すみませんが、しいたけはありますか？ Excuse me, do you sell shiitake?
- はい、あそこにあります Yes, they are over there. (Lesson 34)
- 鶏の胸肉はいくらですか？ How much is the chicken breast? (Lesson 34)
- １００グラム当たり８３円です It is 83 yen per 100 grams.

In Japan they use the metric system: グラム (gram) and キロ (kilo). But be careful when buying fruit: it is so expensive you don't buy it by the gram or the kilo, but by the unit. Asking for りんごを５００グラムください *ringo o gohyaku guramu kudasai* (500 grams of apples, please) is not the done thing. You would normally say りんごを５個ください *ringo o go ko kudasai* (I'll have five apples, please).

🎧 Fast-food outlets

Like almost anywhere in the world, ファストフード chains are a feature in Japan, especially マクドナルド and ケンタッキーフライドチキン. You don't have to struggle much if you go to one of these restaurants, because once you can read カタカナ, you will understand most items on the menu, such as: ハンバーガー, チキンサンドイッチ and コカコーラ. But take care, as "French fries" are called フライドポテト!

- ご注文はお決まりになりましたか？ Have you decided on your order? (lessons 44 and 52).
- これとあれをお願いします (Pointing) I'll have this and that, please. (Lesson 34)
- ハンバーガーとコーラのＬサイズをください A hamburger and large cola, please.
- 玉ねぎ抜きでお願いします Without onion, please.
- お飲み物は何にしますか？ What would you like to drink? (Lesson 34)
- こちらでお召し上がりですか、お持ち帰りですか？ Will you eat here or is it take-out? (lessons 41 and 52)

We recommend you try Japanese ファストフード: chains such as 吉野家 *Yoshinoya* or 松屋 *Matsuya*, which offer dishes like 牛丼 *gyūdon* or カレーライス. They are cheaper and more interesting than マクドナルド, which you can find in your own backyard. (But if you must go there, at least try something you can't find back home!)

🎧 To the restaurant!

There's no shortage of places to eat in Japan, from small ラーメン, そば or うどん noodle eateries to luxurious restaurants. Many restaurants show hyper-real plastic models of the dishes they serve in the window, as well as the price, making it easy to decide where to eat. Once you have decided, open the sliding door, be greeted by the loud いらっしゃいませ from the waiters, and sit down or wait to be taken to a table.

- 何名様ですか？ How many people are you? | ２人です Two people. (Lesson 25)
- ご案内します。こちらです Follow me, please (I'll lead you). This way.

🎧 Meals	
breakfast	朝 食 ｜ 朝ご飯
lunch	昼 食 ｜ 昼ご飯
snack	おやつ
dinner	夕 食 ｜ 夕ご飯

🎧 いただきます！

We are now ready to look at the メニュー.

However, before you actually begin eating, don't forget to say いただきます (Lesson 27)!

- 英語のメニューがありますか？
  Do you have an English menu?
- おすすめ料理は何ですか？
  What dishes do you recommend?
- 定食はありますか？
  Do you have set menus (main dish with rice and miso soup)?
- ラーメンと餃子をお願いします
  I'll have ramen and some gyoza.
- あれと同じものにします
  (Pointing) I want the same as that thing over there.
- 外にある「親子丼定食」をください
  I want the *oyakodon* set outside (in the window).
- 日本酒もお願いします
  Some sake too, please.
- ジュースのお代わりをください
  Another juice, please.
- ごちそう様でした
  Thanks for the meal!

🎧 Paying

In many restaurants, you pay at the cash register near the entrance. Don't wait for the bill: just head to the register, and a member of staff will rush to ring up your bill. In Japan you don't tip, not even in restaurants! When you are given the change, simply keep it if you don't want the waiter to hunt you down in order to give back the money "you forgot." Saying goodbye with a ごちそう様でした *gochisō sama deshita* is good manners. A round of very loud ありがとうございました will ring out as you exit! Let's see a few useful sentences when the time to pay comes (review Lesson 42 too):

- お勘定をお願いします The bill, please.
- 全部でいくらですか How much is it altogether?
- 勘定は別々にしてください We want separate bills.
- ２０００円です It is 2,000 yen.

🎧 Flavors and sensations	
bitter	苦い
hot	熱い
delicious	おいしい
sweet	甘い
cold	冷たい
spicy hot	辛い
salty	塩辛い
sour	すっぱい
bland	味が薄い

🎧 Cooking styles	
grilled	鉄板焼き
to roast, grill	焼く
to cook, simmer	煮る
to steam	蒸す
to deep fry (in oil)	揚げる
to boil	ゆでる
to pickle	漬ける
to stir-fry	炒める

🎧 Vocabulary: Japanese food

	Typical dishes 日本料理 (にほんりょうり)		豆腐 (とうふ)	Tofu
炒飯 (チャーハン)	Chinese style fried rice with egg, vegetables, meat, etc.		豚カツ (とん)	Pork, dipped in a crumb batter and deep-fried, served with a special sauce
団子 (だんご)	Typical Japanese sweet. Three rice-flour balls in sweet sauce		うどん	Udon noodles, usually served in hot soup
どら焼き (や)	Typical Japanese sweet. A small pancake filled with **anko** sweet bean paste		焼き肉 (や にく)	Meat of different kinds, roasted on a hot plate (done by guests)
餃子 (ぎょうざ)	Steamed or fried Chinese dumpling stuffed with meat or vegetables		焼きそば (や)	Fried soba noodles with a special sauce, vegetables and meat
牛丼 (ぎゅうどん)	A bowl of rice topped with beef and onion		焼き鳥 (や とり)	Roasted chicken kebabs
唐揚げ (から あ)	Japanese-style fried chicken		**Ingredients** 日本料理の材料 (にほんりょうり ざいりょう)	
カレーライス	Curry rice (Japanese-style)		あんこ	Sweetened bean paste.
カツ丼 (どん)	A bowl of rice topped with **tonkatsu** and sauce		大根 (だいこん)	Daikon radish
味噌汁 (みそしる)	Miso soup		大豆 (だいず)	Soy bean
餅 (もち)	Rice cake		だし	Dashi stock, the base for many Japanese dishes, made from fish or seaweed
納豆 (なっとう)	Fermented soybeans		ごま	Sesame
おでん	Winter hot pot with daikon radish, **chikuwa** fish cakes, meatballs, etc.		白菜 (はくさい)	Chinese cabbage
お好み焼き (この や)	"Pancake" on a bed of cabbage, to which anything can be added		かつおぶし	Dried bonito flakes
おにぎり	Rice balls, usually with a filling such as tuna, umeboshi plum, salmon, kombu, etc		昆布 (こんぶ)	Kombu, kelp
親子丼 (おやこどん)	Bowl of rice (丼) with chicken (親, the "parent") and egg (子, the "child")		みりん	Mirin rice wine for cooking
ラーメン	Ramen		味噌 (みそ)	Miso paste
刺身 (さしみ)	Sashimi		のり	Nori seaweed
しゃぶしゃぶ	Vegetable and beef stew, with the beef very finely cut and boiled in water		蓮根 (れんこん)	Lotus root
シュウマイ	Steamed meat dumpling, originally from China		しいたけ	Shiitake mushroom
そば	Soba noodles served either in hot soup or cold		醤油 (しょうゆ)	Soy sauce
すき焼き (や)	Vegetable, meat, and tofu stew, cooked by the guests themselves		竹の子 (たけ こ)	Bamboo shoot
寿司 (すし)	Sushi		梅干 (うめぼし)	Pickled plum
たこ焼き (や)	Flour balls stuffed with octopus, typical in the Osaka region		わかめ	Wakame seaweed
天ぷら (てん)	Tempura		わさび	Wasabi horseradish

🎧 Food vocabulary

Vegetables 野菜		Others その他		mayonnaise	マヨネーズ
cabbage	キャベツ	bread	パン	mustard	からし
carrot	にんじん	cake	ケーキ	oil	油
cucumber	きゅうり	cheese	チーズ	pepper	こしょう
eggplant	なす	chocolate	チョコレート	salt	塩
garlic	にんにく	dessert	デザート	sauce	ソース
green pepper	ピーマン	egg	卵 / 玉子	sugar	砂糖
lettuce	レタス	ice cream	アイスクリーム	vinegar	酢
onion	玉ねぎ	omelet	オムレツ	**Drinks 飲み物**	
potato	じゃがいも	pasta	パスタ	alcoholic drink	お酒
pumpkin	かぼちゃ	pudding	プリン	beer	ビール
rice (cooked)	ご飯	soup	スープ	coffee	コーヒー
rice (uncooked)	米	yoghurt	ヨーグルト	black tea	紅茶
salad	サラダ	**Utensils 器具**		green tea	抹茶
scallion	にら	big bowl	丼	juice	ジュース
tomato	トマト	bottle	瓶	milk	牛乳
Meat 肉		bowl	茶碗	coffee with milk	カフェオレ
beef	牛肉	chopstick rest	箸置き	sake	日本酒
chicken	鶏肉	chopsticks	お箸	soft drink	ジュース
ham	ハム	disposable chopsticks	割りばし	tea	お茶
lamb, mutton	羊肉	fork	フォーク	water	水
pork	豚肉	frying pan	フライパン	wine	ワイン
sausage	ソーセージ	glass	グラス / コップ	**Fruit 果物**	
steak	ステーキ	lunch box	弁当箱	apple	りんご
Fish 魚		knife	ナイフ	banana	バナナ
		menu	メニュー	cherry	さくらんぼ
bonito	鰹	napkin	ナプキン	grape	ぶどう
clam	貝	plate	お皿	kiwi	キウイ
crab	蟹	pot	鍋	mandarin	みかん
octopus	蛸	wet hand towel	おしぼり	melon	メロン
prawn, shrimp	海老	spoon	スプーン	orange	オレンジ
salmon	さけ / しゃけ	**Seasonings 調味料**		peach	桃
sardine	鰯	butter	バター	pear	梨
squid	いか	ginger	しょうが	strawberry	苺
tuna	鮪	ketchup	ケチャップ	watermelon	すいか

Cultural Note: Table Manners

It is worthwhile knowing some basic table manners so you don't commit any of the typical mistakes characteristic of 外人 *gaijin* (foreigners).

Let's start with the お箸 *ohashi* (chopsticks) used for almost all meals (except for Western dishes, although seeing someone eating スパゲッティ with お箸 is not unusual). Knowing how to use お箸 is essential if you don't want to starve to death in 日本, and with a little bit of practice one quickly gets used to them.

There are a few taboos with お箸: don't stick them into the ご飯 *gohan* or other food leaving them in a vertical position, or pass food from one diner to another from お箸 to お箸. Why? Both actions are only done at Japanese funerals.

Another custom has to do with alcohol (mainly ビール), which is consumed in great quantities when there are guests. Never serve yourself: you must wait till someone else serves you. Hold up your グラス while being served. Next, the right thing to do is for you to serve the person who has just filled your glass. Take the びん (bottle), with the label facing upward, and make as if you are going to serve: the person will respond at once by holding out their グラス with a wide smile and a loud ありがとう.

Don't be surprised when all the food comes at once, on small plates. The usual thing is to eat a little bit of everything, from one or several shared platters. Also remember it is not rude to noisily slurp スープ and noodles. In fact, slurping indicates one is enjoying the dish, and brings good luck! Last of all, we will mention it isn't bad table manners to raise your 茶碗 *chawan* of スープ or ご飯 to your mouth to make eating easier.

There are many more unfamiliar customs, but you can start with these! いただきます!

Soba noodles can be slurped. (Photo: M. Bernabé)

🎧 漫画例 Manga Examples

This lesson only has three manga examples, due to the long vocabulary tables we have offered in this chapter. It is worthwhile committing all those words and phrases to memory because they are very useful and common in everyday life in Japan. Let's see some examples of their usage in manga.

Manga Example 1: At the store

We start with an everyday scene in any market or shopping area in Japan: a shop clerk trying to attract customers by shouting to each and every passerby about how good her products are. Notice the いらっしゃい, which is just a small distortion of いらっしゃいませ, the greeting used only in shops of any kind and restaurants, usually followed by Ｘはいかがですか？ (How about x?). Remember いかが is the formal version of どう (How about . . . ?, Lesson 34). In this case, the clerk is offering 納豆, extremely smelly and sticky fermented soybeans—very healthy though, or so they say.

To conclude this example, we will show you a little trick that will surely be great for your economy. Supermarkets in Japan usually close at 8 or 9 in the evening, and about half an hour before closing time, the staff start placing discount stickers on fresh produce. You can save a lot of money by shopping at that time! The stickers give the amount of the discount, for example, ２割 *ni wari* (20% off), or even 半額 *hangaku* (half-price) (Lesson 42).

J.M. Ken Niimura

Akiko: いらっしゃい いらっしゃい！ 納豆（なっとう）はいかがですか！
Welcome, welcome! Natto TOP how about be Q?!!
Welcome, welcome! How about some natto?!

Manga Example 2: The complex world of sushi

Gabriel Luque

Here we have a restaurant specializing in sushi. Let's give you a short sushi "guide" to help you learn even more vocabulary. There are two basic kinds of sushi: 巻き寿司 *makizushi* and 握り寿司 *nigirizushi*. The first kind consists of a roll with the ingredient in the middle, surrounded with rice and wrapped in *nori* seaweed (巻く *maku*, to roll). The type known as 鉄火巻き *tekka maki* (tuna rolls) are widely known. The second kind is a thin strip of fish, or other type of ねた (topping), on a ball of pressed rice (握り *nigiri*). In addition to the types of sushi in this manga example トロ (fatty tuna), イカ (squid), and アナゴ (eel), there many others, such as まぐろ (tuna), えび (prawn), しゃけ (salmon), たこ (octopus), 卵焼き *tamagoyaki* (omelet), or たい (sea bream), to name just a few.

Customer 1:	トロにイカね〜	Customer 2:	こっちアナゴ追加
	toro and squid EP		*here eel add*
	One toro and one squid!		I'll have one more eel.
Customer 3:	ビール２本持ってきて〜	Shoji:	はい！
	beer two bring come		*yes*
	Bring two bottles of beer!		Coming!

Manga Example 3: *Katsudon* and *donburi*

This example shows us an informal way of asking what one wants to eat, using the verb もらう ("to receive," Lessons 28 and 45). Notice the usage of でも, studied in Lesson 37.

In less luxurious restaurants there are pieces of paper stuck to the walls with the names of the dishes served and their price. In this example, the customer looks at the pieces of paper

Studio Kōsen

and chooses カツ丼 *katsudon* (deep-fried breaded pork on rice), which, moreover, is 特製 *tokusei* (special). Other dishes on the list include チャーハン (fried rice), 親子丼 *oyakodon* (egg and chicken on rice), and 卵丼 *tamagodon* (egg on rice). The kanji 丼 indicates "bowl of rice on which something is placed."

Terada:	特製カツドン…でももらおうか
	special katsudon . . . or something receive Q?
	Could you bring me . . . a special katsudon?

Exercises 練習

1 What do the following words mean: 夕ご飯 (ゆうはん),
熱 (あつ) い, ゆでる, 甘 (あま) い, 焼 (や) く and 炒 (いた) める?

2 Translate the words "chocolate," "water," "cabbage," "tomato," "prawn," and "omelet."

3 Define these typical Japanese dishes in English: 焼 (や) きそば, おにぎり, 親子丼 (おやこどん) and 天 (てん) ぷら.

4 Name and describe at least five typical ingredients in Japanese cuisine.

5 You are at the market. Ask the stallholder for two onions and a lotus root.

6 You are in a hamburger joint, and the waiter asks you お飲 (の) み物 (もの) は何 (なん) にしますか? What do you answer?

7 You are at a restaurant and you want to order a tempura set menu. How do you ask for it?

8 What does the word いらっしゃいませ mean, and when and where is it used?

9 What are the names of the two main kinds of 寿司 (すし) and why are they thus called?

10 In Manga Example 3 on the facing page, how much does the fried rice cost?

— **Answers to all the exercises can be found online by following the link on page 7.** —

Lesson 48 • 第48課
Compound Sentences (2)

Here is the second of three sections we will devote to the formation of compound sentences. This time we will study expressions of cause/reason, and intention/aim. You should try your best to learn these constructions well: they will be very useful.

🎧 Cause/reason: から

Lesson 41 gave different uses of から: the particle of origin (from), the subordinating conjunction, and the construction 〜てから. Besides other meanings, such as "since" or "considering," から also means "because" in answer to どうして (why?). **Usage:** After a verb or *-i* adjective, nothing is added. *-na* adjectives and nouns take the verb "to be" (です/だ). The structure is usually "cause/reason + から + consequence."

- どうして帰るの？つまらないから帰る Why are you leaving? Because I'm bored.
- この本はもう読んだから、あげる I already read this book, so I'll give it to you.
- ジョンはまじめだから合格するだろう Since John is serious, I'm sure he'll pass.
- 彼は先生だったから、これが分かるはずだ He was a teacher, so he should understand this.

🎧 Cause/reason: ので

ので is similar to から: "cause/reason + ので + consequence." **Usage:** After a verb or *-i* adjective, nothing is added. *-na* adjectives and nouns need な in the present tense, but in the past tense な is replaced with だった. But ので is not used when answering どうして (why?). ので is a weightier expression than から, used when the speaker thinks the reason stated before から is valid and obvious, and that the listener will agree. In principle, using ので is wrong when the first part of the sentence expresses conjecture, invitation, request, personal opinion or wish. But there is a modern tendency, especially among the young, to use ので and から almost without distinction. Still, do bear in mind the slight differences in the meanings between both expressions.

- 雨が降っていたので行けなかった I couldn't go, because it was raining.
- 頭が痛いので仕事が出来ない I can't work because I have a headache.
- この街は安全なので夜によく散歩する Since this town is safe, I usually take walks at night.
- 彼はアホなので謝らないよ Because he is stupid, he won't apologize.

🎧 Aim: ために

ために is used to express intention or aim, meaning "for" or "in order to." **Usage:** After a verb nothing is added, and after a noun we must use の (replaced by だった in the past tense). This form of ために is not used with adjectives of any kind.

- 車を買うためにいっぱい働きます I work a lot in order to buy myself a car.
- 日本人は仕事のために生きているみたいだ It seems the Japanese live to work.
- いい仕事を見つけるために勉強しています I study in order to find a good job.
- 彼女のために何でもやれるぞ I can do anything for my girlfriend.

Sometimes ために is used to express cause/reason, just like から or ので. In this case, it can be used with adjectives. *-i* adjectives don't require anything, while *-na* adjectives require な. This usage of ために is rather formal and seldom used, but it is worthwhile knowing.

- 風邪をひいたために、家で休んでいた Because I caught a cold, I rested at home.
- 家が古いために、修理が必要だ Because the house is old, it needs repairing.

🎧 Aim: のに

のに is like ために, as it expresses an aim and can be translated as "for." のに is nothing more than the phrase nominalizer の, studied in Lesson 40, plus the particle に, which here indicates intention. のに is only used after verbs in the infinitive.

- じゃがいもを切るのに包丁を使った I used a kitchen knife to cut the potato.
- キムチを作るのに白菜が必要だ To prepare kimchi you need Chinese cabbage.
- 秋葉原へ行くのに電車が便利だ To go to Akihabara the train is convenient.
- ＨＰを作るのに二ヶ月もかかった It took me 2 months to make the web page.

Note: There is another completely different usage of のに which indicates "although," "in spite of." We will study this in the next lesson.

🎧 When: 時

Let's go on to study other useful constructions in the formation of complex sentences. The first construction is 時 *toki*, which indicates time or "when." **Usage:** Nothing is added after a verb or an *-i* adjective. With *-na* adjectives, な is required, while with nouns we must add の. In the past tense, however, both do without な and の, respectively, and use だった.

• 韓国に行った時、けっこう暑かったです When I went to Korea it was quite hot.
• 子どもの時、よく友達と遊んでいた When I was a boy, I played with my friends.

You can add に to 時, obtaining 時に. The meaning is the same, although 時に is more emphatic and stronger than just 時.

• 試験の時にすごく緊張していたよ At the time of the exam, I was very nervous.
• 彼が来た時にお姉さんは出かけた When he came, my elder sister went out.

🎧 While: 間に

間に *aida ni* indicates the interval between two points in time (meaning "while" or "during") or in space (meaning "between"). **Usage:** The same as 時.

• 日本にいる間に、空手を習いたい I want to learn karate while I'm in Japan.
• 夏休みの間、よく勉強しました I studied very hard during the summer holidays.
• 日本と韓国の間に日本海がある Between Korea and Japan is the Sea of Japan.

Note: For 間に, the action stated in the main sentence happens "within" the time introduced by the sentence ending in 間に. But 間 on its own indicates both actions happen "during" exactly the same time period.

• 週末の間、京都を歩いた All weekend long I walked through Kyoto.
• 週末の間に京都を歩いた At the weekend (at some point) I walked through Kyoto.

🎧 While: うちに

The expression うちに has an almost equivalent meaning to 間に, and also means "while." Both can be used without distinction in many sentences. But while 間に indicates an interval of time with starting and ending points, which can be measured with a watch, うちに doesn't have that connotation, and merely indicates "time interval not necessarily measurable." **Usage:** Just like 時 and 間に.

• 大学にいるうちに勉強しなさい While you are at university, you must study.
• 雨が降らないうちに終わりましょう Let's finish while it's not raining (before it rains).
• 寿司を新鮮なうちに買いましょう Let's buy sushi while it's fresh.
• お茶を温かいうちに飲んでください Drink your tea while it's hot.

🎧 Before and after

The expressions meaning "before" and "after" are 前に *mae ni* and 後で *ato de*. Nothing is added between the verb and 前に. With nouns, の is required. These expressions are not used with adjectives.

- ジムは家に入る前に「おはよう」と言った Jim said hello before going in the house.
- 昼ごはんの前に君と話したい I want to talk with you before lunch.

Verbs preceding 後で must be in the past tense. Nouns require の. **Note:** Sometimes, in informal register, we can do without the で in 後で.

- ビールを飲んだ後（で）げっぷが出た I burped after drinking the beer.
- 映画を見た後で公園へ行きました After watching a movie, I went to the park.
- 授業の後でゲームセンターに行こうよ Let's go to the game center after class.

🎧 Conjunctions

Let's now see a few more useful conjunctions:

And (later) / and (then) / and (also): そして

- 昨日は遊園地に行った。そして、おいしい夕食を食べた
  I went to an amusement park yesterday. And (later) had a delicious dinner.
- 私はやせたいのでダイエットをしています。そして、運動もしています
  Because I want to lose some weight, I'm on a diet. And (also) I'm taking exercise.

Then / therefore / later / now: それで

- 岩手県で生まれて、愛知県で育った。それで、埼玉県で結婚した
  I was born in Iwate Prefecture and raised in Aichi. Later on, I married in Saitama.
- オレは大学に行けなかった。それで、いい仕事を見つけることが出来なかった I couldn't go to university. Therefore, I couldn't find a good job.

Well / well then / then: それでは（それじゃ）

- もう時間です。それでは、スピーチを始めましょう
  It's time now. Well then, I'll start my speech.

After that / and then / since then: それから

- 5年前、大学を卒業した。それから、彼と全然会っていないな
  I graduated from university five years ago. Since then, I haven't seen him again.

Therefore / that's why / consequently / so: だから

- 先週、旅行に行った。だから、今はとても疲れている
  I went on a trip last week. That's why I'm tired.
- 社長は無駄にお金を使った。だから、会社が倒産してしまいました
  The president squandered money. Consequently, the company went bankrupt.

🎧 Compound sentences (2): General summary table		
～から	Cause/reason. "Since, because, considering"	すしが好きだから、いっぱい食べよう Since I like sushi, I shall eat a lot.
～ので	Cause/reason. "Since, because, considering"	渋谷は人が多いので、迷いやすいです Since there are lots of people in Shibuya, it's easy to get lost.
～ために	Aim/intention. "For"	日本へ行くために3年間も働いた In order to go to Japan, I worked for three years.
～のに	Aim/intention. "For"	すしを作るのに、新鮮な魚がいる To make sushi, you need fresh fish.
～時	"When"	渋谷にいる時、いつも迷ってしまう When I'm in Shibuya, I always get lost.
～間に	Physical or temporal distance between two points. "While, during"	彼が寝ている間に買い物をしに行ってこよう While he's sleeping, I shall go shopping (and come back).
～うちに	Period during which something remains valid. "While, during"	日本にいるうちに北海道へ行きたい While I'm in Japan, I want to go to Hokkaido.
～前に	"Before"	寝る前に歯を磨きなさい Before going to sleep, brush your teeth.
～後で	"After"	買い物に行った後で、魚を食べた After going shopping, I ate fish.

好きな *suki-na* that one likes; いっぱい a lot; 食べる *taberu* to eat; 渋谷 *Shibuya* Shibuya (district in Tokyo); 人 *hito* people; 多い *ooi* a lot of; 迷う *mayou* to get lost; 日本 *Nihon* Japan; 行く *iku* to go; 3年間 *san nen kan* for 3 years; 働く *hataraku* to work; 作る *tsukuru* to make; 新鮮な *shinsen-na* fresh; 魚 *sakana* fish; いつも always; 寝る *neru* to sleep; 買い物 *kaimono* shopping; 北海道 *Hokkaidō* Hokkaido; 歯を磨く *ha o migaku* to brush one's teeth

🎧 漫画例　Manga Examples

As usual, the manga examples will help us see in practice how to use the constructions we have just studied. These panels should help you clarify the explanations on the new structures and give you a more concrete idea of their usage.

Manga Example 1: Cause or reason using *node*

In this first example someone has eaten what was on the table, and the characters are arguing about who's done it. Suddenly, the boy in the panel confesses he is the "guilty" one: he explains the reason in this sentence using の で. Notice how the reason (あんまり腹がへった) precedes the consequence (つい無断でたべちゃった). The verb before の で must be in the simple form. In this case we have 減る *heru* (decrease), which is part of the set phrase 腹が減る *hara ga heru*, which literally means "the stomach decreases," although its real meaning is "to be hungry" (Lesson 27).

　の で is used when the cause or reason expressed by the speaker is clear, and it is assumed the listener will accept it as something understandable and obvious. In our example, the connotation of の で is not that strong, and the almost synonymous word から could have been used instead with no problem. Last of all, it is worth mentioning that の で is used in formal situations more often than から: it sounds more "serious." **Notes:** あんまり is a distortion of あまり which we studied in Lesson 45, used here to mean "so much." Notice the contraction たべちゃった: its non-contracted form is 食べてしまった. Take the opportunity to go back to Lesson 35 and review this last form.

Gabriel Luque

Taku: あんまり腹がへったので、つい無断でたべちゃった。ゆるしてください。

so much stomach SP decrease because, inadvertently without permission. forgive please

I was so hungry I ate it without permission. Please forgive me.

Manga Example 2: Perhaps: Cause or reason tag *kara*

Like ので, the word から is used to indicate cause/reason. Here we see から dangling at the end of the sentence. It could be the answer to a question with どうして (why?), or a simple explanation for why something is done. There is another explanation for this last usage:

sometimes a sentence ends with the tag から, ambiguously implying, by way of excuse, that there is a reason for what one is doing, but without putting forward a specific explanation. Sentences such as 私、もう帰るから ... **Watashi, mō kaeru kara** "I'm going now, (so ...)" or ちょっと忙しいんだから ... **Chotto isogashii n dakara** "I'm a little busy (so ...)" are common. **Notes:** なんにも is the distortion of 何も **nani mo** (nothing, Lesson 37). You should also take this opportunity to review the usage of もう (Lesson 40).

J.M. Ken Niimura

Lin: もう思い残すことなんか、なんにもないから…

any more regret thing (emphasis), nothing there is because ...

So, there is nothing else I can regret ...

Manga Example 3: Idiomatic usage of *dakara*

In this chapter we looked at the expression だから, which is used to state a reason or a cause, as in: 彼は菜食主義者だ。だから、肉を食べない **Kare wa saishokushugi-sha da. Dakara niku o tabenai.** "He is a vegetarian. So he doesn't eat meat." However, in this example, we find a slightly different usage of だから, often seen in spoken language: だから is used at the beginning of a sentence to convey annoyance, or insistence on something. It could be translated as "for goodness sake," "I've already told you ...," "but you ..." **Note:** うん is the informal way of saying "yes," while ううん means "no."

Studio Kōsen

Sayaka: うん…だから土曜日の映画、行けないの

yes ... that's why Saturday pop movie, go ep

Yes ... I've already told you I can't go to the movies on Saturday.

Manga Example 4: Usage of *tame ni*

A few pages ago, we learned that ために means "for" or "in order to": here is a good example of its usage. The speaker indicates the "aim" for which he was born, using ために. However, he says it with the pronoun この (this), and, therefore, unless we know the context, we can't tell what he's talking about. Since he is skating in the image, we can imagine the original sentence could have been something like 俺はスケートをするために生まれてきた (I was born to skate). Using the **kosoado** pronouns (Lesson 34), この (this), その (that), and あの (that over there) in conjunction with grammatical constructions is very common. We will see another instance in Manga Example 6.

Xian Nu Studio

Teruo:	俺はこのために生まれてきた！

I TOP this for born come!

I was born for this!

Manga Example 5: Usage of *toki*

Let's now study how to say "when" in Japanese using 時. As we can see in the example, the process is quite easy: all you need to do is add the word 時 after the sentence with which we want to indicate "when," as in the example, 最後に電話で話した時 (when I last spoke with him on the phone.) Try making your own sentences with 時: it is simple and with practice you will master it. **Note 1:** Depending on the inflection of the verb or adjective preceding 時, the meaning changes. If conjugated in the past tense, it refers to something that happened in a previous stage: 昨日、料理をしていた時、彼が来た **Kinō, ryōri o shite ita toki, kare ga kita** (Yesterday, when I was cooking, he came.) In the infinitive, it refers to something that we know will inevitably happen in the future or something that usually happens: 私は寝る時、悪夢を見てしまう **Watashi wa neru toki, akumu o mite shimau** (Whenever I sleep, I have bad dreams.). **Note 2:** おっしゃる is a formal version of 言う (Lesson 52).

J.M. Ken Niimura

Fletcher: いや、私が先生と最後に電話で話した時、こうおっしゃっていた

no, I SP teacher CP last telephone IP talk when, in this way said

Well, when I last spoke with the teacher on the phone, that's what he said.

Manga Example 6: Usage of *mae ni*

Let's see an example of how to say "before" using the word 前, which we already know. We simply add 前に after a sentence, like in the example: 私を殺す前にキスしてね **Watashi o korosu mae ni kisu shite ne** (Kiss me before you kill me). The opposite of 前に is 後で **ato de** (after).

As mentioned in Manga Example 4, it is common to see the **kosoado** pronouns この, その, and あの together with grammatical constructions: here we have その前に (before that). More examples: この後で (after this), あのように (in that way, Lesson 43), そのはずだ (that is almost certain, Lesson 43), この場合 **kono ba'ai** (in this case, Lesson 46), そのうちに **sono uchi ni** (one of these days, Lesson 48), このまま (just as it is, Lesson 46).

Charlie:	その前にお前の首へし折るぞ
	that before you POP neck break EP
	Before that, I'll break your neck.

Manga Example 7: Usage of *sore de wa*

We will conclude this intense but useful lesson with an example of それでは, which, as we see in this panel, is usually used in speeches or introductions as a sign that we are about to start talking, like our "now" or "well, then."

それでは is also used when saying goodbye, sometimes contracted into じゃ when speaking: one of the first expressions we saw in Lesson 4 was それじゃ、また明日会いましょう **Sore ja, mata ashita aimashō** (Well, let's meet again tomorrow). This expression can be contracted into それじゃ、また明日 (Well, [see you] tomorrow), and even further to じゃね、また (Well, see you), cutting the それ. There is also the concise but extremely common じゃね (literally "well" or "well then," but used to mean "see you later").

Kitano:	えーそれでは新しい人事の発表を―
	er . . . then new staff POP introduction DOP
	Er . . . Well, let's introduce the new staff and . . .

Exercises 練習

(1) Answer the question どうして彼と付き合っているの？ with "Because I like him." (好きな that one likes; 彼 he; 付き合う to go out with)

(2) Translate: "Because I'm thirsty, I (will) drink water." Use both ので and から (to be thirsty のどがかわく; to drink 飲む; water 水)

(3) Translate the sentence: 正男くんにほれたので、別かれましょう。(正男 Masao; ほれる to fall in love; 別れる to split up)

(4) Translate: "To dance, you need a little bit of grace." (to dance 踊る; necessary 必要な; a little bit of 少しの; grace 優雅さ)

(5) Translate: 入院していた時、悲しかったです。(入院する to be hospitalized; 悲しい sad)

(6) Translate: ご飯を温かいうちに食べなさい。(ご飯 food; 温かい warm; 食べる to eat)

(7) Translate: "Kiss me before going to sleep." (to kiss キスする; to sleep 寝る)

(8) Translate: "I went to Thailand. And later, I also went to Vietnam." (to go 行く; Thailand タイ; Vietnam ベトナム)

(9) What does だから mean when spoken at the beginning of a sentence?

(10) Where does the expression じゃね come from, and what does it literally mean? What is its actual meaning?

— **Answers to all the exercises can be found online by following the link on page 7.** —

Compound Sentences (3)

The time has come for the third and final of our intensive series of lessons on compound sentences, this time with a focus on expressing opposition or contrast.

🎧 But / however: けれども/けれど/けど/が

The basic word for "but/however" is けれども, although it is quite formal and is usually reduced to けれど (also formal, but less so). It can be reduced even more to the informal expression けど. We also have が, which has an equivalent meaning (we studied its usage as "but" in Lesson 37, which we advise reviewing). **Usage:** We add nothing after verbs and *-i* adjectives. Nouns and *-na* adjectives need the verb to be in its simple form, だ.

- バイクを運転できるけれども、バイクがありません I can ride a motorcycle, but I don't have one.
- カメラを買いたいけれど、お金がない I want to buy a camera, but I don't have any money.
- ボブは先生だけど、教えるのが嫌いだ Bob is a teacher, but he doesn't like teaching.
- 彼は映画は好きだが、アニメは好きではない He likes films, but not anime.
- 昨日は病気だったけど、今日は大丈夫だ Yesterday I was sick, but today I'm fine.

Just like with が (Lesson 37), sometimes the variations of けれども are used to link sentences and don't necessarily have the meaning "but."

- 後で梅田へ行くけど、美穂も来る？ Later I'll go to Umeda, will you come too, Miho?
- 相談したいんですが、時間がありますか？ I would like to consult with you about something, do you have time?

The same words are used in spoken language to soften sentences, especially when making requests or giving excuses: they are placed at the end, leaving the continuation in the air.

- 今ちょっと忙しいんですけれども . . . Now I'm a little busy, but . . .
- そのパソコンを見たいんだけど . . . I would like to see that computer, but . . .

🎧 Although / despite: のに

This construction has nothing to do with its homophone のに meaning aim/intention (page 165). This のに, like けれども and its "family," means "although" or "despite." The expression のに has a distinct subjective and emotional connotation: we use it to indicate that something that was almost a fact finally has not been possible and provokes in the speaker a feeling of surprise, frustration, or even annoyance. If you want to avoid any subjective or emotional nuance, use けれども, けれど, けど or が. **Usage:** Nothing is added after verbs or *-i* adjectives, while nouns and *-na* adjectives require な.

- ダイエットをしているのに、全然やせない I'm on a diet but despite that, I'm not losing any weight.
- 眠かったのに、徹夜をしました Though I was sleepy, I worked through the night.
- 彼女が好きなのに、告白できない Although I like her, I can't declare my love.
- いい天気なのに、外に出られない Despite this nice weather, I can't go out.

In a colloquial register, sentences that trail off with のに are common. These sentences express displeasure or frustration, and could be translated as "and to think that . . ."

- 彼はすごく金持ちなのに ... And to think that he's so rich ...
- なんでそれが欲しくないの？ただなのに ... Why don't you want that? It's free ...

🎧 Although / in spite of: くせに

くせに is like のに. While のに can be used in formally and colloquially, くせに is colloquial or even vulgar, with pejorative and accusatory connotations. **Usage:** Nothing is added after verbs or *-i* adjectives. With nouns, の needed; with *-na* adjectives, we use な.

- 何も知らないくせに、何を言っているの？ You don't know anything; what are you saying?
- 医者のくせに、病気を治せない Although he's a doctor, he can't cure sickness.

As with のに, we will sometimes find くせに at the end of a sentence that trails off.

- 何だ、その態度？がきのくせに ... What's with that attitude? You're nothing but a little brat ...

🎧 Even / even if: 〜ても

In Lesson 32 we saw the expression 〜てもいい, to ask for permission. We will now study a related expression, since the basic structure is exactly the same: 〜ても, meaning "even" or "even if," in sentences expressing hypothesis or conjecture, unlike のに, which is used with sentences whose certainty is assured. **Usage:** Verbs, nouns, and adjectives of both kinds must be conjugated in the *-te* form (Lesson 35), to which も is added.

🎧 Interrogatives + 〜ても	
何を言っても	No matter what he says . . .
誰に言っても	No matter who he says it to . . .
どう言っても	No matter how he says it . . .
どんな説明をしても	No matter how he explains . . .
どこへ行っても	No matter where he goes . . .
いつ行っても	No matter when he goes . . .
いくら払っても	No matter how much he pays...
言う *iu* to say; 説明する *setsumei suru* to explain; 行く *iku* to go; 払う *harau* to pay	

- 雨が降っても、試合を行います Even if it rains, the match will be held.
- 免許がなくても、このバイクを運転できる Even without a license, you can drive this motorcycle.
- パソコンを買っても仕事ができない Even if I buy a computer, I can't work.
- 難しくても、試験に合格したい No matter how difficult it is, I want to pass the exam.
- この問題、アホでも解ける Even a fool can solve this problem.

If we add an interrogative pronoun or adverb (Lesson 34) to a verb + ても, we obtain sentences such as: "no matter what I do . . ." or "no matter what it is . . ." (see table, above).

- いつ行っても、あの店は閉まっている No matter when I go, that shop is closed.
- 何を言っても、君を許すつもりはない No matter what you say, I won't forgive you.

🎧 Strong recommendation: 〜方がいい

Let's look at some other constructions. 〜方がいい *hō ga ii* , is used to make strong recommendations or suggestions, not quite orders, but almost. **Usage:** This expression is only used with verbs, which must be conjugated in the past tense (except with negative expressions, when verbs are conjugated in the negative of the present tense).

- 彼女に花をあげた方がいいと思うよ I think you should give her some flowers.

- 彼を殺すのをあきらめた方がいいよ If I were you, I'd forget about killing him.
- その水を飲まない方がいいよ I recommend you don't drink that water.
- 腐っているから、みかんを食べない方がいいよ Don't eat the mandarins, because they are rotten.

🎧 More usages of the -ō conjugation

Let's now see two expressions using the -ō conjugation, which we studied in Lesson 34, and which on its own means "let's . . ."

All you need to do is add 〜とする or 〜と思う to a verb in the -ō form to create two new expressions with different meanings, which can be very useful.

We will start with the construction -ō form + とする. It means "to try to" or, more literally, "to be in the process of doing something."

- 私は銀行強盗をしようとしていた I was trying to rob a bank.
- 彼はバスに乗ろうとした時、死んだ As he was going to get on the bus, he died.
- マンガを描こうとしているけど、難しいね I'm trying to draw a comic book, but it's difficult.
- バカなのに大学に入ろうとしている Even though I'm stupid, I'm trying to get into university.

The second new expression -ō form + と思 is used to indicate something like "I think I'm going to . . . ," that is, it is simply the combination of the -ō form ("let's . . . ," Lesson 34) plus と思う ("I think that . . ." Lesson 41).

- 彼女に告白しようと思っています I'm thinking of declaring my love to her.
- 勉強をやめようと思っている I'm thinking about abandoning my studies.
- 鈴木さんは家を買おうと思っている Mr. Suzuki is thinking of buying a house.

🎧 Conjunctions

We will finish this third lesson in our series devoted to the formation of compound sentences by studying a few essential conjunctions. On page 179 you also have a summary table with all the conjunctions we have seen thus far.

But / however / nevertheless: だけれども / だけれど / だけど / でも / しかし

- 社長はとても優しいです。だけれど、その息子は鬼みたいに厳しいです
  The director is very kind. However, his son is so demanding, he's like an ogre.

• 巻き寿司は大好きだ。でも、きゅうりの巻き寿司は大嫌いだ！
  I love makizushi. But I hate cucumber makizushi!

In spite of that / however: それなのに / なのに

• 加藤さんはとても金持ちです。それなのに、非常にけちです
  Mr. Kato is very rich. In spite of that, he is extremely stingy.
• 僕はかっこいい。なのに、女が寄ってこない
  I'm handsome. However, the girls don't come near me.

🎧 Compound sentences (3): General summary table		
〜けれ ども 〜けれど 〜けど 〜が	But / However / Nevertheless (〜けれども: formal, 〜けれど: neutral, 〜けど: informal, 〜が: neutral / formal)	彼は歯科医ですけれども、歯を抜けません He's a dentist, but he can't pull out a tooth. (formal)
		彼は歯科医だけど、歯を抜けない He's a dentist, but he can't pull out a tooth. (inf.)
		彼は歯科医だが、歯を抜けません He's a dentist but he can't pull out a tooth. (neutral / formal)
〜のに	Although / In spite of	彼は歯科医なのに、歯を抜けない Although he's a dentist, he can't pull out a tooth.
〜くせに	Although / In spite of (informal / pejorative)	彼は歯科医のくせに、歯を抜けない Although he is a dentist, he can't even pull out a tooth! (pejorative)
〜ても	Even if / Although (In hypothetical sentences)	彼は歯科医でも、歯も抜けない Even if he is a dentist, he can't pull out a tooth.
〜方が いい	You had better / You should (Strong recommendation or suggestion)	歯が痛いだろう？歯科医に行った方がいいよ Your tooth is painful, isn't it? You should go to the dentist.
〜おう とする	To try to / To be in the process of doing something"	歯科医が歯を抜こうとしていた The dentist was trying to pull out a tooth.
〜おう と思	I think I'm going to …	歯が痛いから、歯科医に行こうと思っている Since my tooth is hurting, I think I'm going to go to the dentist.

彼 *kare* he; 歯科医 *shikai* dentist; 歯 *ha* tooth; 抜く *nuku* to pull out; 痛い *itai* painful;
行く *iku* to go

L.46	例えば	For example	花が好きです。例えば、桜や椿が大好きです I like flowers. For example, I like sakura and camellias very much.
L.46	ところで	By the way	いい天気だね。ところで、桜はもう咲いた？ Isn't the weather fine? By the way, have the sakura bloomed yet?
L.46	それに	Besides	椿は満開です。それに、桜もきれいです The camellias are in full bloom. And besides, the sakura are pretty too.
L.48	そして	And later / And then	昼ご飯を食べた。そして、桜を見に行った I ate lunch. And then, I went to see the sakura.
L.48	それで	Then / Therefore	今日、昼ご飯を食べなかった。それで、今とてもお腹がすいている I haven't had lunch today. Therefore, I'm very hungry now.
L.48	それでは	Well then / Then	おはようございます！それでは、桜を見に行こう！ Good morning! Well then, let's go and see the sakura!
L.48	それから	After that	今日は桜を見に行きます。それから、昼ご飯を食べるつもりです Today, I'm going to see the sakura. After that, I intend to have lunch.
L.48	だから	Therefore	桜が咲いた。だから、見に行きました。 The sakura have bloomed. Therefore, I went to see them.
L.49	だけれども だけれど だけど でも しかし	But However Nevertheless	椿はもう咲いています。だけれども、桜はまだ咲いていません The camellias have already bloomed. However, the sakura haven't bloomed yet. もう昼ご飯を食べた。でも、まだお腹がすいている I have already had lunch. But I'm still hungry. 今日はいい天気です。しかし、明日は雨が降るそうです Today the weather is fine. But, apparently, it is going to rain tomorrow.
L.49	それなのに なのに	Despite that/ However	桜が咲いている。なのに、見に行けない The sakura have bloomed. However I can't go to see them.

Summary table: Conjunctions (Lessons 46, 48 and 49)

花 *hana* flower; 好きな *suki-na* that one likes; 桜 *sakura* cherry blossom (sakura); 椿 *tsubaki* camellia; いい *ii* fine; 今 *ima* now; 天気 *tenki* weather; 咲く *saku* to bloom; 満開 *mankai* full bloom; きれいな pretty; 昼ごはん *hiru gohan* lunch; 食べる *taberu* to eat; 見に行く *mi ni iku* to go to see; 今日 *kyō* today; お腹がすく *o naka ga suku* to be hungry; 明日 *ashita* tomorrow; 雨が降る *ame ga furu* to rain

🎧 漫画例 **Manga Examples**

We've really stepped up the pace in the last few lessons as we study more and more complicated aspects of the language and we hope that you can feel your Japanese rapidly improving. Don't give up now, you are doing very well!

Manga Example 1: Sentence-ending *kedo* and usage of *no ni*

We get to see two expressions in this example. To start with, take a look at the clerk's first sentence, それなら 安 く しとく けど and the けど closing it. The meaning of this けど is not exactly "but" (as usually is the case in the word's most orthodox usage); it is more a way of leaving the sentence unfinished, thus softening the statement and perhaps implying something unspoken (in this case something like "but why on earth would you want to buy something like that?!")

Regarding the のに in あんた外国人なのに, notice that as it is placed after a noun 外国人, it needs the help of な. Here, the speaker expresses some surprise, therefore, it is not unusual that he uses のに, as you will remember that this construction has a relevant ingredient of subjectivity. Here, のに can be translated as "despite." **Notes:** The prefix お before the word いくら (how much) is honorific and implies respect (Lesson 52). The 〜とく in 安くしとく is a spoken contraction of 〜ておく (Lesson 35). The adjective 妙な *myō na* (written here in katakana) is difficult to translate: it has the connotation of "strange" or "unexpected." もん is the colloquial contraction of the word 物 *mono* (thing).

George: これ、おいくらですか？
this, how much be Q?
How much is this?

Man: それなら安^{やす}くしとくけど…
that if cheap put but . . .
I can make that cheap for you . . .

George: あんた外国人^{がいこくじん}なのに、ミョウなもんに興味^{きょうみ}あるんだね。
you foreigner although, strange thing IOP interest there are be EP
Despite being a foreigner, you are interested in very strange things, aren't you?

Manga Example 2: *Shikashi* and *no ni* at the end of a sentence

Here we also have two expressions to comment on. The first one is しかし meaning "but," "however" or "nevertheless." It is certainly a very useful word, although in colloquial register でも (but) is used more often.

The second expression is のに, closing the panel and leaving the sentence's conclusion in the air. Its meaning could be translated as "although" but in this context we can interpret it as "To think it hasn't rained . . ." or "But it hasn't rained . . ." **Note:** 降っちゃいない is the contraction of 降ってはいない. Notice the emphatic particle も in this construction: go back to Lesson 37 to review its usage.

Gabriel Luque

Satoru: しかし…どうしてこんなに水がにごっているのだろう…？

however . . . why like this water SP muddy POP be . . . ?

However . . . I wonder why the water is so muddy?

大雨も降っちゃいないのに…

heavy rain neither fall although . . .

But it hasn't rained that heavily . . .

Manga Example 3: The pejorative expression *kuse ni*

We have learned how the expression くせに means "although," "despite," but with a pejorative nuance. With this same pejorative intention, we have translated the 何もできないくせに part, literally "In spite of not being able to do anything," as "Despite his incompetence," because the word "incompetence" implies that the speaker is superior or disdainful. **Note:**

The construction 〜やがる shows violence, extreme roughness, or a threat. We will study it in Lesson 53. As you have probably noticed, using くせに and やがる in the same sentence gives it a layer of "threat" or "disdain" almost impossible to convey in a translation.

Xian Nu Studio

Kisaki: 何もできないくせに…妙に人の心を動かしやがる…

nothing can in spite of… strange person POP heart DOP move (vulgar)

Despite his incompetence . . . he can oddly move people . . .

Manga Example 4: Expressing "even" with *-temo*

It is now time to review the usage of the construction *-te* form + も (or 〜ても as we saw earlier in this chapter) which, you will remember, has the meaning of "even" or "although," and is used in sentences expressing hypothesis. In this sentence, the speaker expresses the hypothesis 死んでも, and then the result if that supposition finally became true: 後悔はしない. **Notes:** Notice the usage of ために (for), which in this case comes with the *kosoado* その (that), forming そのために (for that), as we saw in Lesson 48. Notice, too, the emphatic usage of the particle は in 後悔はしない (I won't regret it) (Lesson 37).

Xian Nu Studio

Tetsuya: そのために死んでも後悔はしないぞ！

that for die regret TOP do not EP!

Even if I die for that, I won't regret it!

Manga Example 5: No matter how . . .

In this chapter we also saw that we combine an interrogative plus a verb and the 〜ても construction, we obtain sentences such as: "no matter what I do . . ." Here we have one of them: いくら電話しても (no matter how much I call . . .). Usually, いくら has the meaning of "how much" when talking about quantity of money, but here it is used for a more general meaning of "how much / many." Another option would be 何回電話しても *nan kai denwa shitemo* (no matter how many times I call . . .). **Notes:** Take the opportuni-

Studio Kōsen

ty to review ので ("since," "because," Lesson 48), and notice as well the 〜てみる construction (giving the nuance of "try to do something," Lesson 35) of きてみた. Last of all, the んだ closing the sentence is the typical tag used to give "security" or to "soften" the sentence, which we studied in Manga Example 4 in Lesson 40.

Seiji: いくら電話しても出ないので、心配になって来てみたんだ

how much telephone do go out since worry become come try be

Since no matter how much I called no one answered, I got worried and came.

Manga Example 6: *Hō ga ii* for strong suggestion

And now we focus on 〜方がいい *hō ga ii,* used to give suggestions or advice and rather strong; not quite an order, but it comes very close. Usually, 〜方がいい is used to advise other people. However, we see here a slightly different usage: the speaker is consulting about something that she thinks might be necessary for her to do: あたしは死んだほうが

Studio K'osen

いいのか？ Remember that the verb before 〜方がいい must be conjugated in the past-affirmative (死んだ方がいい) or present-negative (死なない方がいい). **Note:** やっぱり has no direct translation: it's something like "after all" or "I knew that."

Chie: あたしやっぱり死んだほうがいいんかなぁ

I after all die better if Q? EP

After all, it is better if I die, isn't it?

Manga Example 7: Usage of *-ō to suru*

The final manga example in this lesson lesson will help illustrate the usage of the 〜おうとする construction (to try to, to be in the process of doing something). In our sentence, Noriko says 逃げようとしている. In order to master this construction, you should thoroughly review the *-ō* form (Lesson 34). **Note:** Notice the いつかのように part. いつか means "sometime." (Lesson 41). のように is a comparative (like) we briefly saw in Lesson 43, and which we will study in depth in Lesson 54. いつかのように means "like (I did) some other time."

Gabriel Luque

Seiji: ああわたしは…わたしはまたいつかのように逃げようとしている…

aah I TOP . . . I TOP again someday like in the process of . . .

Aah, I . . . I'm trying to escape, like some other time . . .

Exercises 練習

(1) Translate into formal Japanese: "I'm hungry, but I don't have any money." (to be hungry: お腹がすいている , money お金)

(2) What differences in formality are there between the expressions: けれども, が, けど and けれど?

(3) What is けど used for in the sentence すみません、これが欲しいんだけど ...? (すみません : excuse me, 欲しい : to want)

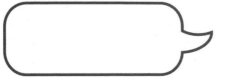

(4) Translate: 魚 は好きなのに、どうして寿司は嫌いなの？ (魚 : fish, 好きな : that one likes, 寿司 sushi, 嫌いな : that one dislikes)

(5) Translate this sentence: 彼女 は大人のくせにそんな 服を着ている。(彼女 : she, 大人 adult, 服 clothes, 着る : to wear)

(6) Translate: "Even if I go to Japan, I won't learn Japanese." (to go: 行く , Japan: 日本 , to learn: 習う , Japanese: 日本語)

(7) Translate: "No matter how much I study, I don't learn anything." (to study: 勉強 する , to learn: 習う , nothing: 何も)

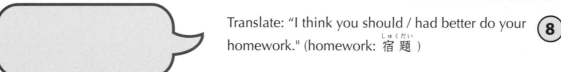

(8) Translate: "I think you should / had better do your homework." (homework: 宿題)

(9) Translate: 山本 さんは 論文 を書こうとしている。(山本 : Yamamoto, 論文 : thesis, 書く : to write)

(10) Translate into colloquial Japanese: "There's a party today. But you should not go." (today: 今日 , party: パーティー , to go: 行く)

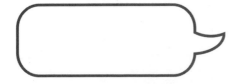

— **Answers to all the exercises can be found online by following the link on page 7.** —

Lesson 50 • 第50課

Relative Clauses

In this lesson we will learn how to give more depth to our sentences by means of relative clauses to provide additional information about a noun.

🎧 What is a relative clause?

Relative clauses give extra information about a noun, for example: "The **house** <u>which is near the school</u> is blue," "That **man** <u>who is walking in the town</u> is my uncle," or "The **dog** <u>whose fur is black</u> is big." The relative clauses we have underlined give extra information about the nouns "house," "man," and "dog," respectively.

Notice how in English we use relative pronouns such as "which" or "whose" to introduce these kinds of clauses. In Japanese, we don't need any such pronoun, although we must bear in mind that the order in these kinds of sentences is often the total reverse of the English order: the noun comes last.

* <u>あの学校に近い</u>家は青いです The house <u>that is near the school</u> is blue.
* <u>街を歩いている</u>あの男は叔父です That man <u>who is walking around the town</u> is my uncle.
* <u>あの黒い毛の</u>犬は大きいです The dog <u>with black fur</u> / <u>whose fur is black</u> is big.

🎧 How to form relative clauses

Forming relative clauses is not difficult, but you must bear in mind the following rules:

⇒ The noun about which information is offered must go <u>after</u> the relative clause.

⇒ If the relative clause ends in a verb or an **-i** adjective, these must be conjugated in the simple form. With **-na** adjectives, we require な, and with nouns, we must add の. But in the past tense or the negative, they both need the verb to be conjugated in the simple form.

⇒ The subject in a relative clause is never marked with the topic particle は: the subject particle が is compulsory, unless we are looking to add emphasis. For example:

* <u>猫が食べた</u>魚は高かった The fish <u>that the cat ate</u> was expensive. (With は after 猫 we would explicitly express that it was the cat and no one else who ate the fish.)

⇒ When there is nothing between the subject and the verb of the relative clause, the が (indicating subject) can be replaced by の without distinction. For example:

* <u>車が / の通った</u>道路は狭い The road <u>where the car passed</u> was narrow.

🎧 "Internal" relative clauses

Let's look at two kinds of relative clauses: "internal" and "external." "Internal" relative clauses are those where the noun (about which information is provided) is part of the original sentence from which the relative clause is derived. Refer to the table and you'll get a clearer idea: 少年 **shōnen**, 倉庫 **sōko**, 友達 **tomodachi** and 本 **hon** are part of a basic hypothetical phrase, and they can all be "embellished" by the other words in order to "stand out." Let's now see a few example sentences of this kind:

🎧 Relative clauses
Basic sentence: 少年は倉庫で友達に本を見せた The boy showed a book to his friend in the warehouse
"Internal" relative clauses
倉庫で友達に本を見せた 少年 <u>The boy</u> who showed a book to his friend in the warehouse
少年が倉庫で本を見せた 友達 <u>The friend</u> to whom the boy showed a book in the warehouse
少年が倉庫で友達に見せた 本 <u>The book</u> which the boy showed to his friend in the warehouse
少年が友達に本をみせた 倉庫 <u>The warehouse</u> where the boy showed a book to his friend
"External" relative clauses
少年が倉庫で友達に本を見せた 日 <u>The day</u> when the boy showed a book to his friend in the warehouse
少年が倉庫で友達に本を見せた という 理由 <u>The reason</u> why the boy showed a book to this friend in the warehouse
少年が倉庫で友達に本を見せた という こと <u>The fact</u> that the boy showed a book to his friend in the warehouse
少年 **shōnen** boy; 倉庫 **sōko** warehouse; 友達 **tomodachi** friend; 本 **hon** book; 見せる **miseru** to show; 日 **hi** day; 理由 **riyū** reason

• <u>日本語を習っている</u> あの女性は親切だ That woman <u>who is learning Japanese</u> is kind.

• 彼が使ったタオルは洗濯機に入れた
I put the towel <u>that he used</u> in the washing machine.

• <u>日本語が上手だった</u>人は少なかった
There were few people <u>who were good at Japanese.</u>

• <u>汚れた服の</u>女はどこに行った？
Where has the woman <u>whose clothes were dirty</u> gone?

• <u>センスがよくない人が集まる</u>場所に行かなければならない
I must go to a place <u>where people who don't have style meet</u>. (two relative clauses)

🎧 "External" relative clauses

There are also relative clauses where the noun (about which information is provided) is not a part of the basic hypothetical phrase (see table on the facing page). Some of these nouns cannot be directly linked to the sentence; to do so, they require という (or って in its colloquial form).

Never take という: nouns expressing feelings (音 *oto* sound, 匂い *nioi* smell, 痛み *itami* pain); nouns perceived by the senses (写真 *shashin* photo, 音楽 *ongaku* music).

- 腐った魚の匂いがひどいです The smell <u>of rotten fish</u> is disgusting.
- ビートの強い音楽が好きだ I like music <u>with a strong beat</u>.

Always take という: abstract concepts expressing thoughts or assertions (うわさ rumor, こと fact / thing, 意見 *iken* opinion, 理由 *riyū* reason, 考え *kangae* thought . . .).

- 政府が悪いという意見はありますか Is your opinion <u>that the government is bad</u>?
- 彼らがラスベガスで結婚したいってうわさは本当かな？

  Is the rumor <u>that they want to get married in Las Vegas</u> true?

In other cases, it doesn't matter whether we use という or not:

- マンガを翻訳する（って）仕事は楽しい The job <u>of translating manga</u> is fun.
- 男が自殺した（という）事件があった There was an incident <u>in which a man died</u>.

🎧 The many usages of よう

In Japanese several expressions and grammatical constructions use よう. Let's start by reviewing the よう constructions seen in Lesson 43. First, we have ようだ at the end of a sentence to mean "apparently," when the speaker's degree of certainty is high:

- 天気が崩れたようだね Apparently, the weather has worsened.
- 彼女の弟さんは背が高いようだ Apparently, her younger brother is tall.
- 先生は娘をしかったようです Apparently, the teacher scolded my daughter.

We also have the ような and ように variations, which act as simile (Lesson 54):

- あの鬼のような先生が嫌いだ I hate that teacher who is like an ogre.
- 彼は政治家のようにうそをつくね He lies (tells lies) like a politician.

🎧 In order to: ように

ように after verbs (only), usually in the simple form, indicates "in order to" or "so that," to express that a certain action be implemented to obtain a desired outcome.

　The structure of this kind of sentence is always "[result] ように [action]." That is, before ように we specify the result we want to obtain and, afterward, we detail the action or actions that must be done to achieve it.

- 日本へ行けるように働いている I'm working in order to go to Japan.
- 猫が魚を食べないように隠そう I shall hide the fish so that the cat doesn't eat it.
- 合格できるように祈りたい I want to pray so that I can pass.
- 事故がないように気をつけてください Be careful (in order) not to have an accident.
- 父が怒らないように謝ろう I shall apologize so that my father doesn't get angry.

🎧 Soft command or request: ように + verb

The expression ように combined with a verb like 言う *iu* (to say), 頼む *tanomu* (to ask), or 命令する *meirei suru* (to command) is a way of asking someone to do something. You can't make a direct request or order with this structure. ように + verb is normally used either to indicate what kind of order or request oneself or a third person has received, or to describe an order or request in an indirect way or which was performed in the past:

- 先生は私に本を読むように言った The teacher told me to read a book.
- 社長は山崎にやめるように言った The president told Yamazaki to resign.
- 彼女はあそこで待つように僕に頼んだ She asked me to wait there.
- 川井にオフィスへ来るように言ってください Please tell Kawai to come to the office.
- 私は息子に勉強するように命令した I ordered my son to study.

Note: Since we are talking about orders, you can review Lesson 30, where the imperative is explained, as well as the usage of 〜てくれ, which we studied in Lesson 45.

🎧 To get to the point of: ようになる

ようになる usually indicates gradual change or the end of processes that are usually long. It means "to get to the point of . . . ," "to finally manage to . . ." or "to become able to . . ." This expression can only be used with verbs conjugated in the simple form.

- 彼は泳ぐようになった He managed to (learn to) swim.
- 日本語を話せるようになりたい I want to become able to speak Japanese.
- タバコを吸わないようになった I managed to not smoke. (I managed to quit smoking.)
- やっと統計が分かるようになった I have finally managed to understand statistics.

🎧 To try to do something: ようにする

The last よう expression we will see is ようにする, used to express an intention or decision. An exact translation of this expression is very difficult to suggest, but we could define ようにする more or less as "to decide to do something...," "to try to do something...," "to have the intention of using all the necessary means to do something...," etc.

- 毎朝、運動するようにしたい I want to try to exercise every morning.
- 彼はあまり食べないようにしている He is trying not to eat much.
- 明日、十時に来るようにしてください Tomorrow, make sure you come at 10.
- 政治家はうそをつかないようにしないといけない Politicians must try not to lie.

🎧 Usages of よう		
ようだ (Lesson 43)	Apparently	彼は城に行ったようだ Apparently, he went to the castle.
ような (Lesson 43 / 54)	Simile	彼は城のような家に住んでいる He lives in a house that looks like a castle.
ように (1)	Adverbial form of よう	あの家は城のように広い That house is as spacious as a castle.
ように (2)	In order to / so that	城に行けるように地図を書こう I'll draw you a map so that you can go to the castle.
ように (3)	Order / Request	彼は地図を書くように言った He told / asked me to draw a map.
ようになる	To get to the point of ...	彼は地図を書けるようになった He has got to the point of being able to draw a map.
ようにする	To try / decide to do something"	毎日、城まで走って行くようにする I'm going to try to run to the castle every day.

彼 *kare* he; 城 *shiro* castle; 行く *iku* to go; 家 *ie* house; 住む *sumu* to live; 広い *hiroi* spacious, wide; 地図 *chizu* map; 書く *kaku* to write, to draw; 言う *iu* to say; 毎日 *mainichi* every day; 走る *hashiru* to run

🎧 漫画例 **Manga Examples**

These manga examples will help you review relative clauses and give you a clearer idea of the numerous usages of よう**.**

Manga Example 1: A simple relative clause

This manga is written in hiragana, in the style of children's stories, because children can't read kanji. The sentence should be: 目の大きな人はお腹がすいて死にそうです. The relative clause is 目の大きな, and it provides information about the noun 人. Notice that as we saw earlier in this chapter, the subject particle が is sometimes replaced with の. Therefore, 目が大きな人 (the man with big eyes) would also be valid.

   In Japanese the concepts of restrictive and non-restrictive relative clauses don't exist. The sentence 目の大きな人は親切だ *me no ooki-na hito wa shinsetsu da* can mean both "the man, who has big eyes, is kind" (non-restrictive) and "the man who has big eyes is kind" (restrictive). In this case, the relative clause is restrictive. **Notes:** Notice how the sentences お腹がすいている (to be hungry) and 死にそうです (he looks like he is going to die) are linked by the *-te* form (lessons 35 and 46). Notice, too, the usage of the suffix for conjecture 〜そうだ in 死にそうです.

めのおおきなひとは、おなかがすいてしにそうです

Xian Nu Studio

Narrator: めのおおきなひとは、おなかがすいてしにそうです
eye POP big person TOP, stomach SP empty die be
The man who had big eyes was starving to death.

Manga Example 2: An "internal" relative clause

J.M. Ken Niimura

Here the relative clause: ミュンヘン大学の図書館で私が銃で撃った describes the noun 男. It is an "internal" relative clause because the noun 男 is part of the basic phrase 私はミュンヘン大学の図書館で私が銃で撃った. **Note:** The subject of the relative clause (in this case 私) never takes は; it needs が.

Zange: 彼は、ミュンヘン大学の図書館で私が銃で撃った男だ！！

he TOP, München university POP library PP I SP gun IP shoot man be

He is the man I shot with a gun in the library of the University of Munich!!

Manga Example 3: An "external" relative clause

Studio K'osen

Here is an "external" relative clause, meaning the noun about which the information is given is totally independent, not part of a basic hypothetical phrase. Here, the noun is 噂, and the relative clause is おまえがムコ候補に肩入れしている.

We mentioned that some nouns require という when linked to a relative clause where the noun expresses an abstract concept, like thoughts or assertions. 噂 is such a concept, so we will use either という or the shorter colloquial form って, as here.

Sayama: おまえがムコ候補に肩入れしているって噂は聞いてるぜ

you SP son-in-law candidate support do say rumor TOP hear EP

I have heard the rumor that you support him as a candidate for son-in-law.

Manga Example 4: Two usages of *yō*

In this manga example we have two different usages of よう. In 食欲もそこそこ出てきたようだ, we have ようだ meaning "apparently" (Lesson 43). In 会話もできるようになった, we see ようになる, indicating a gradual change, literally, "She has become able to hold a conversation [after an adaptation period which has taken place gradually and which has already concluded]." **Note:** し is used to indicate "not only X, but also Y" (Lesson 46).

Xian Nu Studio

Doctor:　彼女、食欲もそこそこでてきたようだし、会話もできるようになった

she appetite too a little go out apparently besides, conversation too to get to

Apparently, she has recovered some of her appetite and, what's more, she is able to talk now.

Manga Example 5: In order to, using *yō ni*

Here, ように expresses "so that" or "in order to." The aim is お客様に良いことがたくさんあります and the action to be performed to achieve it is ここで見守って. The phrase ように is placed in the middle, after the clause indicating the aim, to link both clauses and convey the meaning "in order to." **Note:** Before ように the verb is usually in the simple form, but since the register here is formal, she has chosen to leave the verb あります in the *-masu* form.

Gabriel Luque

Boss:　お客様に良いことがたくさんありますようにここで見守ってね！

Mr. client IOP good thing SP many there is so that here PP pay attention EP!

Stay here and pay attention in order to make sure the clients have everything they need!

Manga Example 6: Request, using *yō* + verb

In this request we see the construction ように + verb for soft requests or orders.

The phrase 待つように言った is obviously a request. Other possible phrases could have been: 待つように頼んだ ***matsu yō ni tanonda*** (you asked him to wait) or 待つように命令した ***matsu yō ni meirei shita*** (you ordered him to wait), etc. **Note:** The expression 〜そうだ here is different to the one in Lesson 43, Manga Example 1 (to give information obtained from another source). Thus, 待つように言ったそうだ literally means "I've heard / been told that you have told him to wait."

Man:	お母さん、銀行の支店長に融資を待つように言ったそうだね

mom, bank POP branch director IOP funds DOP wait (request) say looks like be EP

Mom, you've told the bank manager to wait for the funds, haven't you?

Manga Example 7: To try to do something, using *yō ni suru*

ようにする has the nuance of "try to" or "decide to do something." The sentence 彼女と話すようにしたい has the connotation of either "I want to try to talk with her" or "I want to have the intention of doing all I possibly can to talk with her." That is, using ようにする is more or less the same as a declaration of intent. **Note:** これから (literally, "from this") means "from now on," "after this."

Naoya:	これから、彼女と話すようにしたいなぁ…

this from, her CP talk try to want EP . . .

From now on, I want to try to talk to her . . .

Exercises 練習

1 Which is the relative clause in this sentence? "The man who loved Makiko is called Koji."

2 Translate the sentence in question 1. (man 男^{おとこ}; to love 愛^{あい}する; Makiko 真紀子^{まきこ}; Koji 浩二^{こうじ})

3 Translate: "The motorcycle Akira bought is very fast." (motorcycle バイク; to buy 買^かう; Akira 明^{あきら}; very とても; fast 速^{はや}い)

4 Are these sentences correct? Why/why not? 彼^{かれ}が売^うっている梨^{なし}が甘^{あま}い。彼の売っている梨が甘い。(彼 he; 売る to sell; 梨 pear; 甘い sweet)

5 Translate: 彼^{かれ}がヤクザから賄賂^{わいろ}をもらったという事件^{じけん}は本当^{ほんとう}ですか (彼 he; 賄賂 bribe; もらう to receive; 事件 case; 本当 true)

6 In Japanese temples, people write down prayers, such as 合格^{ごうかく}するように . What does this sentence mean? (合格する to pass an exam)

7 Translate: "The customer told the sales clerk to shut up." (customer お客^{きゃく}さん; to tell 言^いう; sales clerk 店員^{てんいん}; to shut up 黙^{だま}る)

8 Translate: "I want to be able to read a book." (to read 読^よむ; book 本^{ほん})

9 Translate: 毎日^{まいにち}、8 時間^{じかん}は寝^ねるようにしています。(毎日 every day; 時間 time; 寝る to sleep)

10 Does Japanese distinguish between restrictive and non-restrictive relative clauses? Explain using an example.

— **Answers to all the exercises can be found online by following the link on page 7.** —

Exercises 練習

1 Which is the relative clause in this sentence? "The man who loved Makiko is called Koji."

2 Translate the sentence in question 1. (man 男（おとこ）; to love 愛（あい）する; Makiko 真紀子（まきこ）; Koji 浩二（こうじ）)

3 Translate: "The motorcycle Akira bought is very fast." (motorcycle バイク; to buy 買（か）う; Akira 明（あきら）; very とても; fast 速（はや）い)

4 Are these sentences correct? Why/why not? 彼（かれ）が売（う）っている梨（なし）が甘（あま）い。彼の売っている梨が甘い。(彼 he; 売る to sell; 梨 pear; 甘い sweet)

5 Translate: 彼（かれ）がヤクザから賄賂（わいろ）をもらったという事件（じけん）は本当（ほんとう）ですか (彼 he; 賄賂 bribe; もらう to receive; 事件 case; 本当 true)

6 In Japanese temples, people write down prayers, such as 合格（ごうかく）するように . What does this sentence mean? (合格する to pass an exam)

7 Translate: "The customer told the sales clerk to shut up." (customer お客（きゃく）さん; to tell 言（い）う; sales clerk 店員（てんいん）; to shut up 黙（だま）る)

8 Translate: "I want to be able to read a book." (to read 読（よ）む; book 本（ほん）)

9 Translate: 毎日（まいにち）、8 時間（じかん）は寝（ね）るようにしています。(毎日 every day; 時間 time; 寝る to sleep)

10 Does Japanese distinguish between restrictive and non-restrictive relative clauses? Explain using an example.

— **Answers to all the exercises can be found online by following the link on page 7.** —

今日の朝と午後、ヌリアは
元気に写真をとったり、
散歩をしたりした。

Review for Lessons 46–50

Answers to all the review exercises can be found online by following the link on page 7.

🎧 *KAGE* – New vocabulary 新しい単語

遅い (おそい)	slow / late	のんきな	carefree
うそ	lie	ラブホテル	love hotel
他の	other	勝手にする	to do as one pleases, to do what one likes

1. According to what you have read in the fourth episode of *Kage*, what is the name of the young man who helped Nuria the day before? What does he suggest they do when they leave the manga store? Once they finally have a date, what does he suggest after leaving the restaurant?

2. Nuria had gone into a store to do something. What?

3. What do Nuria and her companion end up ordering at the restaurant?

4. What food doesn't the young man like? How about Nuria?

5. Why do they both laugh when they find out what food the other doesn't like?

6. Mina calls Nuria to give her a message. Who is the message from, and what is its approximate content?

7. What does のに indicate in the following sentences?

a) 写真をとるのにこの店に入った　_____

b) 日本人なのに寿司（すし）が好きじゃない　_____

8. In this episode of *Kage*, there are two sentences with conjuctions that have a similar meaning to the two examples of のに in question 7, above. Find them.

a) _____.

b) _____.

9. Translate into English the following sentences from the text of **Kage**.

a) しゃべっているうちにとても遅<small>おそ</small>くなった。

_____.

b) 彼<small>かれ</small>がヌリアのカメラを取<small>と</small>ろうとしたので、オレは助<small>たす</small>けようと思った。

_____.

c) ヌリアは元気に写真をとったり、散歩<small>さんぽ</small>をしたりした。

_____.

d) ヌリアの送った写真はあまりよくない。

_____.

e) 他<small>ほか</small>の人を送った方がいいかもね！

_____.

10. Why do we find the particle の in the sentence ヌリアの送った写真はあまりよく ない？Could we use the particle は instead? How about the particle が？

11. In this episode of the manga we see several sentences ending in けど or in が , such as あ、オレは達也<small>たつや</small>だけど… or あたしはトマトが嫌<small>きら</small>いだけど… or お酒<small>さけ</small>を 飲んでいる場合<small>ばぁい</small>じゃないと思いますが… What is the meaning of these けど or が at the end of the sentences?

12. Place each word from the box on the facing page into the correct place in the chart, ac-cording to its category.

Utensils	
Herbs and spices	
Fruit	いちご
Vegetables	

Meat	
Fish	
Drinks	

いちご　　酢^す　　紅茶^{こうちゃ}　　ワイン　　牛肉^{ぎゅうにく}　　トマト　　にんじん

貝^{かい}　　キウイ　　さくらんぼ　　ステーキ　　ジュース　　鶏肉^{とりにく}　　ナイフ

豚肉^{ぶたにく}　　茶碗^{ちゃわん}　　かつお　　かつお　　水　　カフェオレ　　なす

びん　　にんにく　　塩^{しお}　　なべ　　ハム　　桃^{もも}　　コーヒー

ビール　　オレンジ　　バナナ　　お箸^{はし}　　お皿^{さら}　　フォーク　　にら

日本酒^{にほんしゅ}　　グラス　　たこ　　じゃがいも　　キャベツ　　いか　　まぐろ

なし　　ソーセージ　　羊肉^{ひつじにく}　　みかん　　いわし　　ケチャップ　　油^{あぶら}

13. Link each Japanese dish with its corresponding description.

a) ご飯^{はん}の上に牛肉^{ぎゅうにく}を置^おいたもの

b) ご飯^{はん}に野菜^{やさい}を入れて、炒^{いた}めたもの

c) ご飯^{はん}の上に生^{なま}の魚を握^{にぎ}ったもの

d) 肉^{にく}を焼^やいたもの

e) ご飯^{はん}の上に鶏肉^{とりにく}と卵^{たまご}を置^おいたもの

f) 野菜^{やさい}や魚をたくさんの油^{あぶら}で揚^あげたもの

1) 焼肉^{やきにく}

2) 牛丼^{ぎゅうどん}

3) 天ぷら

4) 親子丼^{おやこどん}

5) 寿司^{すし}

6) チャーハン

14. Fill in the blanks with the most suitable word from the box at the end of the exercise.

a) お茶^{ちゃ}が＿＿＿＿＿＿＿＿＿＿＿＿＿＿ので、甘^{あま}いおかしも食^たべましょう。

b) 十二時になりました。＿＿＿＿＿＿＿＿＿＿を一緒^{いっしょ}に食べましょうか？

c) 私は辛いものはだめなので、すしを＿＿＿＿＿＿＿＿なしにしてください。

d) ご飯を食べる前に、＿＿＿＿＿＿＿＿＿＿で手をきれいにしてください。

e) もちは＿＿＿＿＿＿＿＿＿＿＿＿＿＿＿＿＿＿＿＿＿＿＿＿から作ります。

f) 日本人は白い＿＿＿＿＿＿＿＿＿＿＿＿＿＿＿＿＿＿＿＿をよく食べます。

g) ヨーグルトは＿＿＿＿＿＿＿＿＿＿＿＿＿＿＿＿＿＿＿＿から作ります。

h) ワインは＿＿＿＿＿＿＿＿＿＿＿＿＿＿＿＿＿＿から作る飲み物です。

i) 暑いの？じゃ、あの店で＿＿＿＿＿＿＿を買って、散歩しながら食べよう！

j) 中国人はナイフとフォークを使わないよ。＿＿＿＿＿＿＿＿＿を使うよ。

ぶどう	昼ご飯	お箸	米	アイスクリーム
牛乳	ご飯	わさび	苦い	おしぼり

15. Choose the most suitable answer for each sentence.

a) 日本人はいつも１２時ごろに＿＿＿＿＿＿＿＿＿＿＿を食べます。
　　1. 昼食　2. 朝食　3. 夕食　4. おやつ

b) どらやきは＿＿＿＿＿＿＿＿＿＿＿＿＿＿＿＿＿＿＿＿食べ物だ。
　　1. すっぱい　2. 塩辛い　3. 甘い　4. 苦い

c) カフェオレは＿＿＿＿＿＿＿＿＿と＿＿＿＿＿＿＿＿の飲み物です。
　　1. 水　2. 日本酒　3. ビール　4. コーヒー
　　1. ジュース　2. 牛乳　3. ワイン　4. 抹茶

d) レモンの味は＿＿＿＿＿＿＿＿＿＿＿＿＿＿＿＿＿＿＿＿です。
　　1. すっぱい　2. 塩辛い　3. 甘い　4. 苦い

e) 昨日は＿＿＿＿＿＿＿＿＿＿を一個切ったので、たくさん泣きました。
　　1. きゅうり　2. キウイ　3. 玉ねぎ　4. りんご

f) 醤油は＿＿＿＿＿＿＿＿＿＿＿＿＿＿＿＿＿＿＿＿＿＿＿です。
　　1. 野菜　2. 調味料　3. 飲み物　4. 器具

16. Form nouns using the adjectives from the box below and place them in the most suitable sentence.

a) 彼女の顔の＿＿＿＿＿＿＿＿＿＿はプレタポルテのモデルのようだ。

b) 部屋の＿＿＿＿＿＿＿＿＿＿をみてから、「ここにすみたい」と決めた。

c) 私はタイ人だから、札幌の冬の＿＿＿＿＿＿＿＿が大嫌いです。

d) ボブは走ったり、サッカーをやったりする。あの人の＿＿＿＿＿＿＿＿はせごいね！

e) この大変な仕事を始める前に、仕事の＿＿＿＿＿＿＿＿＿＿が分かってほしいです。

f) この書類の＿＿＿＿＿＿＿＿＿＿＿＿＿＿＿をわすれないでください！書類を守ってください！

たいせつ 大切な	あか 明るい	げんき 元気な	うつく 美しい	きけん 危険な	さむ 寒い

17. This conversation is out of order. Rewrite it in the correct order.

1) じゃ、お勧め料理は何ですか？

2) すき焼きですか？いいですね！それをください！

3) 今日の寿司はとてもおいしいですよ。お勧めします！

4) そうですか？じゃ、寿司ではなくて、すき焼きをお勧めします。

5) ごめんなさい、英語のメニューがありません。しかし、私は説明できます。

6) しかし、僕たちは生の魚を食べられないんですよ。

7) いらっしゃいませ！何名様ですか？

8) ３人ですが、英語のメニューはありますか？

店員さん：＿＿＿＿＿＿＿＿＿＿＿＿＿＿＿＿＿＿＿

お客さん：＿＿＿＿＿＿＿＿＿＿＿＿＿＿＿＿＿＿＿

店員さん：＿＿＿＿＿＿＿＿＿＿＿＿＿＿＿＿＿＿＿

お客さん：＿＿＿＿＿＿＿＿＿＿＿＿＿＿＿＿＿＿＿

店員<ruby>店員<rt>てんいん</rt></ruby>さん： ＿＿＿＿＿＿＿＿＿＿＿＿＿＿＿＿＿＿＿＿

お<ruby>客<rt>きゃく</rt></ruby>さん： ＿＿＿＿＿＿＿＿＿＿＿＿＿＿＿＿＿＿＿＿

店員<ruby>店員<rt>てんいん</rt></ruby>さん： ＿＿＿＿＿＿＿＿＿＿＿＿＿＿＿＿＿＿＿＿

お<ruby>客<rt>きゃく</rt></ruby>さん： ＿＿＿＿＿＿＿＿＿＿＿＿＿＿＿＿＿＿＿＿

18. Complete the following dialogue held at a restaurant.

Waiter: いらっしゃいませ。

Client: こんにちは。<ruby>夕方<rt>ゆうがた</rt></ruby>の８時なので、⁽¹⁾＿＿＿＿＿＿＿＿を食べたいです。

Waiter: <ruby>大丈夫<rt>だいじょうぶ</rt></ruby>ですよ。⁽²⁾＿＿＿＿＿＿＿＿＿＿＿＿＿＿＿＿＿ですか？

Client: 一人です。

Waiter: じゃ、こちらです。⁽³⁾＿＿＿＿＿＿＿＿はお<ruby>決<rt>き</rt></ruby>まりになりましたか？

Client: はい、<ruby>寿司<rt>すし</rt></ruby>を<ruby>お願<rt>おねが</rt></ruby>いします。

Waiter: どんな<ruby>寿司<rt>すし</rt></ruby>ですか？

Client: はい、そちらにあるまぐろの<ruby>巻き寿司<rt>まきずし</rt></ruby>を２つください。

Waiter: まぐろの<ruby>巻き寿司<rt>まきずし</rt></ruby>ですか？あ、⁽⁴⁾＿＿＿＿＿＿＿＿＿＿ですね！

Client: そうです。後は、えびやしゃけの⁽⁵⁾＿＿＿＿＿＿＿＿をください。

Waiter: <ruby>ご飯<rt>はん</rt></ruby>の上に魚を<ruby>握<rt>にぎ</rt></ruby>る<ruby>寿司<rt>すし</rt></ruby>のことですね？

Client: はい、そうです。しかし、私は<ruby>辛<rt>から</rt></ruby>い食べ物が好きじゃないんですよ。

Waiter: じゃ、⁽⁶⁾＿＿＿＿＿＿＿＿＿＿＿＿＿＿＿＿<ruby>抜<rt>ぬ</rt></ruby>きにしますか？

Client: はい。あと、<ruby>米<rt>こめ</rt></ruby>から作る日本の<ruby>有名<rt>ゆうめい</rt></ruby>な飲み物も飲んでみたいです。

Waiter: あ、⁽⁷⁾＿＿＿＿＿＿ですね！熱いのと⁽⁸⁾＿＿＿＿＿＿＿＿＿のがありますが...

Client: じゃ、冬だから、⁽⁹⁾＿＿＿＿＿＿＿＿＿にします。体を温めなきゃね！

＊＊＊　三十分後　＊＊＊

Client: あ、とてもおいしかったです！⁽¹⁰⁾＿＿＿＿＿＿＿＿＿をお願いします。

Waiter: どうもありがとうございました。１２４０円です。

Client: はい、どうぞ。(goes out) ⁽¹¹⁾＿＿＿＿＿＿＿＿＿＿＿＿＿＿＿＿！

Waiter: ありがとうございました！

19. Fill in the blanks with the most suitable expression from the box below.

a) この仕事が終わった＿＿＿＿＿＿＿＿＿＿＿＿＿＿たくさん遊ぼうね！

b) 今日は遅くまで仕事をしなければならない＿＿＿＿＿＿、行けないよ。

c) あの人はかっこいい＿＿＿＿＿＿＿＿＿＿、彼女が全然できない。

d) 車を買う＿＿＿＿＿＿＿＿＿＿＿＿非常にがんばっています。

e) 私は大阪に住んでいた＿＿＿＿＿＿＿、よくたこ焼きを食べに行った。

f) 私は少年マンガは好きだ＿＿＿＿＿＿＿＿、少女マンガは嫌いだ。

g) 生きている＿＿＿＿＿＿＿＿、たくさんの国へ旅行するつもりです。

くせに	から	ために	時	うちに	後で	けど

20. Fill in the blanks with the most suitable expression from the box below.

a) くそ！山へ散歩をしに行きたかった＿＿＿＿＿＿＿、雨が降っている！

b) 大阪に住んでいる＿＿＿＿＿＿＿＿＿、いろいろな料理を食べたいなぁ！

c) 先生はバカな学生に日本語を教え＿＿＿＿＿＿としている。かわいそう...

d) あのバカな学生に日本語を教え＿＿＿＿＿＿＿＿＿、だめだと思うよ。

e) 新しいパソコンを買いたい＿＿＿＿＿＿、秋葉原まで電車で行きました。

f) パソコンを買う＿＿＿＿＿＿＿＿、クレジットカードで払えるかどうか聞いてね。

ので	のに	前に	よう	間	ても

21. Fill in the blanks with the most suitable expression from the box below.

a) 大学へ入る＿＿＿＿＿＿＿＿＿＿＿＿＿＿＿＿＿＿、すごく勉強しました。

b) ミホちゃんが来た＿＿＿＿＿＿＿、パーティーに誰も来ていませんでした。

c) 明日は大学へ行った＿＿＿＿＿＿＿＿＿＿＿よ。試験があるんだから ...

d) 試験がある＿＿＿＿＿＿＿＿＿＿＿＿＿＿＿＿＿、大学へ行きました。

e) 私は若い＿＿＿＿＿＿＿＿＿＿＿＿＿＿＿結婚したいと思います。

f) 私は彼女と結婚したかった＿＿＿＿＿＿＿＿＿、彼女は「嫌だ」と言った。

g) 午後に、おじいさんと散歩をし＿＿＿＿＿＿＿＿＿＿＿と思います。

よう	方がいい	ので	けれど	ために	時	うちに

22. Link these sentence fragments so they form full valid sentences.

a) 彼女は結婚したくないので、 | 1) 彼女とたくさんの子どもを作りたい！
b) 彼は日本語の先生のくせに、 | 2) あきらめた方がいいよ。
c) おいしい料理を作るのに、 | 3) 漢字が読めないよ。
d) 私は彼女と結婚しているうちに、| 4) いい材料が必要です

i) この難しい本を読む前に | a) たくさんの単語を覚えてください
ii) 僕は日本へ行きたいけど、 | b) 何も分からなかったよ
iii) この映画を見るのに、 | c) ＤＶＤプレーヤーが必要だよ
iv) この映画を見たのに、 | d) 航空券のためのお金がない

1) いくら勉強しても、 | i) パーティーをやろうと思うよ！
2) 彼は何も勉強しなかったくせに、| ii) たくさん勉強しなきゃならない
3) 東京大学へ入りたいので、 | iii) 東京大学に入れないよ
4) 東京大学に入った後で、 | iv) 東京大学へ入れたよ

23. As shown in the example, make only one sentence from the two provided, applying what you have learned in Lesson 50.

a) 川口先生はとてもやさしいです　／　川口先生は大学で働いている

大学で働いている川口先生はとてもやさしいです。

b) あの犬は黒いです　／　あの犬はいつも寝ている

_____。

c) 友達はとても頭がいいです　／　友達が結婚した

_____。

d) ヤクザは人を殺した　／　ヤクザは走っていた

_____。

e) 私は妻を愛している　／　妻はいつもおいしい料理を作ってくれる

_____。

f) 妻は天ぷらを作った　／　天ぷらはとてもおいしかった

_____。

g) 友達は小説を書いた　／　小説はおもしろかった

_____。

24. Choose the most suitable answer for each sentence.

a) 私は弟にその自転車を_____ので、今その自転車は私のだよ！

1. もらった　2. あげた　3. くれた　4. くださった

b) 私は社長にその自転車を_____ので、今その自転車は私のだよ！

1. もらいた　2. あげた　3. くれた　4. いただいた

c) 私は弟にその自転車を_____ので、今その自転車は弟のだよ！

1. もらった　2. やった　3. くれた　4. くださった

d) 弟は私にその自転車を_____ので、今その自転車は私のだよ！

1. くださった　2. やった　3. くれた　4. いただいた

e) 私は友達に雑誌を＿＿＿＿＿＿＿＿＿＿＿＿のに、「欲しくないよ」と友達が言った。

   1. さしあげた　2. くれた　3. あげた　4. もらった

f) 社長はママに新しい車を買って＿＿＿＿＿＿＿。どうしてパパは怒っているの？

   1. あげた　2. くださった　3. もらった　4. やった

g) 山本くんは犬にご飯を＿＿＿＿＿＿＿＿＿＿＿＿＿＿＿＿。

   1. くれた　2. もらった　3. さしあげた　4. やった

h) ケイコさんは新しいゲームを＿＿＿＿＿＿＿よ！すごくうれしいです！

   1. くれました　2. あげました　3. やりました　4. いただきました

i) 先生、明日のパーティーに来て＿＿＿＿＿＿＿＿＿＿＿＿か？

   1. くださる　2. いただけます　3. やれます　4. あげます

25. Correct the mistakes in the following sentences.

a) 今日、青山さんの犬は静かのに、カラスがうるさいね。

b) 車を買うためにとてものお金が必要ですね。

c) 昨日、私はエリコさんの家へ掃除をしに行ってくれました。

d) お母さんは作った親子丼はまずかった。

e) ご飯を食べる後で、買い物をしに行きましょう。

f) あの泥棒はレンブラントの絵を盗みようとしているぞ！

26. Choose the most suitable answer for each sentence.

a) 映画を見に行きましょうか？＿＿＿＿＿＿、どんな映画が見たいの？

   1. それに　2. ところで　3. なのに　4. ところは

b) 社長＿＿＿＿お金をたくさんくださいましたよ、父＿＿＿＿＿＿＿。

   1. は／に　2. から／は　3. に／は　4. は／から

c) ね、ね！天ぷらの＿＿＿＿＿＿＿＿＿＿＿＿＿＿を教えてください！

　　1. 作り方　2. 作る方　3. 作ら方　4. 作った方

d) 彼女は大学へ行ける＿＿＿＿＿＿＿＿＿＿＿＿、非常にがんばりました。

　　1. けれど　2. ように　3. ので　4. っても

e) あの家へ＿＿＿＿＿＿＿＿＿＿＿＿＿方がいいよ。危ない犬がいるから！

　　1. 入る　2. 入った　3. 入らない　4. 入って

f) パトリックくんは漢字が読める＿＿＿＿＿＿＿＿＿＿＿、書けない。

　　1. けど　2. ので　3. ても　4. ために

g) お母さんは弟に部屋の掃除を＿＿＿＿＿＿＿＿＿＿＿ように命令した。

　　1. して　2. しろ　3. した　4. する

h) オレは車に乗る＿＿＿＿＿＿＿＿＿＿＿＿＿、いつも速く走るぜ！

　　1. ても　2. 時　3. けれども　4. ように

i) 今、この本を作る＿＿＿＿＿＿＿＿、たくさんの練習問題を考えている。疲れるぜ！

　　1. くせに　2. よう　3. ために　4. から

j) あの人はいくら＿＿＿＿＿＿、いつも「お腹が減ったよ」と言っている。

　　1. 食べた　2. 食べるので　3. 食べても　4. 食べるために

k) アキラくんはレンブラントの絵を盗める＿＿＿＿＿＿＿＿＿＿＿＿。

　　1. ようになった　2. ようにした　3. ようとする　4. ようと思う

l) 彼は日本人＿＿＿＿＿＿＿＿＿＿＿＿＿＿＿、漢字が書けない。

　　1. くせに　2. にくせに　3. がくせに　4. のくせに

m) 昨日はインド料理のレストランへ行った。＿＿＿＿＿＿＿＿＿＿＿、カラオケへも行った。

　　1. それなのに　2. だから　3. それから　4. それでは

Kanji

肉	茶	味	飯	料	理	堂	寺	代	銀	音
(171)	(172)	(173)	(174)	(223)	(224)	(183)	(186)	(206)	(185)	(257)
映	画	毎	週	曜	夕	長	黒	色	特	紙
(198)	(244)	(192)	(193)	(194)	(195)	(201)	(199)	(200)	(187)	(259)

27. Link each kanji with its most common reading.

音	いろ		黒い	あじ
肉	おと		味	ちゃ
週	はん		茶	ながい
銀	しゅう		夕	くろい
色	ぎん		長い	ゆう
飯	にく		寺	てら

28. Choose the correct kanji or kanji combination for each reading.

a) 私は<u>まいしゅう</u>、<u>ぎんこう</u>のとなりにある店に<u>おちゃ</u>を飲みに行きます。

　　まいしゅう：1. 毎週　2. 毎月　3. 毎日　4. 毎年

　　ぎんこう：1. 金行　2. 飯行　3. 銀行　4. 食行

　　おちゃ：1. お余　2. お傘　3. お茶　4. お米

b) 明日は友達_{ともだち}と大学の<u>しょくどう</u>で<u>りょうり</u>をします。

　　しょくどう：1. 食堂　2. 飲堂　3. 銀堂　4. 飯堂

　　りょうり：1. 物理　2. 料理　3. 心理　4. 地理

c) 京都_{きょうと}には平安_{へいあん}<u>じだい</u>のきれいな神社_{じんじゃ}と<u>てら</u>がたくさんあります。

　　じだい：1. 寺代　2. 時代　3. 持代　4. 侍代

　　てら：1. 待　2. 時　3. 侍　4. 寺

d) あの方はいつも<u>がか</u>を守っている。<ruby>彼<rt>かれ</rt></ruby>らの<u>みかた</u>だそうですよ。

　　がか：1. 画家　2. 映画　3. 画内　4. 画肉

　　みかた：1. 味方　2. 見方　3. 未方　4. 和方

29. Choose the correct reading for each kanji combination.

a) 月曜日に<u>白黒</u>写真の本を大学の<u>食堂</u>で見ました。

　　月曜日：1. げつよび　2. げつゆうび　3. げつようび　4. げつゆび

　　白黒：1. はくこく　2. しろくろ　3. はくごく　4. しろぐろ

　　食堂：1. しょくとう　2. しょくどう　3. しょっどう　4. しょっとう

b) <ruby>昨日<rt>きのう</rt></ruby>、私は<u>社長</u>が安い<u>飯屋</u>に入るのを見ました。

　　社長：1. しゃちょ　2. しゃなが　3. しゃちょう　4. じゃなが

　　飯屋：1. はんや　2. はんじょう　3. めしじょう　4. めしや

c) タイ人は日本語の<u>母音</u>の<u><ruby>発<rt>な</rt></ruby>音</u>に慣れていないみたい。

　　母音：1. ぼいん　2. ぼおん　3. ははおと　4. ぼおと

　　発音：1. はついん　2. はつおん　3. はつおと　4. はっおん

30. Write the kanji for the given *furigana*.

a) 土 _____<ruby>日<rt>よう</rt></ruby>は彼女（<ruby>かのじょ</ruby>）と_____（<ruby>えいが</ruby>）を見に行きます。

b) お姉さんは_____（<ruby>いろ</ruby>）っぽくて、_____（<ruby>くろ</ruby>）い服を着ています。

c) 今日の_____（<ruby>ゆうがた</ruby>）に_____（<ruby>なが</ruby>）い_____（<ruby>てがみ</ruby>）を書くつもりです。

d) 神戸（<ruby>こうべ</ruby>）の_____（<ruby>にく</ruby>）は_____（<ruby>とく</ruby>）においしいと皆（<ruby>みな</ruby>）は言う。

e) 彼女（<ruby>かのじょ</ruby>）は_____（<ruby>まいにち</ruby>）、苦い（<ruby>にが</ruby>）お_____（<ruby>ちゃ</ruby>）を飲みます。

f) _____（<ruby>ぎんこう</ruby>）の中でご_____（<ruby>はん</ruby>）を食べてはいけないですか？

Lesson 51 • 第51課

Unexpected Events and Accidents

In this lesson we will learn how to face theft, accidents and sickness along with a lot of useful new vocabulary.

🎧 The role of the police

Japan is very safe and the possibilities of being robbed or attacked are slim. The role of the Japanese police tends to be watching traffic, taking care of lost children or objects, giving directions, etc. Each neighborhood has a 交番 *kōban*, a mini-police station with only two or three policemen, who see to the safety in the neighborhood. If you ever get lost, go to the closest 交番: there they will kindly and diligently help you find your way.

🎧 Emergencies	
accident	事故
ambulance	救急車
bag	バッグ
emergency	緊急
injured person	けが人
injury	けが
pickpocket	スリ
police	警察官
to rob	盗む
thief	泥棒
wallet	財布
witness	目撃者

- すみませんが、道に迷ってしまいました Excuse me, I'm lost. (Lessons 35 and 37)
- ここは何という町ですか？ What is this city called? (Lesson 41)
- この住所はここから近いですか？ Is this address near here? (Lesson 41)
- 電車の駅へ行く道を教えてください Please tell me the way to the railway station.
- 東京タワーに行きたいんですが I'd like to go to Tokyo Tower (Lessons 37 and 40)
- 代々木公園まで歩いて行けますか？ Can I walk to Yoyogi park?

🎧 Theft

As we have just mentioned, to be the victim of theft in Japan is extremely rare. Nevertheless, let's look at a few sentences to practice vocabulary and grammar.

- 一番近い交番はどこですか？ Where is the closest koban?
- 誰かが私の財布を盗んだ Someone has stolen my wallet. (Lesson 41)
- 泥棒が私のバッグをひったくって逃げた The thief snatched my bag and ran off.

- リュックには財布とクレジットカードが入っています
  My wallet and my credit cards are in my (stolen) backpack.
- 盗難証明書を作ってください Fill in the theft report, please.

🎧 Losing something

The Japanese are very considerate when they find lost property, and usually take it to the closest 交番. If the lost object is a wallet with money that is returned intact, it is customary to give 10% of the money as a token of gratitude to the person who found it.

- ここに財布がありませんでしたか？ Wasn't there a wallet here?
- 忘れ物係はどこですか？ Where is the lost and found office?
- 地下鉄にカメラを忘れてしまいました I left my camera on the subway.
- どんなカメラですか？ What kind of camera is it?
- 銀色で、メーカーはカシオです It's silver and its make is Casio. (Lessons 35 and 46)
- 見つかった場合、連絡してください If you find it, let me know, please. (Lesson 46)
- パスポートをなくしました。再発行していただきたいのですが...
  I have lost my passport. I would like you to reissue it . . . (Lessons 35, 31 and 45)

🎧 What's wrong with me, Doctor?

Let's turn our focus to visits to the doctor and hospitals.

- 気分が悪いですが I don't feel good. (Lesson 37)
- 医者 (救急車) を呼んでください Call a doctor (an ambulance), please.
- 病院に連れていってください Take me to a hospital, please. (Lesson 35)
- 診療の予約をとってくれますか？ Can you make me an appointment for a consultation, please? (Lesson 45)
- どんな症状ですか How do you feel? | What symptoms do you have?
- お腹が痛いです I have a stomachache. (Lesson 26)
- 風邪をひいたようです I think I've caught a cold. (Lesson 43)
- 熱があります I have a fever.
- せきが止まりません I can't stop coughing. (lit. The cough doesn't stop)
- 転んで腕を痛めました I've fallen and hurt my arm.
- 手をやけどしました I've burnt my hand.
- 足首をねんざしました I've sprained my ankle.

- ペニシリンのアレルギーがあります I'm allergic to penicillin.
- 毎日この薬を飲んでいます I take (lit. drink) this medicine every day.
- 生理中です I have my period.
- どのくらいで治りますか？ How long will I take to recover?
- 旅行は続けられますか？ Can I continue my trip? (Lesson 32)
- 処方せんを書いてもらえますか Could you write me a prescription? (Lesson 45)

🎧 Talking with the doctor

Let's look at some typical things a doctor might say:

- いつからその症状がありますか？ How long have you had those symptoms? (Lesson 41)
- どこが痛いですか？ Where does it hurt you?
- 横になってください Lie down, please.
- シャツを脱いでください Take your shirt off, please.
- 深呼吸をしてください Breathe deeply.
- 血液 (尿) 検査が必要です You need to have a blood (urine) test. (Lesson 37)
- アレルギーはありますか？ Do you have any allergies?
- 血圧 (体温) を測りましょう I'll take your blood pressure (temperature). (Lesson 34)
- 大したことはありません It's nothing serious.
- この処方せんをもって薬局に行って、薬を買って飲んでください
  Take this prescription, go to the pharmacy, buy the medicine and take it. (Lessons 35 and 46)

🎧 Accidents

We will conclude this section with some useful phrases in case of a traffic accident.

- 交通事故があって、けがをしています There was a traffic accident, and I'm hurt.
- 友達が車にはねられました My friend has been run over by a car.
- 救急車が来るように電話してください Call an ambulance, please. (Lesson 50)
- 警察も呼んでください Call the police as well. (Lesson 37)
- 右腕を折ったみたいです I think I've broken my right arm. (Lesson 43)
- 出血が激しくて止められない I am bleeding heavily and I can't stop it.
- 事故証明書を書いてください Fill in the accident report, please.

🎧 Medical vocabulary

Basic vocabulary

doctor	医者（いしゃ）
hospital	病院（びょういん）
hospitalization	入院（にゅういん）
insurance	保険（ほけん）
leaving the hospital	退院（たいいん）
medicine	薬（くすり）
pain	痛み（いた）
patient	患者（かんじゃ）
pharmacy	薬局（やっきょく）or 薬屋（くすりや）
surgery	手術（しゅじゅつ）
symptom	症状（しょうじょう）

Sickness 病気（びょうき）

allergy	アレルギー
anemia	貧血（ひんけつ）
appendicitis	盲腸炎（もうちょうえん）
asthma	ぜんそく
bronchitis	気管支炎（きかんしえん）
bruise	打撲（だぼく）
burn	やけど
cancer	癌（ガン）
cold	風邪（かぜ）
diabetes	糖尿病（とうにょうびょう）
diarrhea	下痢（げり）
food poisoning	食中毒（しょくちゅうどく）
fracture	骨折（こっせつ）
gastric ulcer	胃潰瘍（いかいよう）
gastritis	胃炎（いえん）
inflammation of the ear	中耳炎（ちゅうじえん）
influenza	インフルエンザ
hepatitis	肝炎（かんえん）
high blood pressure	高血圧（こうけつあつ）
indigestion	消化不良（しょうかふりょう）
low blood pressure	低血圧（ていけつあつ）
pneumonia	肺炎（はいえん）
rheumatism	リューマチ
rhinitis	鼻炎（びえん）
sprain	ねんざ
sunstroke	日射病（にっしゃびょう）
tetanus	破傷風（はしょうふう）

Parts of the body 部位（ぶい）

bone	骨（ほね）
blood	血（ち）or 血液（けつえき）
blood vessel	血管（けっかん）
heart	心臓（しんぞう）
intestines	腸（ちょう）
joint	関節（かんせつ）
kidney	腎臓（じんぞう）
liver	肝臓（かんぞう）
lung	肺（はい）
muscle	筋肉（きんにく）
skin	皮膚（ひふ）
urine	尿（にょう）

Types of doctor 医者（いしゃ）

dentist	歯科医（しかい）
gynecologist	婦人科医（ふじんかい）
internist	内科医（ないかい）
ophthalmologist	眼科医（がんかい）
otolaryngologist	耳鼻咽喉科医（じびいんこうかい）
pediatrician	小児科医（しょうにかい）
surgeon	外科医（げかい）

Miscellaneous

bandage	包帯（ほうたい）
blood pressure	血圧（けつあつ）
breathing	呼吸（こきゅう）
injection	注射（ちゅうしゃ）
pulse	脈拍（みゃくはく）
temperature	体温（たいおん）
X-ray	レントゲン

Cultural Note: Japanese Addresses

One of the most surprising things in 日本 *Nihon* is that the vast majority of streets don't have names, and houses don't have numbers. The question is obvious: how do the poor postmen find their way around? And, if we want to go to a specific address (住所 *jūsho*), how will we find it? Let's look at a typical Japanese address, in this case, that of the famous Nintendo head office, in Kyoto:

〒 **601-8501** 京都府京都市 南 区上鳥羽鉾立 町 １ １ 番地１　任天堂株式会社.

If you get lost, go to the *kōban*!
(Photo: M. Bernabé)

The first number (601-8501) is the zip code (the sign 〒 means "zip code"). Then, we have the prefecture 京都府 *Kyōto-fu* (府 *fu*: prefecture, only when used with Kyoto and Osaka, with other prefectures we use 県 *ken*, except for Tokyo, which is 都 *to*, and Hokkaido, which is 道 *dō*), the city 京都市 *Kyōto-shi* (市 *shi*: city), the district 南区 *Minami-ku* (区 *ku*: ward, district), the town 上鳥羽鉾立町 *Kamitoba Hokodate-cho* (町 *cho*: neighborhood), the block within the neighborhood, *11-banchi* (番地), and, finally, the plot number, 1. At the end, we have the name of the person or company, 任天堂株式会社 *Nintendō Kabushikigaisha* (株式会社 *kabushikigaisha*: public corporation). Notice how everything is the other way round compared to Western addresses: in Japan, they start from the prefecture and work their way down until they reach the plot of land. Following Western criteria, we would have something like Nintendo, 1-11 Kami-toba Hokodate-cho, Minami-ku, Kyoto-shi, Kyoto-fu 601-8501. That is, we would have to reverse the order of the elements, because we start from the plot and we finish with the prefecture or state.

So, to find an address, we must have a good map, and look for the city first, then the district, then the town / neighborhood, etc. It is no wonder the Japanese draw maps (usually from the nearest train or subway station) when they want to indicate the location of a place. But if you ever get lost or can't reach your destination, you can always go to the closest 交番 *kōban* (police box) and ask the 警察官 *keisatsukan* (police officer). They are prepared for this, and will be glad to help you.

🎧 漫画例 Manga Examples

Although, ideally, you should never have to use the language you have learned in this chapter in real life, it will certainly be useful if you want to understand the jargon which appears in the thousands of comics and movies involving policemen or doctors. Let's see some examples.

Manga Example 1: Police jargon

In this first example we find two different things. First, there is quite a lot of police-related vocabulary, which is essential if you want to enjoy watching police or yakuza movies and reading detective manga. Useful police- and crime-related vocabulary that you can find in this manga example includes 本部 (headquarters), 不審 (suspicious), 人物 (person), 至急 (immediately) and 応援 (reinforcements). Other typical words in police jargon—which you won't usually find in dictionaries —include デカ, a colloquial word used when referring to a 刑事 *keiji*, (police officer, detective), ガイシャ (a contraction of 被害者 *higaisha* "victim"), ホシ (another word for 犯人 *hannin*, meaning "criminal"), and チャカ ("gun," which has many other names in Japanese, including 銃 *jū*, 拳銃 *kenjū*, ピストル and ハジキ).

This manga example also gives us the opportunity to review the subject of addresses studied in the Cultural Note on the facing page. Here you will notice how the policeman indicates his location: 本町３丁目付近: "in the vicinity of the 3rd block of Honmachi."

えー本部本部
本町３丁目
付近に不審人物
発見至急応援を—

Xian Nu Studio

Police.: えー本部本部本町３丁目付近に不審人物発見　至急応援を—
(ほんぶ　ほんぶ　ほんまちさんちょうめふきん　ふしん　じんぶつはっけん　しきゅうおうえん)

err . . . headquarters headquarters Honmachi 3 block vicinity PP *suspicious man discover immediately reinforcements* DOP *. . .*

Err . . . Headquarters, headquarters. I've discovered a suspicious man in the vicinity of the 3rd block of Honmachi. Send reinforcements immediately . . .

Manga Example 2: Asking for directions

This time we see a man who wants to ask for directions and goes to a 交番 *kōban* (police box) to do it. He first breaks the ice with すいません (a colloquial version of すみません, "excuse me"), and then he asks his question. At the end of the sentence he adds the の です tag (Lesson 40), and a が (Lesson 37), all in order to make the question less brusque.

すいません
ちょっと道を
ききたい
のですが…

This is a very common way of expressing oneself in Japanese. Observe now the ちょっと. It literally means "a little," as in ちょっと待って *chotto matte* (wait a little), but it really has countless usages: to call for attention, ちょっとすみません (excuse me a minute), to soften something difficult to say: ちょっと無理ですね *chotto muri desu ne* (I'm afraid that's impossible) or as an "aid" when asking ちょっと道をききたい as in this example.

Gabriel Luque

Man:	すいません　ちょっと道をききたいのですが…
	excuse me a little way DOP ask be but . . .
	Excuse me, I would like to ask for directions . . .

Manga Example 3: Calling the police

Here's what to say if we witness an accident and we want to call the police. By the way, the number of names that exist for policemen is fascinating. The generic name for the police is 警察 *keisatsu*, from which the word 警察官 *keisatsu kan* (police officer) is derived. Other words for police officer are 巡査 *junsa*, the colloquial 警官 *keikan*, デカ, or お巡りさん, like in this example. The word 刑事 *keiji* means "detective." A criminal's most typical word for a police officer is サツ (from 警察), or ポリ.

早く
きて！

お巡り
さん
事故
です‼

J.M. Ken Niimura

Note: The telephone number for emergencies in Japan is 110番 *hyakutōban* (be careful with the irregular reading).

Man:	お巡りさん　事故です！！　早くきて！
	police SUF accident be! quickly come!
	Officer, there's been an accident! Come quickly!

Manga Example 4: Calling the hospital to report an emergency

Let's now enter the doctors' world. In this example, we can see that the doctor is being informed on the phone about a patient who has just been hospitalized. Since the sentence

itself has no difficulty, we will focus on the grammar. We can see in the 打って portion two sentences linked with the *-te* form (Lessons 37 and 46). We can also see an adverb (Lesson 22) formed from the *-i* adjective うまい. うまい is the colloquial version of いい (good), therefore, うまくできない means "cannot do it well." And, finally, notice the expression using the conjecture そうです (Lesson 43), used to give information obtained from another source (similar to "I've been told that . . .").

Tel.:	事故です！患者は胸を打って呼吸がうまくできないそうです！
	accident be! patient TOP *chest* DOP *hit breathe* SP *well can looks like be!*
	It's an accident! The patient has hit himself on the chest and can't breathe well!

Manga Example 5: A demanding patient

Another medical example. This time we have a 患者 *kanja* (patient) asking the nurse for 薬 *kusuri* (medicine). Notice the word 痛み止め, literally something that stops (止める *tomeru*) the pain (痛み), and then we have the verb "drink" (飲む) for taking medicine. By the way, the verb 効く means "to take effect."

Regarding grammar, we have a sentence linked with the *-te* form (Lessons 35 and 46) using 飲んで, and a construction with けど (Lesson 49), indicating "but." **Note:** ブスコパン is a brand of painkiller.

Miura:	痛み止め飲んで２時間たったけど効かないよ。ブスコパン頼むよ
	painkiller drink 2 hours pass but take effect EP. *Buscopan ask* EP
	Two hours have passed since I took the painkiller, but it doesn't take effect. Come on, give me some Buscopan.

Manga Example 6: Names of illnesses

Gabriel Luque

Here we find some names of illnesses (病気 *byōki*), including 食あたり (the term 食中毒 *shokuchūdoku* is also used). Notice the suffix 炎 *en*, the equivalent of the English suffix "–itis" (meaning "inflammation"). Thus, 肺炎 *haien* is "pneumonia" or "lung (肺) inflammation (炎)," 扁桃腺炎 *hentōsenen* is "tonsillitis" or "tonsil (扁桃腺) inflammation (炎)," and 胃炎 *ien* is "gastritis" or "stomach (胃) inflammation (炎)," etc. There are more suffixes, like 病 *byō*, indicating "disease": 心臓病 *shinzōbyō* means "heart disease," and アルツハイマー病 is "Alzheimer's disease."

Doctor: 肺炎_{はいえん}じゃない…食_{しょく}あたりじゃない…扁桃腺炎_{へんとうせんえん}でもない…

pneumonia not be . . . food poisoning not be . . . tonsillitis neither be . . .

It's not pneumonia . . . or food poisoning . . . or tonsillitis . . .

Manga Example 7: Tests and hospitalization

To conclude, here is a good example of medical jargon: notice how the doctor tells the patient she must be hospitalized (入院する) so that she can take some tests (検査を受ける), and that they will know more when they obtain the results (結果). On the grammatical level, notice the 〜てもらう form (Lesson 45), which adds the nuance that the listener will perform the action for the benefit of the speaker. There is also an example of the *-ō* form (Lesson 34) in 入院しましょう. Last of all, notice the usages of から as the particle "from" (Lesson 41) (これから and 明日から), and as a connector indicating cause/reason (Lesson 48) (わかりますから).

Xian Nu Studio

Doctor: これからいろいろ検査_{けんさ}を受_うけてもらいます

this from several tests DOP take (receive)

From now on, we will have you take several tests.

くわしくは結果_{けっか}でわかりますから 明日_{あした}からさっそく入院_{にゅういん}しましょう

in detail TOP result IP understand because tomorrow from immediately hospitalize

The results will give us more details, so tomorrow we shall hospitalize you.

Exercises 練習

(1) Translate the following words: 財布 , 事故 , 熱 ,
薬局 , レントゲン , 心臓 and 痛み .

(2) Translate the following words: "doctor," "hospital," "injury," "ambulance," "cough" and "cold."

(3) You go into a 交番 to report that you've lost
a ring. What do you say? (to lose 失くす ; ring
指輪)

(4) Translate: "I've got a headache, a fever, and I
can't stop coughing."

(5) Translate: ただのインフルエンザかもしれないが、
血液 検査 が 必要 です。 (ただの a simple . . .)

(6) Translate this address: 〒 100-8280   東 京   都
千代田区神田駿河台 町 4 丁目 6 番地。

(7) How words do you know for "gun"? And
"policeman"? List them.

(8) Translate: ちょっと分からないので、 説明 して
ください。 (分かる to understand; 説明する to
explain)

(9) Translate: "I'm taking medicine because I have a
headache." (painful 痛い ; head 頭 ; medicine
薬)

(10) What does the suffix 炎 mean? Write at least four
words with 炎 that we have studied and give their
meanings.

— **Answers to all the exercises can be found online by following the link on page 7.** —

Formal Language

Japanese has formal language to show respect and to enable us to speak in a polite way. There are three modes of honorific speech, which we will study in this chapter.

Honorific speech

Japanese honorific speech is called 敬語 *keigo*. We use 敬語 when speaking with or about people superior to us (bosses, teachers or elders), with people we have just met, and in formal situations such as speeches, weddings, work meetings and dealing with clients. In Japanese, there are three kinds of 敬語. These are 尊敬語 *sonkeigo* (language of respect), 謙譲語 *kenjōgo* (language of modesty), and 丁寧語 *teineigo* (polite speech). Take care not to mix them up!

🎧 *Sonkeigo*: The language of respect

尊敬語 literally means "language (語) of respect (尊敬)." We use 尊敬語 when talking <u>with</u> or <u>about</u> another person, raising his or her position to express our respect. The subject of the action is always the other person. To be formal in English, we use certain polite words and address people by their title, such as Mr. or Ms. But Japanese formal language, however, has other grammatical and lexical changes. The table (right) gives 尊敬語 and 謙譲語 versions of verbs you already know. Let's see some examples:

	🎧 Special verbs		
	Normal	*Sonkeigo*	*Kenjōgo*
to do	する	なさる	いたす
to be	いる	いらっしゃる	おる
to go / come	行く | 来る	いらっしゃる	参る | 伺う
to eat / drink	食べる | 飲む	召し上がる	いただく
to see	見る	ご覧になる	拝見する
to borrow	借りる	―	拝借する
to know	知っている	ご存知だ	存じている
to die	死ぬ	お亡くなりになる	―
to say	言う	おっしゃる	申す | 申し上げる
to give	くれる	くださる	―
to give (2)	あげる	―	さしあげる
to receive	もらう		いただく

- 田中さん、何をなさっていますか？ What are you doing, Mr. Tanaka?
- ご希望をおっしゃってください Please tell me what you wish.
- 鈴木さんはもうご存知です Ms. Suzuki already knows.
- 先生は（私に）本をくださった The teacher gave me a book. (Lesson 45)

Conjugation お + **Root** + になる: Take the root of any verb (Lesson 31), add お at the beginning and になる at the end. For example, 書く *kaku* (to write) ⇒ *-masu* form: 書きます ⇒ (without ます): 書き ⇒ add お and になる: お書きになる. **Note:** This conjugation is not used with *suru* verbs (with those verbs we use なさる. For example, 勉強する *benkyō suru*⇒ 勉強なさる to study).

- 先生はお手紙をお書きになった The teacher wrote a letter.
- すみません、お立ちになってください Excuse me, please stand up.
- この本をお読みになっていないと思います I don't think you've read this book.

🎧 The 〜られる form

Sonkeigo has a special conjugation (see table, right). Group 1 verbs replace the last *-ru* with *-rareru*, and Group 2 verbs replace the last *-u* with *-a* and add *-reru*. (See Lesson 19 for a definition of Group 1 and Group 2 verbs.) Thus, *kaku* ⇒ *kak-* ⇒ *kaka-* ⇒ *kakareru*. Note 買う *kau* becomes *kawareru* (not *kaareru*), and 待つ *matsu* becomes *matareru* (not *matsareru*).

	Simple f.	Meaning	Rule	*Sonkeigo*
Group 1	教える	to teach	−るられる	教えられる
	起きる	to wake up		起きられる
Group 2	貸す	to lend	−すされる	貸される
	待つ	to wait	−つたれる	待たれる
	買う	to buy	−うわれる	買われる
	帰る	to return	−るられる	帰られる
	書く	to write	−くかれる	書かれる
	急ぐ	to hurry	−ぐがれる	急がれる
	遊ぶ	to play	−ぶばれる	遊ばれる
	拒む	to refuse	−むまれる	拒まれる

- 清水さんは本を書かれたそうです Apparently, Mr. Shimizu wrote a book.
- (あなたは) 仙台へ行かれましたか？ Did you go to Sendai?
- (あなたは) 英語を教えられていますか？ Do you teach English?
- 木村さんは結婚されていますか？ Mr. Kimura, are you married?

Notice the table has no verbs ending in ぬ, nor the irregular verbs する (to do) or 来る *kuru* (to come). There is only one regular verb ending in ぬ, and that is 死ぬ *shinu* (to die), which already has its own 尊敬語 version: お亡くなりになる *onakunari ni naru* (see table, facing page). Even though する and 来る have a *-rareru* version (される and 来られる *korareru*), they also have 尊敬語 versions: なさる and いらっしゃる, respectively.

🎧 Important observation

If talking <u>with</u> someone equal <u>about</u> someone hierarchically superior, use the strategies we have seen to show respect to the superior person but with the verb in the simple form:

- 先生はいらっしゃらないぞ (Talking with a classmate) The teacher is not here.

In the previous sentence, we are talking about someone we respect (先生), so we use the verb いらっしゃる (to be), but in the simple form because we are talking to an equal, a classmate. We have also added the colloquial end-of-sentence particle ぞ. Other examples:

- 社長はもうお帰りになったよ The president has already gone.
- 加藤さんは大学まで歩かれたよね Mr. Kato walked to university, didn't he?

🎧 *Kenjōgo*: The language of modesty

Let's look at 謙譲語 *kenjōgo*, literally "language (語) of modesty (謙譲)" used when talking <u>with</u> a person we consider superior, lowering our position to indirectly raise the other person's position. The subject of the action is always "I" or someone in the *uchi* group. We never use 謙譲語 to refer to actions by someone who is not "I" or not in the *uchi* group, as it would sound as if we were degrading the other person. As with 尊敬語, there are "modest" versions of several of the most common verbs (see the first table in this lesson).

- 私はアルゼンチンから参りました I come from Argentina | I'm from Argentina.
- 妹は医者と結婚いたしておます My sister is getting married to a doctor.
- すみませんが、社長は出かけております I'm sorry, the president has gone out.*

*The company president is hierarchically superior, but he belongs to the speaker's *uchi* group. When talking with someone *soto* about anybody in our *uchi* group, we use 謙譲語.

Conjugation: お + **Root** + する/いたす: Take the root of any verb (Lesson 31) and add お at the beginning and する or, more formally, いたすat the end:書く *kaku* (to write)⇒ -*masu* form: 書きます ⇒ root (without ます): 書き ⇒ add お and する: お書きする. **Note:** Some suru verbs add ご (not お) at the beginning, for example: ご案内する *go annai suru* (I'll guide you).

- 先生の本をお読みしたいです Professor, I'd like to read your book.
- ご相談したいと思っております I'd like to consult with you.

🎧 Observations

If talking to somebody equal or inferior about an action we did in the interest of somebody superior, or in their presence, we use 謙譲語 in its simple form:

- 私は先生に本をさしあげたよ (To a classmate) I gave the teacher a book.
- 社長の計画書を拝見したぞ (To a colleague) I've seen the president's project.

The respectful prefix お or ご is used with nouns or adjectives. お is used before words of Japanese origin, usually written with one kanji: e.g., お早い *ohayai* (early), お車 *okuruma* (car) etc., and ご before words of Chinese origin, which usually have two or more kanji: ご家族 *gokazoku* (your family), ご心配 *goshimpai* (worry). Exceptions include お食事 *oshokuji* (meal), お元気 *ogenki* (healthy) and お電話 *odenwa* (telephone).

🎧 *Teineigo*: Polite speech

丁寧語 *teineigo* means "polite language," perhaps the closest in usage to our English use of Mr., Mrs., etc., and the corresponding polite language. It is merely polite, involving no special hierarchies and is based on always using the です and 〜ます verb forms.

- 私は脳外科医です I'm a neurosurgeon.
- ここには亀がいます There is a turtle here.

To be politer, use ございます for ある and いる, and でございます for です.

- 私は脳外科医でございます I'm a neurosurgeon.
- ここには有名な絵がございます There is a famous picture here.

In 丁寧語, the prefixes お〜 and ご〜 are profusely used before nouns and adjectives, although it is women who, by far, tend to use them more often:

- 社長の奥様、お美しいですね (To the company president) Your wife is beautiful.
- お店でご飯を食べてきました I have had lunch in the shop.

		🎧 Formal language: Summary	
そんけいご **尊敬語** *(language of respect)*	We raise somebody else's position.	1. Special verbs.	先生、何かおっしゃいましたか？ Did you say something, teacher?
		2. お + Root + になる	三浦さんはお待ちになっています Mr. Miura is waiting.
		3. 〜られる	三浦さんは待たれています Mr. Miura is waiting.
けんじょうご **謙譲語** *(language of modesty)*	We lower our position.	1. Special verbs	その本を拝見しました I saw that book.
		2. お/ご+ Root + する	あ、お待ちしておりました Oh, I was waiting for you.
ていねいご **丁寧語** *(polite speech)*	Formal language.	1. Use of the *-masu* form	三浦さんは待っています Mr. Miura is waiting.
		2. Use of でございます, よろしい, etc.	これは先生の本でございます This is the teacher's book.
		3. お〜/ご〜 before nouns and adjectives	先生のご意見は何ですか？ What's the teacher's opinion?

🎧 漫画例   **Manga Examples**

Mastering the usage of Japanese honorific speech can be tricky and takes time. For the moment, try to concentrate only on understanding what you are being told in formal Japanese; as your language skills improve and you become more confident, you can try using it yourself.

Manga Example 1: *Sonkeigo*

Our first example gives us an instance of the usage of the language of respect or 尊敬語 ***sonkeigo***. The normal version of the sentence in this panel would be 何をしているのですか？ ***Nani o shite iru no desu ka?*** Notice how the verb なさる is used here, it being the "respectful" version of する (to do). An important point is that even when forming the gerund (Lesson 24), which is usually formed with the ***-te*** form and the verb いる (to be), the latter is sometimes replaced with its respectful version いらっしゃる. Thus, the している part (to be doing) finally becomes なさっていらっしゃる.

  It is worth mentioning that the verbs いらっしゃる, なさる, おっしゃる and くださる are slightly irregular, because their ***-masu*** forms are, respectively, いらっしゃい<u>い</u>ます, なさ<u>い</u>ます, おっしゃ<u>い</u>ます and くださ<u>い</u>ます. That is, before the final ます we add an い which, according to the rules, should not be there. Therefore, if we changed the sentence we are now examining into the ***-masu*** form, we would obtain 何をなさっていらっしゃ<u>い</u>ますか.

Likewise, it is essential to know that there are "formal" versions of some words. The most typical examples are 方 ***kata*** (replacing 人 ***hito*** "person"), どなた (formal version of 誰 ***dare*** "who?"), or the adjective よろしい (instead of いい, "good"). Likewise, in formal language, we opt for the ***kosoado*** こちら, そちら and あちら instead of ここ, そこ and あそこ (Lesson 34).

Studio Kōsen

Man:　…お客様。なにをなさっていらっしゃるのですか…？
　　　. . . customer SUF *what* DOP *do be be* Q*? . . . ?*
　　　Madam, what are you doing?

Manga Example 2: *Sonkeigo* in the simple form

In this example we see two instances of the formal language of respect or 尊敬語 *sonkeigo*. First, we have the special verb いらっしゃる, here replacing 来る *kuru* (to come). The speaker also uses the *-rareru* form of the *suru* verb 執刀する *shittō suru* (to operate), that is, 執刀される. In this last case, 執刀なさる could have been used as well (remember なさる is the respectful version of する), with hardly any nuance differences.

   Notice how in the sentence, the speaker talks <u>about</u> 堀部教授, who is someone he respects, someone superior to himself: that's why he uses 尊敬語 when speaking. However, since he is talking <u>with</u> someone who is his equal or inferior, he deliberately leaves his verbs in the simple form to denote familiarity toward them.

Doctor: 間もなく堀部教授がいらっしゃる
soon Horibe professor SP come
Professor Horibe will come soon.
今日は教授みずから執刀されるとの事だ
today professor himself operate do SBP NOM be
The professor himself will operate today.

Manga Example 3: *Sonkeigo* and *kenjōgo* in the same sentence

The languages of respect and modesty can be used at the same time, combining forms as we see here. Yoshida is talking with a stranger, so he uses the respectful form (尊敬語 *sonkeigo*) of the verb おっしゃる (to say), with which he raises the position of the person he is talking to. But when speaking about himself, he uses the modest form (謙譲語 *kenjōgo*) of the verb to be, おる, lowering his position to indirectly raise that of the person he is talking to. Notice how in 謙譲語 the gerund 〜ている is changed into 〜ておる (〜て

おります in the *-masu* form). **Notes:** We studied the 〜ても form (although) in Lesson 49. The verb わかる (to understand) is usually written 分かる, but, sometimes, either for style reasons or because of the author's preference, 判る is used.

Yoshida: 何もおっしゃらなくても、すべて判っております。
nothing say (although), everything know be
Even if you say nothing, I know everything.

Manga Example 4: Honorific prefixes and *kenjōgo*

In all three modes of formal language the honorific prefixes お〜 and ご〜 are very frequent. You can see quite a few in this manga example. By the way, there are some very common words in Japanese that always use honorific prefix, even when talking in colloqui-

al Japanese: お茶 **ocha** (tea), お金 **okane** (money), ご飯 **gohan** (rice, meal), お湯 **oyu** (hot water), お菓子 **okashi** (cake), お風呂 **ofuro** (bath), etc. **Notes:** Sometimes we find the ご〜 or お〜 prefix in kanji: 御〜. Also notice in this sentence how the customer (客) is addressed as お客様, with the suffix of highest respect 〜様 (Lesson 15), and that's because, as you know, the customer is "god" in Japan.

Xian Nu Studio

Kumi: あのーお客様、ご出発までの間お休みできる

well ... customer SUF, departure until NOM recess rest can

If you please ... Ladies and gentlemen, I'll get a room ready at once ...

お部屋をご用意致しますので、どうぞ。

room DOP prepare do because, go ahead

... where you can rest until departure time. Come in, please.

Manga Example 5: The *uchi–soto* relationship in formal language

As we saw in Lesson 45, the difference between one's own group (**uchi**) and those outside it (**soto**) is very important. Here, Chiaki says "Kawai is coming" using the verb 参る **mairu** (to come), which belongs to the language of modesty (謙譲語 **kenjōgo**). Moreover, for extra "humbleness," she doesn't use the honorific 〜さん after Kawai's name, something

surprising if we think that he is actually Chiaki's boss, whom we would expect her to treat with respect. Chiaki considers Kawai as an **uchi** member when talking to a visitor from another company who clearly belongs to the **soto** group, and that's why she uses 謙譲語.

Xian Nu Studio

Chiaki: ただいま川井が参りますので…

now Kawai SP come because ...

Kawai will come right away ...

Manga Example 6: A new form

There is a very common request form which, despite being quite formal, is not considered part of 敬語 *keigo*: it is お + Root + ください, equivalent to the request made with 〜てください (Lessons 24 and 35), but more formal. This construction is formed by placing お (or ご with *suru* verbs) in front of the root of the verb (Lesson 31), and placing ください after it. In this panel we see お待ちください (wait, please), which comes from the verb 待つ (to wait).

J.M. Ken Niimura

Other examples would be: お書きください *okaki kudasai* (please write), お座りください *osuwari kudasai* (please sit down), or ご注意ください *go chūi kudasai* (please be careful), which come from the verbs 書く (to write), 座る (to sit) and 注意する (to be careful) respectively. Learn this form well, because you will find it more than once. In the panel we also have お調べ致します (I check), an instance of the structure お + Root + いたす, from the verb 調べる. Notice how いたす is sometimes written 致す in kanji, as in the example.

Receptionist:	ただ今お調べ致しますので少々お待ち下さい。

now investigate do because a little wait please

I'll check it at once. Wait a minute, please.

Manga Example 7: *Teineigo*

Finally, we will see an instance of polite speech or 丁寧語 *teineigo*: notice how Aiko uses the verb でございます instead of です. The usage of でございます is one of the most common characteristics of 丁寧語.

For the moment, you don't need to master honorific speech. If it is any consolation, many native Japanese, especially the young, find these forms difficult to use. However, recognizing the different patterns of usage will be helpful, because they are widely used in daily life, mainly in sales clerk-customer relationships.

Gabriel Luque

Aiko: はい。こちら伊丹空港の受付でございます。

yes. here Itami airport POP reception be

Yes? This is Itami airport reception office.

Exercises 練習

1 What are the three kinds of honorific speech in Japanese, and when do we use each of them?

Give the 尊敬語 version of the verbs 言う, 知っている, 飲む, あげる and 行く. **2**

3 To what normal verbs do these 謙譲語 verbs correspond: 申す, いただく, いたす, 拝見する and 伺う?

Translate: 野村先生は記事をお書きになっている.
(野村 Nomura; 先生 teacher; 記事 article; 書く to write) **4**

5 Conjugate the following verbs in the ～られる form: 歩く (to walk), 寝る (to sleep), 殺す (to kill), and 走る (to run).

Translate: 私は本の内容を存じております。(私 I; 本 book; 内容 contents) **6**

7 Is the following sentence correct: 私は映画をご覧になっております? Why/why not? If not correct, correct it. (私 I; 映画 movie)

Translate: そちらにおいしいお魚のお店がございます。(おいしい tasty; 魚 fish; 店 shop) **8**

9 When would you use this sentence? 先生はご質問したいと申し上げました. Translate it. (先生 teacher; 質問する to ask a question)

Translate: そちらのいすにお座りください。 Which of the three kinds of 敬語 does it correspond to? (いす chair; 座る to sit) **10**

— **Answers to all the exercises can be found online by following the link on page 7.** —

Casual Speech

After the intense formal language lesson, let's look at the other side of the coin: casual speech—the spontaneous street language essential for understanding manga!

Overview

There are several registers of casual speech, but we will focus on the colloquial and vulgar. Colloquial language can be used with close friends, but avoid vulgar language, mostly used in movies and manga; in real life you will seldom hear it. We'll use (C) to indicate "colloquial" and (V) for "vulgar." Let's look at the characteristics of Japanese casual speech.

🎧 Particles

One characteristic of spoken and spontaneous Japanese is the frequent omission of grammatical particles, which you will have seen in the manga in this book:

- マリア、帽子買ったわ Maria bought a hat. (female C)
- 映画館、行きたいんだよ I want to go to the movies. (C)

In the first sentence the topic particle は that should follow マリア is omitted (Lesson 37), as is the direct object particle を (Lesson 40) after 帽子. In the second sentence, the direction particle に (or へ, Lesson 38) after 映画館 has been left out. End-of-sentence particles are frequent in casual speech. The first sentence above has the female emphatic particle わ; the second, statement particle よ and emphatic tag んだよ (Lesson 40).

🎧 Imperative, swearwords and dislocations

Japanese vulgar language (and sometimes the colloquial) is almost the only register that uses the direct imperative studied in Lesson 30 (plus the 〜てくれ form in Lesson 45), and the various swearwords we saw back in Lesson 23:

- 日本へ行けよ、バカ野郎！ Go to Japan, you stupid ass! (V)
- 貸してくれよ、その辞書 Come on, lend it to me, that dictionary. (C/V)
- 行きたくないんだよ、クソ学校へ I don't want to go to the damn school. (V)

Notice how we often find dislocated phrases, like the second and third ones, where the usual order of the elements has been changed to highlight a certain part of the sentence.

🎧 The most common contractions			
Normal ⇒ Colloquial	**Type**	**Normal form**	**Colloquial version**
-t/de iru ⇒ *-t/deru* (Lesson 35) 　　　*-t/den*	(C) (V)	食べている	食べてる 食べてん（だ）
-t/de iku ⇒ *-t/deku* (Lesson 35)	(C)	飲んでいく	飲んでく
-t/de oku ⇒ *-t/doku* (Lesson 35)	(C)	食べておく	食べとく
-t/de ageru ⇒ *-t/dageru* (Lesson 45)	(C)	食べてあげる	食べたげる
-t/da darō ⇒ *-t/darō* (Lesson 43)	(C)	飲んだだろう	飲んだろう
-te shimau ⇒ *-chau* (Lesson 35)	(C)	食べてしまう	食べちゃう
-de shimau ⇒ *-jau* (Lesson 35)	(C)	飲んでしまう	飲んじゃう
-te wa ⇒ *-cha* (Lesson 32)	(C)	食べてはいけない	食べちゃいけない
-de wa ⇒ *-ja* (Lesson 32)	(C)	飲んではいけない	飲んじゃいけない
-nai ⇒ *-n* (except: しない ⇒ せん)	(V)	食べない	食べん
-nakereba naranai ⇒ *-nakya* (Lesson 32)　　　　　*-nakya nannai*	(C)	飲まなけれ ばならない	飲まなきゃ 飲まなきゃなんない
-reba ⇒ *-rya* (Lesson 56)	(C)	食べれば	食べりゃ
-nakereba ⇒ *-nakya* (Lesson 56)	(C)	食べなければ	食べなきゃ
to iu ⇒ *tte* | *teyuu* | *ttsuu* (Lesson 41)	(C)	彼という	彼って | 彼ってい う | 彼っつう
-ai | *-oi* ⇒ *-ee*	(C)	高い | すごい	たけえ | すげえ
食べる *taberu* to eat; 飲む *nomu* to drink; 彼 *kare* he; 高い *takai* expensive, high; すごい cool, amazing, fantastic			

🎧 Contractions

The table above shows common colloquial and vulgar contractions. If you find a written contraction not in the table, read it aloud: you may be able to figure out where it came from

- ビール、買っといたぞ！ I've bought beer (just in case)! (C)
- 食べちゃっていいの、ケーキ？ Can I eat it, the cake? (C)
- 大阪って街、面白くてたまらん The city of Osaka is great fun. (V)
- 明日、すげえ雑誌を読んじゃおう Tomorrow I'll read a fantastic magazine. (C)
- 何遊んでんだ？働けって言ったろう？ What are you doing, playing? I've told you to work, haven't I? (V)

Other contractions include 何か **nani ka** ⇒ なんか (something, Lesson 41); どこか ⇒ どっか (somewhere, Lesson 41); これは/それは/あれは ⇒ こりゃ/そりゃ/ありゃ (this, that, that over there, Lesson 34); こちら/そちら/あちら ⇒ こっち/そっち/あっち (this way, that way, that way over there, Lesson 34); 仕方がない **shikata ga nai** ⇒ しょうがない (it's no use / it can't be helped).

🎧 Shortenings

A characteristic of casual speech is shortening certain words or phrases, such as もの ⇒ もん (thing, Lesson 57); ところ ⇒ とこ (place, Lesson 58); かもしれない ⇒ かも (perhaps, Lesson 43); のだ ⇒ んだ (emphatic tag, Lesson 40). Notice the omission of the potential form ら of Group 1 verbs: 食べられる **taberareru** ⇒ 食べれる (Lesson 32).

- どっかいいとこ行かなきゃ We must go somewhere good. (C)
- おっす！ピーマン 食べれる？ Hey! Can you eat (do you like) green pepper? (C)
- 俺んちには面白いもんがあるかも In my house there might be something cool. (C)

In the second sentence, おっす is short for おはようございます (good morning). 俺んち **orenchi** in the third sentence is short for 俺の家 **ore no uchi** (my house).

🎧 Colloquial vocabulary					
Nouns		奴 **yatsu**	guy / man	**Verbs**	
こいつ	this guy	野郎 **yarō**	guy / moron	エッチする	to have sex
そいつ	that guy	**Adjectives**		なめる	to take for a fool
あいつ	that guy there	エッチな	sexy	ナンパする	to pick up
ガキ	kid / brat	かっこいい	handsome, cool	びびる	to be scared stiff
きさま	you (threat)	かっこわるい	not cool	ふざける	to mess around
ちび	kid / midget	すごい	grcat; cool	むかつく	to get angry
チャリ	bicycle	せこい	stingy	**Expressions**	
つら	face / mug	ださい	tacky	こら！	hey! (threat)
てめえ	you (threat)	でかい	huge	ざまあみろ	serves you right
変態 **hentai**	weird / pervert	ひどい	horrible	超 **chō**	super (very)
マジ	truly	やばい	risky; dicey	めっちゃ	very

🎧 Grammatical patterns

The table on the right shows grammatical patterns in colloquial or vulgar language. For instance, 〜てやがる is a vulgar verb ending with a nuance of contempt; 〜てたまるか means "I'll be damned if . . ." and ぶっ〜 adds menace to words like 殺す *korosu* (to kill).

🎧 Patterns in casual Japanese		
〜てやがる	(V)	歩いてやがる He's walking
〜たまるか	(V)	飲んでたまるか I won't drink it
ぶっ〜	(V)	ぶっ殺す I'll kill you
すごく	(C)	すごく高い Really expensive
すごい	(C)	すごい高い Really expensive
歩く *aruku* to walk; 飲む *nomu* to drink; 殺す *korosu* to kill; 高い *takai* expensive, high; すごい cool, terrific		

- てめえ、なめてやがんのかぁ！ You, do you take me for a fool?! (very V)
- この試合、負けてたまるかよ！ I'll be damned if I lose this match! (V)
- 何を笑ってんだ？ぶっ殺すぞ！ What you laughing at? I'm gonna kill you! (very V)

The adverb すごく comes from すごい, a colloquial adjective meaning "fantastic, cool," etc. すごく means "very," synonymous with とても (Lesson 45). Often すごい is used instead of すごく even though it is grammatically wrong.

- すごく／すごい甘いんだね、このりんご！ It's real sweet, this apple, isn't it? (C)

There are also words whose main consonant is "doubled" in casual register: ばかり ⇒ ばっかり (only, Lesson 58); やはり ⇒ やっぱり (I knew it); あまり ⇒ あんまり (not much, Lesson 45); さき ⇒ さっき (a while ago); まま ⇒ まんま (as it is, Lesson 47).

- 文句ばっかり言うなよ、お前 Don't just complain (don't complain so much), man! (C)
- ごめんね、友達のまんまでいたいけど I'm sorry, but I want to stay friends. (C)

🎧 Questions in the negative

In English, we can make a request in the form of a question using a negative verb as a soft-ener (Won't you come?) In Japanese this is frequent and in all registers, including formal, colloquial and vulgar.

- こちらへ来ていただけませんか？ Could you come here, please? (Formal)
- 私と一緒に博物館へ行かない？ Won't you come with me to the museum? (C)
- 君、電話に出てくれない？ You, how about answering the phone? (C)
- 遠いんじゃないの、それ？ Isn't that very far? (C/V)

Notice the end-of-sentence tag じゃない？ The more colloquial じゃん is used mainly in Tokyo.

- 彼女のかばん、高いんじゃない？ Her bag is very expensive, don't you think?
- あのマンガ、面白いじゃん？ That manga is interesting, isn't it?

🎧 Answering yes / no questions

In English if asked "You're not hungry?," and we are not hungry, we answer "No." In Japa-nese, we answer "Yes" (Yes, it's true that I'm not hungry.) If we are hungry, we answer "No" (No, it's not true that I'm not hungry), i.e., denying a negative, which gives an affirmative.

- お肉を食べたくないんですか？ | はい（食べたくない）
  You don't want to eat meat? | Yes (I don't want to eat).
- 真理子が好きじゃないの？ | いいえ、違う（好きだ）
  You don't like Mariko? | No, you're wrong (I like her).

🎧 漫画例 Manga Examples

Let's look at some manga examples that will clarify the usage of colloquial and vulgar language that we've studied so far in this chapter. A word of advice: take this lesson only as a simple guide to casual speech that will help you understand comic books and movies. In real life, avoid using this kind of Japanese whenever you can.

Manga Example 1: Vulgar language

This panel contains some of the most vulgar Japanese there is, full of contractions, rough words and even special grammatical constructions. Notice first the words うるせえ and 関係ねえ *kankei nee*, very vulgar versions of the words うるさい (noisy) and 関係がない (having no relation to). Originally, contracting the last part of words ending in *-ai* and *-oi* into *-ee* was a characteristic of the vulgar dialect in Tokyo, but it has spread all over Japan and is often used in comic books and movies.

The word てめえら is the plural of てめえ, a vulgar way of saying "you," with a strong nuance of threat and insult. てめえ is a distortion of 手前 *temae* (a form of address used by men to address an inferior). In this example we have a contraction we haven't studied: it is にゃ, its normal form being に and は together.

Notice the final 〜てやがれ, the imperative form of 〜てやがる, a rough and rude form of the gerund 〜ている. You will find 〜てやがる in manga, but never in real life.

Gabriel Luque

Katsuichi: うるせえ！てめえらにゃ関係ねえ話だ！引っ込んでやがれ！

noisy! you IOP relation there isn't topic be! withdraw (vulgar)!

Shut up! This has nothing to do with you! Out!

Manga Example 2: Threats

Here is another instance of vulgar language. Notice first, at the end, じゃねえ, a vulgar contraction of じゃない, or the more orthodox form ではない. では is usually contracted in all registers in Japanese into じゃ, and the ねえ at the end is a rough contraction of ない. In this example we also have the prefix ぶっ〜, which adds brusqueness to a word. By adding ぶっ〜 to the verb 殺す *korosu* (to kill), the speaker is strengthening his sentence and adding, as well, the nuances of "threat" and "resolve."

Last of all, the 〜てやる form is common in vulgar language to indicate disdain toward the other person or to sound more macho; it has little to do with the meaning of "give or do a favor to someone inferior" of the 〜てやる we saw in Lesson 45.

Xian Nu Studio

ぶっ殺してやる

おどしじゃねーぞ

Kaneshiro: ぶっ殺してやる

(prefix) kill (give)

I'm gonna kill you.

おどしじゃねーぞ

threat not be EP

And I'm not bluffing.

Manga Example 3: A belligerent girl

Generally, a girl would never use this type of vulgar language, because this register is too rough and "macho" for a woman. However, in this example, we have quite an exception. The girl uses two very vulgar words: the verb ふざける (to mess around, to bug), and the noun 野郎 *yarō* (guy, man). The word デブ (fat guy) is slightly less vulgar.

The word ふざけん is a vulgar contraction of ふざける (the る becomes ん when talking very fast), and the な, as we have seen before, is used to form the direct negative imperative. Therefore, ふざけんな means "Don't bug me." As a curiosity, we will mention that in the most gangster-like register in Japanese some speakers roll their "r," like in Spanish.

ふざけんな デブ野郎〜〜〜っ

Studio Kōsen

Tokiwa: ふざけんな デブ野郎————っ

lark around (negative imperative), fat guy

Stop fucking with me, fat-ass!!

Manga Example 4: A very vulgar negative imperative

Here we have a negative imperative of the kind exclusively used in vulgar register: "verb + んじゃない."

Take a look at the example: いい気になる *ii ki ni naru* is a set phrase with the meaning of "to get smart with, to be stuck up." じゃねえ is the distortion of じゃない. Therefore,

いい気になってんじゃねえ (its non-distorted version being いい気になっているんじゃない) means more or less "don't get smart." More examples of this kind of (very) vulgar negative imperative are: ケーキを食べるんじゃない！ *Kēki o taberu n ja nai!* (Don't eat the cake!), こっちで遊ぶんじゃない！ *Kotchi de asobu n ja nai!* (Don't play here!), マンガを読むんじゃない！ *Manga o yomu n ja nai!* (Don't read manga!)

Kumasaka:　いい気になってんじゃねえ！
good feeling become not be!
Don't get smart with me!

Manga Example 5: Using the negative to ask

Here is an example of a question in the negative. Notice how, despite conjugating the verb in the **-masu** form (ありません), Asakawa omits all grammatical particles: a very obvious characteristic of spoken language. In its most orthodox form the sentence would be この４人に見覚えがありませんか？ *Kono yonin ni mioboe ga arimasen ka?* Here, however, the speaker has avoided the particles に, が and か, something we don't generally recommend.

Notice the negative form of the question: its literal translation would be "Don't these 4 people ring a bell?" In Japanese, the negative is often used when asking things, since it a "softens" a direct question.

Asakawa:　この４人 見おぼえありません？
this 4 people see remember not there are?
Do these 4 people ring a bell?

Manga Example 6: A tag for agreement

The tag じゃない at the end of a sentence used with an interrogative intonation, is a way of looking for the other person's agreement.

This example offers us a peculiar instance of this. The sentence seeking agreement is アンタのせいじゃない (it's not your fault). If we add the colloquial expression for statement じゃない, we obtain アンタのせいじゃないじゃない？, as in the example. This gives us two じゃない together, something that may sound really strange but which is not unusual in colloquial language. Therefore, the literal translation of this sentence is "It's not your fault, isn't it?" Giving this last じゃない an interrogative tone is very important, because, otherwise, the other person would interpret it as a negative. The tag じゃない？ is extremely common in spoken Japanese.

Kawami: だから…自分を責めないでよ…アンタのせいじゃないじゃない…？

so . . . yourself DOP attack EP . . . you POP fault not be not be . . . ?

So . . . don't blame yourself . . . It wasn't your fault, right?

Manga Example 7: Answer to a question in the negative

We will conclude with an example of something which might confuse you. Take a look at the conversation in the panel: literally, it would be "You can't see me?" and then the answer "Yes."

In English, we would interpret that he can see him, but in Japanese we are saying "indeed, I <u>cannot</u> see you." That is, in Japanese we corroborate the speaker's words "you can't see me." In our final translation, however, we have followed the English convention, and have answered "No." Don't feel discouraged if you are not grasping this immediately, this is a concept that takes a while to master!

Man 1: え？オレが見えない？

hey? I SP not see?

Hey? Can't you see me?

Man 2: はい

yes

No.

Exercises 練習

1 To what forms are these contractions equivalent:
～ちゃう, ～てゆう and ～なきゃ?

2 Give the casual or vulgar version of 買っておく,
行きたい and 遊んではだめだ。(買う to buy; 行く
to go; 遊ぶ to play)

3 Translate: 買ってくれよ、車！
(買う to buy; 車 car)

4 Translate: なんか言えよ、これってつまらないん
だよ.(言う to say; つまらない boring)

5 What do we use the construction ～てやがる for?
Form a sentence with it.

6 Is the following sentence grammatically correct:
あの家、すごいでかいね？Why/why not?
(家 house)

7 Translate: あいつ、めっちゃむかつくんだ、すぐ
びびりやがって . . . (すぐ at once)

8 Translate "Can you give me a hand?" using the
negative and the ～てくれる form (Lesson 45). (to
give a hand 手を貸す)

9 Translate: 舞子ちゃん、やせたじゃん？(舞子
Maiko; やせる to lose weight)

10 You <u>don't</u> have a stomachache and someone asks
you お腹、痛くない？What do you answer?
(お腹 stomach; 痛い painful)

— **Answers to all the exercises can be found online by following the link on page 7.** —

Lesson 54 • 第54課
Comparatives

After studying informal and formal registers in Japanese, let's return to our grammar studies to see how to form comparative and superlative sentences.

🎧 As . . . as

In Lessons 43 and 50, we said that ようだ means "apparently . . . ," and that a small variation of this expression could be used to form comparative sentences: "A is as . . . as B." The basic structure of this kind of sentences is "AはBのように . . ."

Usage: After verbs and **-i** adjectives, we add nothing. **-na** adjectives keep the な, and we add の between nouns and ように. **Be careful:** ように is an adverbial form that modifies verbs and adjectives, but never nouns.

- 彼はきつねのようにずるいです He is as sly as a fox.
- この家は宮殿のように広い This house is as roomy as a palace.
- 今は夏のように暑いです It is now as hot as in summer.
- 美穂は宇多田ヒカルのように歌えるよ Miho can sing like Hikaru Utada.

To establish a comparison between nouns, we use the adjectival form ような.

- 彼は宮殿のような家に住んでいる He lives in a house that is like a palace.
- 舞子の彼氏はゴリラのような男だ Maiko's boyfriend is a man like a gorilla.

Finally, we can also make metaphors and similes with ようだ:

- 舞子の彼氏はゴリラのようだ Maiko's boyfriend is (looks like) a gorilla.

Remember, as we saw in Lesson 43, みたいに and みたいな are the colloquial versions of ように and ような, respectively. **Usage:** We don't need to add or eliminate anything.

- 彼はきつねみたいにずるいです He is as sly as a fox.
- 彼は宮殿みたいな家に住んでいる He lives in a house that is like a palace.
- 舞子の彼氏はゴリラみたいだ Maiko's boyfriend is (looks like) a gorilla.

🎧 More . . . than

The basic structure to form this kind of sentence is "AはBより . . ." **Usage:** Don't add anything after a simple-form verb, *-i* adjective, or noun. *-na* adjectives take な. **Be careful:** "AはBよりも . . . ," with identical meaning and usage, is another valid form, as well as the dislocated forms "BよりAは . . ." or "BよりもAは . . ."

- 日本語は英語より難しいだろう Japanese is probably more difficult than English.
- 美穂は宇多田ヒカルよりうまく歌える Miho can sing better than Hikaru Utada.
- この仕事は地獄よりも大変だ This job is tougher than hell.
- アニメよりマンガは面白いと思う I think manga is more interesting than anime.
- 寿司よりもスパゲッティを食べたいな More than sushi, I want to eat spaghetti.

Note: "AはBより . . ." is only used when we know what we are talking about: the subject has already been raised in the conversation or all parties know about it (Lesson 39). If the subject is unknown, we must use the expression "AのほうがBより . . ." The dislocated form "BよりAのほうが . . ." is also possible.

- ジョンのほうがマイクよりハンサムだ John is more handsome than Mike.
- 天ぷらのほうがカレーよりおいしい Tempura is nicer than curry.
- 九州より四国のほうが静かだ Shikoku is quiet, more so than Kyushu.

🎧 Not as . . . as

In Japanese there is no way of saying "A is less . . . than B," maybe due to the Japanese aversion to stating things clearly. The closest expression is "AはBほど + negative," which literally means "A is not as . . . as B" **Usage:** B is only used with simple-form verbs and nouns. The overall sentence must compulsorily be in the negative.

- 英語は日本語ほど難しくない English is not as difficult as Japanese.
- カレーは天ぷらほどおいしくない Curry is not as nice as tempura.
- マイクはジョンほどハンサムじゃない Mike is not as handsome as John.
- 歌うのは踊るほど疲れない Singing is not as tiring as dancing.
- 富士山はエベレストほど高くない Mount Fuji is not as high as Mount Everest.

🎧 Adverbs of gradation

Adverbs of gradation are usually used in sentences of the kind "more . . . than" and "not as . . . as." They follow より and ほど, and give different gradations to our comparisons:

1) やや: slightly
- 秀は知宏よりやや背が高い Hide is slightly taller than Tomohiro.

2) 少し/ちょっと: a little (ちょっと is more informal than 少し)
- 秀は知宏よりちょっと背が高い Hide is a little taller than Tomohiro.

3) かなり/ずいぶん: quite (ずいぶん is somewhat stronger than かなり)
- 秀は知宏よりかなり背が高い Hide is quite taller than Tomohiro.

4) ずっと: much more
- 秀は知宏よりずっと背が高い Hide is much taller than Tomohiro.

The adverb もっと (more) can also form comparative sentences:
- この本はもっと高いよ This book is more expensive.
- 彼(のほう)がもっと頭がいいです He is more intelligent.

🎧 The same . . . as / As . . . as

The structure A は B と同じぐらい **A wa B to onaji gurai** is used to form sentences of the kind "A is more or less the same . . . as B," or "A is as . . . as B." The word 同じ means the same as, and the adverb ぐらい (Lesson 40), means more or less or about. **Usage:** Only nouns or noun phrases are used for B. **Be careful:** Although grammatically correct, the structure "Aは B と同じ . . . ," that is, without ぐらい, is hardly ever used in real life.

- 秀は知宏と同じぐらい背が高い Hide is more or less the same height as Tomohiro.
- ジョンはマイクと同じぐらいハンサムだ John is more or less as handsome as Mike.
- 天ぷらはカレーと同じぐらいおいしい Tempura is more or less as nice as curry.
- 数学は化学と同じぐらい嫌いです I hate math more or less the same as chemistry.
- そのパソコンは車と同じぐらい高い That computer is more or less as expensive as a car.

🎧 Questions

Let's look at the question "Which is more . . . , A or B?" The basic structure in Japanese is "A とBではどちらが . . . ?" **Be careful:** in this kind of sentence always use the interrogative pronoun どちら or its colloquial version どっち (which?); never use 誰 **dare** (who?), どれ (which?), or 何 **nani** (what?).

- 日本語と英語ではどちらが難しいか？ Out of Japanese and English, which is more difficult?
- 日本語は英語と同じぐらい難しい Japanese is more or less as difficult as English.
- 秀と知宏ではどっちが背が高いの？ Who is taller: Hide or Tomohiro?
- 知宏は秀ほど背が高くない Tomohiro is not as tall as Hide.
- 天ぷらとカレーではどちらがおいしいの？ Which is tastier: tempura or curry?
- 天ぷらはカレーよりずっとおいしい Tempura is much tastier than curry.

🎧 Superlatives

There are two ways of forming superlative sentences ("A is the most (adj.) in . . ."). Both structures must always be used with an adjective, and never with a noun or an adverb.

The first is "A は . . . (の中で / で) 一番 (adj.)" ***A wa . . .(no naka de/de) ichiban*** (adj). **Note:** で is used when we are talking about places, and の中で is used when we are talking about groups of something. However, both are often used without distinction.

- 富江はクラスの中で一番頭のいい人です Tomie is the most intelligent in the class.
- エベレストは世界で一番高い山です Everest is the highest mountain in the world.
- 世界で一番安全な国は日本でしょう Japan might be the safest country in the world.

The second structure for superlatives is "A は . . . (の中で / で) 最も (adj.)" ***A wa . . . (no naka de/de) mottomo*** (adj). We use it just like its "sibling" 一番 .

- 富江はクラスの中で最も頭のいい人です Tomie is the most intelligent in the class.
- エベレストは世界で最も高い山です Everest is the highest mountain in the world.
- 世界で最も安全な国は日本でしょう Japan might be the safest country in the world.

Note: 一番 means the first or sometimes the best (for example, 彼は一番だ ***kare wa ichiban da***, He is the first / the best), while 最も is an adverb meaning the most (something).

🎧 Too (much)

The English adverbs "too" and "too much" modify adjectives and verbs. In Japanese we must form compound verbs and adjectives with the auxiliary verb 〜すぎる. For verbs, add 〜すぎる to the root: 働く ***hataraku*** (work) ⇒ Root:働き ⇒ add 〜すぎる:働きすぎる (work too much). For *-i* and *-na* adjectives: replace い or な with 〜すぎる:広い ***hiroi*** (wide) ⇒ 広すぎる (too wide) | 静かな ***shizuka-na*** (quiet) ⇒ 静かすぎる (too quiet).

- あの人はいつも話しすぎますね That man always talks too much, doesn't he?
- 昨日はお酒を飲みすぎた Yesterday, I drank too much (alcohol).
- このサンドイッチはまずすぎるな This sandwich tastes really bad.

Exceptions: いい (good) ⇒ よすぎる (too good) | Negative: 〜ない ⇒ 〜なさすぎる

- 君は勉強しなさすぎるんじゃない？ Don't you study too little?

🎧 Comparative and superlative expressions		
A は *B* のように...	*A* is as ... as *B*	百合は天使のようにきれいです Yuri is as beautiful as an angel.
A は *B* みたいに...	*A* is as ... as *B* (colloquial)	百合は天使みたいにきれいだ Yuri is as beautiful as an angel.
A は *B* より...	*A* is more ... than *B*	百合は久美よりきれいだ Yuri is more beautiful than Kumi.
A のほうが *B* より...	*A* (new topic) is more ... than *B*	百合のほうが久美よりきれいだ Yuri is more beautiful than Kumi.
A は *B* ほど... (neg.)	*A* is not as ... as *B*	久美は百合ほどきれいじゃない Kumi is not as beautiful as Yuri.
A は *B* と同じ ぐらい...	*A* is more or less the same ... as *B*	百合は久美と同じぐらいきれいだ Yuri is more or less as beautiful as Kumi.
...の中で/で一番 (Adj.)	the most (adj.) in ...	百合は会社の中で一番きれいだ Yuri is the most beautiful in the company.
...の中で/で最も(Adj.)	the most (adj.) among ...	百合は会社の中で最もきれいな女性だ Yuri is the most beautiful woman in the company.
〜すぎる	too much ...	百合は背が低すぎる Yuri is too short.
天使 ***tenshi*** angel; きれいな beautiful; 会社 ***kaisha*** company; 女性 ***josei*** woman; 背が低い ***se ga hikui*** short		

🎧 漫画例 Manga Examples

And now let's get on with the manga examples, which, as usual, will help us study in greater depth some of the points we have studied in this chapter. We will also expand on what we've already learned with some new expressions or nuances.

Manga Example 1: The comparative "more than"

This is an example of the "A is more . . . than B" kind. The basic structure in Japanese is "Aは Bより . . ." However, this structure is only valid if both speakers are familiar with the subject they are talking about.

   If you want to introduce a new topic in a comparative sentence of the "more than" kind, then remember that you must use the "Aのほうがより . . ." structure, as in the example here (Notice ほう is written in kanji [方] here, a perfectly valid option and very common in written Japanese.) If the sentence in the manga example had been preceded by the question この薬は効くね (This pill is effective, isn't it?) the response wouldn't use の方が because the pill has previously appeared in the conversation, and it has become the topic in it. You can review the concept of "topic" in Lesson 37. **Note:** かもしれない (Lesson 43), means "perhaps" or "maybe." It is always placed at the end of the sentence.

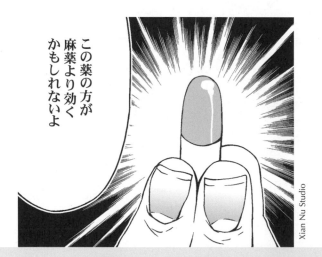

George: この薬の方が麻薬より効くかもしれないよ

this medicine on its part SP *drug more than effective perhaps*

This pill might be more effective than a drug.

Manga Example 2: The comparative "to be like"

The construction "to be like" is formed with the adverbial form ように (before verbs and adjectives) and the adjectival form ような (before nouns). There are colloquial versions, which are, respectively, みたいに and みたいな.

In our sentence, Haruki states that 女王のように見える, literally, "She is seen like (as if she were) a queen." Remember that between the noun and ように or ような, we must add の. A more colloquial version of this sentence would be 女王みたいに見える. (Be careful, with みたいに and みたいな, we don't need の).

Notice, too, the word まるで, which means something like "completely," "utterly," or "just like," and is often used in these kinds of sentences to strengthen them rhetorically.

Studio Kōsen

Haruki: まるで女王のように見える

completely queen like see

She looks just like a queen.

Manga Example 3: A special usage of *yori*

Just as we said in Manga Examples 4 and 6 in Lesson 48, finding grammatical structures that are used with the ***kosoado*** pronouns (Lesson 34) is quite common. The case of より is somewhat special, because it is usually seen only with それ (that), as in the example

here, and is hardly ever combined with other ***kosoado*** pronouns. それより is used when changing subject suddenly in a conversation; its literal translation is something like "more than that." This expression is very difficult to translate directly, although we could paraphrase it with expressions such as "aside from that" or "I agree with what we've just said, but now we must talk about . . ."

Gabriel Luque

Jun: それより後半も今までの調子でいこうぜ！ 勝てるぞ みんな！

this more than 2nd part too now until POP way IP let's EP! win EP everybody!

Aside from that, in the second part we must play the way we've been playing until now! We can win, guys!

Manga Example 4: The comparative "not as"

We saw earlier in this chapter that in Japanese there are no comparative expressions of the "less than" kind, and that we must use subtleties such as "not as much as." The basic structure of this kind of sentence is "AはBほど . . . (negative)." In the manga-example sentence here, there is no comparative element because it has previously appeared in the conversation. Probably, the original sentence said by this man was something like ウチの雪子 ほど太っていない *uchi no Yukiko hodo futotte inai* (She is not as fat as my Yukiko). That would justify Yukiko's rage in the example! Remember that the verb or adjective to

be compared (太っている in this case) must be in the negative. **Note:** ウチ (in kanji 内), is a multipurpose word that can be used when referring to oneself (particularly in the case of women), to one's family, or to close friends: it is the same concept of **uchi** that we analyzed in Lesson 45.

Hiroshi:	ウチの雪子(ゆきこ)ほどじゃないけどな
	inside POP Yukiko so much as not be but EP
	Although she's not as much as my Yukiko.

Manga Example 5: The superlative *ichiban*

Let's review the superlative, expressions of "the most . . ." kind. There are two ways of forming superlative sentences: one is using 一番, like in this panel, and another is with 最も *mottomo*. The basic structure is "Aは . . . の中で/で *no naka de/de* 一番 (adj.)."

In our sentence, それが一番大事なこと (That is the most important thing), the area the speaker is referring to is not mentioned, and the subject is replaced with the pronoun それ (that). To study this structure further, we could change the sentence to 合格する のは 人生で一番大事なこと *Gōkaku suru no wa jinsei de ichiban daiji-na koto* (Passing the exam is the most important thing in life), that is, with a word naming a specific area

(人生で, "in life"), and replacing the pronoun それ with 合 格する (to pass an exam). **Note:** The adverb きっと (surely, undoubtedly) comes at the end of the sentence here. This is a common characteristic of the colloquial language (Lesson 53).

Yūji:	それが一番(いちばん)大事(だいじ)なコトだよ、きっと
	that SP the most important thing be EP, sure
	That's the most important thing, surely.

Manga Example 6: Superlative words

Besides the superlatives 一番 *ichiban* and 最も *mottomo*, there are compound words with superlative meaning, formed by the kanji 最 *sai* plus another kanji. Notice how 最も and 最 have the same kanji, but their reading is different. Other superlative words of this kind are 最良 *sairyō* (the best), 最悪 *saiaku* (the worst), 最新 *saishin* (the newest), 最高 *saikō* (the best / the tallest), 最愛 *saiai* (the most loved), 最強 *saikyō* (the strongest), 最終 *saishū* (the last / the final), 最適 *saiteki* (the most appropriate / the ideal), and many more. Also worth mentioning are 最初 *saisho* (the beginning), 最後 *saigo* (the end), as well as the adverb 最近 *saikin* (lately, recently).

In this example we have the word 最低, which literally means "the lowest," but which is quite often used as an insult hurled mainly by women, with the meaning of "you are scum," "you are pathetic," or even "you are despicable."

鈴木さんなんか大ッキライ！

最低オトコです！

Studio Kōsen

Shigeko: 鈴木さんなんか大ッキライ！ 最低オトコです！

Suzuki SUF (emphasis) hate! the lowest man be!!

I hate you, Suzuki! You scumbag!

Manga Example 7: Too much

The final panel offers an instance of how to form sentences with the meaning of "too much." If we have the verb 知る and we want to say "to know too much," we must add the auxiliary verb 〜すぎる to its root, thus obtaining the verb 知りすぎる. Compound verbs with 〜すぎる can be conjugated just like any other verb: 知りすぎない (negative), 知りすぎなかった (past negative), 知りすぎて (-*te* form), etc. Here, for example, we have the past form 知りすぎた, working as a relative clause that modifies the noun 男. Therefore, 知りすぎた男 means "The man who knew too much." Review Lesson 50 to brush up on the subject of relative clauses.

Gabriel Luque

Title: 第4章 知りすぎた男

number 4 chapter know too much man

Chapter 4: The man who knew too much

Exercises 練習

1 What differences of register and usage are there between the expressions ように and みたいに?

2 Translate: "This house is as big as a cathedral."
(house 家 ; big 大きい ; cathedral 大聖堂)

3 Translate: "This house is bigger than a cathedral."

4 Translate: "This house is not as big as a cathedral."

5 Translate: "This house is more or less as big as a cathedral."

6 Translate: "This house is much smaller than a cathedral."

7 Translate: "Between this house and a cathedral, which is bigger?"

8 Translate: "This cathedral is the biggest in the world." (world 世界)

9 Translate: "This house is too big."

10 What do the following words mean? 最悪 , 最初 , 最良 and 最低 ? What do you think the words 最大 and 最小 could mean?

— **Answers to all the exercises can be found online by following the link on page 7.** —

Lesson 55 • 第 55 課

Sightseeing

In this lesson we will introduce some language that is useful when sightseeing in Japan, and, in doing so, review some of the previous conversation-based lessons we have studied so far.

🎧 Asking for directions

In Lesson 51 we studied how to ask for directions at the 交番 **kōban** police box. Let's learn how to ask directions from people in the street:

- すみませんが、横浜ランドマークタワーへ行く道を教えていただけませんか？ Excuse me, how do I get to Yokohama Landmark Tower? (Lessons 45 and 54)
- 次の角を右へ曲がってください。そしてまっすぐ行ってください Turn right on the next corner. Then, go straight on. (Lesson 48)
- すみませんが、浅草寺は近いですか？ Excuse me, is Sensoji temple close by?
- 歩くには遠すぎるので、地下鉄に乗った方がいいですよ
  It's too far to walk, so I recommend taking the subway. (Lessons 48, 49 and 54)
- この近くにバス停はありますか？ Is there a bus stop near here?
- はい、あの映画館の隣にあります Yes, it is next to that cinema.
- 奈良の見所は何ですか？ What places are worth seeing in Nara?
- 東大寺には大仏があるし、それに春日大社と奈良公園も面白いですよ。
  There is the great image of Buddha in Todaiji temple, and then Kasuga-taisha shrine and Nara Park are also interesting. (Lessons 35 and 48)
- 市内地図をいただけますか？ Could you give me a map of the city? (Lesson 45)
- この辺には商店街がありますか？ Is there a shopping district around this area?
- 二番目の信号を左に曲がってください Turn left at the second traffic light.
- こちらの方向でいいですね？ This is the right way, isn't it?
- 東寺は京都駅の裏側にありますよ The Toji temple is behind Kyoto Station.

🎧 Giving and receiving directions			
behind	〜の裏側に	that way	あちらへ
to go straight on	まっすぐ行く	to the left	左側に
in front of . . .	〜の前に	to the right	右側に
next to . . .	〜の隣に	to turn left	左へ曲がる
on the corner of . . .	〜の角に	to turn right	右へ曲がる
on the opposite side of . . .	〜の向かい	to go 3 blocks	3 ブロック行く

🎧 Taking photos

Sometimes we might want to ask someone to take our photo. Or we may want to take photos of other people—after asking their permission, of course!

- すみません、写真を撮っていただけますか？ Excuse me, could you take a photo (of me)? (Lesson 45)
- もう一枚お願いします One more, please. (Lesson 40)
- (あなたの)写真を撮ってもいいですか？ Could I take a photo of you? (Lesson 32)
- あなたと一緒に写真を撮りたいんですけど I'd like to have my photo taken with you.
- ここで写真を撮ってもいいですか？ Can I take photos here? (Lesson 32)

🎧 At the museum

The sentences below will help you when touring Japanese museums. You can expand them using words from the tables on these pages and grammar patterns we have studied. がんばってね!

- 東京国立博物館の開館時間を教えていただけませんか？
  Could you tell me what time the Tokyo National Museum opens? (Lessons 45 and 54)
- 東京国立博物館は9時半から17時まで開いております
  The Tokyo National Museum opens from 9:30 am to 5 pm. (Lessons 41 and 52)
- しかし、休館日は月曜日ですので、お気をつけください
  However, please be aware that they are closed on Mondays. (Lessons 48 and 52)
- 入場料はいくらですか How much is it to get in?
- 学生割引はありますか？ Is there a student discount?
- 大人2枚と子ども1枚ください Two adult (tickets) and one child, please.

- 館内ツアーはありますか？ Is there a guided tour of the museum?
- 江戸時代の浮世絵はどこにあるんですか？ Where are the Edo period ukiyo-e?
- 絵葉書を買えますか？ Can I buy postcards? (Lesson 32)
- トイレを使ってもいいでしょうか？ Can I use the toilet? (Lesson 32)

🎧 Sightseeing vocabulary

In the city (市内で)

aquarium	水族館	direction	方向	Shinto shrine	神社
art museum	美術館	garden	庭園｜庭	shopping street	商店街
botanical garden	植物園	market	市場	statue	像
Buddhist temple	お寺	movie theater	映画館	street	通り
castle	城	museum	博物館	theater	劇場
city hall	市役所	monument	記念碑	traffic lights	信号
corner	角	park	公園	zoo	動物園

In the countryside (田舎で)

bay	湾	island	島	sea	海
cape	岬	lake	湖	valley	谷
coast	海岸	mountain	山	volcano	火山
harbor	港	peninsula	半島	waterfall	滝
hill	丘	river	川	wood	森

At the museum (博物館で)

adult	大人	exhibition	展示	painting	絵画
child	子ども	exit	出口	price of admission	入場料
entrance	入口	guided tour	館内ツアー	sculpture	彫刻

🎧 Mailing things

And last of all, some useful phrases for the post office:

- 切手（きって）はどこで買（か）えますか？
  Where can I buy stamps? (Lesson 32)
- アメリカまで手紙（てがみ）を出（だ）したいが、いくらですか？
  I want to send some letters to the US. How much is it?
- １１０円（ひゃくじゅうえんえん）です
  It is 110 yen.
- じゃ、１１０円（ひゃくじゅうえんえん）の切手（きって）を ５枚（ごまい）ください
  Then please can I have five 110-yen stamps.
- 航空便（こうくうびん）でお願（ねが）いします
  By air mail, please.
- 船便（ふなびん）でチリに着（つ）くまで何日（なんにち）ぐらいかかりますか？
  How many days will it take to Chile if I send it by sea mail?
- 中身（なかみ）は本（ほん）だけですが、何（なに）かの割（わ）り引（び）きはありますか？
  (The packet) only contains books, is there a discount?

🎧 Post office	
address	住所（じゅうしょ）
envelope	封筒（ふうとう）
fragile (item)	割（わ）れ物（もの）
mailbox	ポスト
packet	小包（こづつみ）
postcard	絵葉書（えはがき）
post office	郵便局（ゆうびんきょく）
registered mail	書留（かきとめ）
special delivery	速達（そくたつ）
stamp	切手（きって）
zip code	郵便番号（ゆうびんばんごう）

Cultural Note: Shrines and Temples

The various Buddhist temples (お寺 *otera*) and Shinto shrines (神社 *jinja*) dotting the most historical Japanese cities, such as 京都 *Kyōto*, 奈良 *Nara* and 鎌倉 *Kamakura*, are fascinating and exotic to Western eyes, but what are the differences between the places of worship of the two main religions in Japan, Buddhism (仏教 *bukkyō*) and Shinto (神道 *shinto*)?

There is a great difference in color: whereas お寺 are not painted and keep the original color of the wood, 神社 are often painted in bright red.

At 神社 we will see 鳥居 *torii* gates, which separate the earthly and spiritual worlds and which mark the entrance to sacred land, often protected by a fierce 狛犬 *komainu* watchdog on each side. You can go to the 神社 to pray for anything, such as success in your career or studies, finding a boyfriend or girlfriend, or recovery from illness. In fact, the sale of お守り *omamori* (amulets) and 絵馬 *ema* (votive tablets on which you write your wishes and then hang) are an essential source of income for the 神社. You'll also find おみくじ, little bits of paper that tell your fortune for a reasonable price.

To pray at a 神社, first purify yourself (rinsing your mouth with water and washing your hands), sound a bell to alert the gods (神 *kami*) to your presence, throw a coin into the offertory box (賽銭箱 *saisenbako*), bow twice, clap twice, bow again, and finally pray.

お寺 are more frugal in appearance than 神社. Here we can find beautiful pagodas (塔 *tō*) and huge bells (鐘 *kane*), and people light aromatic incense (お香 *okō*) to pray to the Buddha. There are many statues of the different Buddhas: (如来 *nyorai*), the bodhisattva (菩薩 *bosatsu*), the 明王 *myōō* (fierce beings who protect the teachings of the Buddhas), and the 仁王 *niō*, two huge statues of angry warriors who guard the temple gates: the one called 阿 *a* has his mouth open, and the other called 吽 *un*, has his mouth closed, as an allegory of the characters opening and closing the Sanskrit alphabet, "a" and "hum," and which, together, represent the beginning and end of all things.

A *torii* gate at Kasuga Jinja (Nara), guarded by a *komainu*
(Photo: M. Bernabé)

🎧 漫画例 Manga Examples

We will say goodbye to conversational lessons with a few manga panels, of course, where some of the topics we have seen in this lesson will be illustrated. We will also see quite a few new things related to Japanese culture, so be sure to read carefully.

Manga Example 1: Going to the post office

The panel opening the manga examples section shows us a boy going to the post office (郵便局) at his mother's request, to hand in a letter (手紙) for special delivery (速達). Ordinary mail would be 普通 *futsū*, and registered mail 書留 *kakitome*. Besides helping us review useful post-related vocabulary, this panel also reviews some grammar seen in previous lessons. For instance, the で in 速達で corresponds to the use of the particle で

we studied in Lesson 38: it indicates "how." Likewise, take a look at the って placed just after the phrase in quotation marks (「」): it is the colloquial version of the "quote" usage of the particle と we studied on page 81, Lesson 41. **Note:** The boy repeats the sentence twice, but in his speech bubble no kanji are used. Sometimes, we will find words or sentences fully written in hiragana when children repeat them: this is a strategy to let the reader know that the child is only repeating sounds and doesn't really understand the meaning of what he's saying.

Kimie: 郵便局の人に「速達でお願いします」って言うのよ

post office POP person IOP "special delivery IP please" say EP EP

And you tell the man at the post office "by special delivery, please," OK?

Kazuhiro: そくたつでおねがいします そくたつでおねがいします

special delivery IP please special delivery IP please

By special delivery, please. By special delivery, please.

Manga Example 2: Asking to have a photo taken

Here we find the most common sentence when asking someone to take a photo of us. Notice how questions with 〜ていただきます (Lesson 45) are often inflected in the potential form (Lesson 32), that is, 〜ていただけます, literally, "could you do me the favor of . . . ?" Peculiarities about photos in Japan: almost all Japanese have the odd habit of posing for photos making the V sign for victory (Vサイン) with the index and middle fingers, a truly compulsive habit. By the way, the word they use to urge someone to smile when taking their photo is チーズ (cheese), just like us in English. **Note:** The man's answer, somewhat unsociable, is へい, a distortion of はい, denoting certain indifference and even annoyance.

Gabriel Luque

Couple:	すみませーん シャッター押していただけます？
	excuse me shutter press (do a favor)?
	Excuse me, could you take a photo of us?

Manga Example 3: A telephone conversation

This is a telephone conversation between a mother and her daughter. As you can see, it is a short conversation: typical in Japan. We will highlight the もしもし, the Japanese equivalent to our "hello?" or "yes?," from the verb 申す *mōsu* ("to say," Lesson 52), which belongs to the formal language of modesty. Seemingly, when the telephone was first introduced in Japan, people needed to make sure they were being heard "from the other side" and so they repeated the verb 申す twice, obtaining something like "I say, I say." This expression has taken root and has become the actual もしもし used today. Notice, too, うん, a colloquial word used to say yes, and the じゃね at the end, used to say goodbye.

Studio Kōsen

Yuki:	もしもし… あ ママ？ うん… 今 友達 来てる そう… じゃーね
	hello . . . oh, Mom? yes . . . now friend come that's right . . . bye-bye
	Hello? Oh, Mom? Yes . . . I have a friend over now. Yes . . . Bye-bye.

Manga Example 4: Zen Buddhism

In this example we have a conversation where a Buddhist monk (お坊さん *obōsan* or 坊主 *bōzu*) remarks to Jim that "doughnuts have holes," and he replies asking whether it is a 公案. You probably know the word 禅 *zen*, which designates a very widespread branch of Buddhism (仏教 *bukkyō*) in Japan. Among the 禅 practices we have 座禅 *zazen*, in which the student sits in meditation for hours (in an uncomfortable position) and contemplate riddles called 公案, which help the student reach enlightenment (悟り *satori*). Probably, the most famous 公案 is the enigmatic 片手ではどんな音がする？ *Katate*

de wa donna oto ga suru? (What is the sound of one hand clapping?) **Note:** In the next panel, the monk says that when you eat a doughnut, the hole disappears, and he wonders where that hole goes to. A very 禅 reflection, no doubt!

Xian Nu Studio

Monk:	ジムさん、ドーナツには穴（あな）がありますね	Jim:	はあ…公案（こうあん）ですか
	Jim SUF, doughnuts PP TOP hole there is EP		*ah . . . koan be Q?*
	Mr. Jim, doughnuts have holes, don't they?		Ah, is this a koan?

Manga Example 5: *Omikuji* fortune telling

We see in this panel a man in a Shinto shrine (神社 *jinja*), who puts a coin in a box with a sign reading おみくじ, takes out a piece of paper reading 大吉, and rejoices at it. Why? Well, the おみくじ tells you what your fortune will be for the year, and there are several kinds. From the best to the worst: 大吉 (great good luck), 中吉 *chūkichi* (medium good

luck), 小吉 *shōkichi* (little good luck), 末吉 *suekichi* (so-so luck), 小凶 *shōkyō* (little bad luck), 半凶 *hankyō* (medium bad luck), 大凶 *daikyō* (great bad luck). **Note:** Other typical things we can see here are a big rope of straw (しめなわ), zigzag-shaped paper decorations (四手 *shide*), and 破魔矢 *hamaya* arrows, which frighten evil spirits and devils away, and are sold during 初詣 *hatsumōde*, the first temple visit of the New Year.

Gabriel Luque

Man:	今年（ことし）のうんせいは…	Box:	おみくじ	Paper:	大吉（だいきち）
	this year POP fortune TOP . . .		*fortunes*		*great good luck*
	Let's see my fortune for this year . . .		Fortunes		Great good luck

Manga Example 6: Praying at a Shinto shrine

母さん、神様に千円もふるまって、なに祈願したの？

Xian Nu Studio

In this example, which also takes us to a 神社 *jinja*, we have a conversation between a mother and a daughter. The mother is praying before an offertory box (賽銭箱 *saisenbako*), which is where prayer money is thrown and where the prayer ritual we saw in the Cultural Note on page 257 takes place. The daughter asks why she has donated so much as 1,000 yen to the gods (神様); because, usually, one throws in 10, or 50 or 100 yen coins, at the most. Larger offerings are only made when you are asking the 神 for something especially important. Notice the use of the particle も, which in this case indicates the idea of "no less than" (Lesson 37).

Michiko: 母さん、神様に千円もふるまって、なに祈願したの？

Mom, god SUF IOP *1000 yen very much donate, what prayer do* EP?

Mom, you've just given 1000 yen to the gods, what have you prayed for?

Manga Example 7: Festivals

We could not conclude this lesson without mentioning the variety of bustling Japanese festivals (祭 *matsuri*). In this example, we see an image of a 山鉾 *yamaboko* float, from one of the most famous festivals in Japan: the 祇園祭, held in the beautiful city of 京都 **Kyōto** throughout the month of July, with its main events on the 17th and 24th. They say this festival has a history of more than one thousand years! It is one of the three most famous festivals in Japan along with the 天神祭 *tenjin matsuri* (in the city of 大阪 **Ōsaka**, on July 25), and the 神田祭 *Kanda matsuri* (in 東京 **Tōkyō**, on May 15), which are all worth seeing. **Notes:** Here you can also see an example of the superlative 一番 *ichiban* (in hiragana here), which we saw in Lesson 54, in the relative clause いちばんもりあがる日 (Lesson 50).

祇園祭３日め、いちばんもりあがる日。

「宵山」とは、

J.M. Ken Niimura

Tomo: 「宵山」とは、祇園祭３日め、いちばんもりあがる日。

"Yoiyama" (definition), Gion festival day 3 (ordinal), the most liven up day

The "Yoiyama" is on the third day of the Gion Festival, the liveliest day.

Exercises 練習

1 Translate the following words: 動物園 (どうぶつえん), 切手 (きって), 城 (しろ), 展示 (てんじ), テレホンカード, 住所 (じゅうしょ) and 美術館 (びじゅつかん).

2 Translate the following words: "flash," "garden," "direction," "street," and "traffic lights."

3 You are heading for the Atsuta Jingu shrine (熱田神宮) (あつた)(じんぐう) in Nagoya (名古屋) (なごや), but you don't know how to get there. Ask somebody.

4 Translate the answer to the previous question: この通りをまっすぐ行って、そして右へ曲がってください。交番の隣にあります。(とお)(い)(みぎ)(ま)(こうばん)(となり)

5 Translate: "Walk two more blocks, and then turn right before the third traffic lights."

6 Ask someone if you can take their photo. If they agree, don't forget to ask them to smile!

7 You are going to the museum, and you need to buy tickets for an adult and three children. What do you say?

8 Translate: スペインまで手紙を出すのに 110 円の切手が必要です。(必要な necessary) (てがみ)(だ)(ひゃくじゅう)(えん)(きって)(ひつよう)

9 What is the process to follow when praying at a 神社 (じんじゃ)? What are 絵馬 (えま), and what are they for?

10 What are 禅, 公案 (ぜん)(こうあん), and the practice of 座禅 (ざぜん), and what is their aim?

— **Answers to all the exercises can be found online by following the link on page 7.** —

づぼらや
〒556-0002　大阪府浪速区
恵比寿東2丁目5番地
Tel 06-6633-5529

お、このレストランはとても有名ですよ。

はい、お乗りになってください。

こんにちは、この住所にあるレストランへ行きたいのですが…

いや、お上手で！ところで、その店のふぐは、他の店のふぐよりおいしいと皆さんおっしゃいます。私も一回食べに参りましたが、やはりとてもおいしかったですよ。

あ、私はスペインから参りました。

いいえ、日本語は運転手さんが言うほど上手ではありませんよ。

どこから来られましたか？日本語が本当にお上手ですね。

そうですか、いいところですよ。

あ、もうお店に到着いたしました。1240円でございます。

はい、行きたいですよ、もちろん。

え？行きたくないですか？

はい、行ってみたいですが、時間がありません。

ところで、大阪と東京ではどちらがお好きですか？

そうですか？大阪では住吉大社という神社をお勧めいたします。行ってみたくないですか？

大阪は東京と同じぐらい好きだと思いますよ！

ピーポー

ピーポー

お!

あ、あんたは上野でぶつかった奴だ!すげえ偶然だな。ね、このダサいペンダント、あんたのもんだろう?

あたしは別に何も怖くないし、逃げてもいないよ。いつも逃げちゃってるよ。何から逃げてるの!?問題から?

あんた、何か怖いのか?なんでそんなことを言うの?

じゃ、ありがとう。

あたしのペンダントだ!!あなたが盗んだの!?

何言ってんだよ?盗んできたねぇペンダント。

あの時、お前が落したので、オレ拾っといただけだ。

お前、問題から逃げてるんだと思う。問題から逃げるのはやばいし、かっこわるいぜ。問題に立ち向かわなきゃ、解決しないんだよ。わかった?

問題に立ち向かう?…そうだね…

考えといてよ!問題をなめるんじゃねぇよ!

はい!分かりました!ありがとうございます!!

ペコリ

まもなく、電車が到着します。ご注意ください。

Review for Lessons 51–55

Answers to all the review exercises can be found online by following the link on page 7.

🎧 *KAGE* – New vocabulary 新しい単語

ふぐ	blowfish	汚い	dirty
運転手	driver	拾う	to pick up
ごみ箱	trashcan	問題	problem
ぶつかる	to crash	立ち向かう	to face
偶然	chance, coincidence	解決する	to solve

1. In this fifth episode of **Kage**, what register of Japanese speech (vulgar, formal, etc.) does the taxi driver use? Why do you think he uses this register?

2. What register of speech does the beggar Nuria meets in the park use? Why do you think he uses this register?

3. What is the specialty of the restaurant Nuria wants to go to? According to the taxi driver, are dishes in this restaurant more delicious than in other restaurants or not?

4. Which city does Nuria like better, Tokyo or Osaka?

5. What illness is the beggar who faints in the park afraid of having? Does he have a fever? What illness does Nuria suggest he might have, and how does she deduce this?

6. Why is Nuria so happy after talking with the beggar? What has she discovered?

7. The taxi driver is visibly surprised when he asks Nuria 行ってみたくないですか? and she answers はい、行ってみたいけど、あまり時間がない. What do you think causes the taxi driver's confusion and his subsequent repetition of the question?

8. What form of **keigo** is used in these phrases: **sonkeigo** (S), **kenjōgo** (K) or **teineigo** (T)?

a) お乗りになってください (S / K / T)

b) 私も一回食べに参りました (S / K / T)

c) １２４０円でございます (S / K / T)

d) 住吉大社という神社をお勧めいたします (S / K / T)

e) どこから来られましたか？ (S / K / T)

9. Change the following sentences from **Kage** into polite Japanese (**desu-masu** form).

a) あんたは上野でぶつかった奴だ！すげぇ偶然だな。

_____ .

b) 何言ってんだよ？盗んでねぇぞ、このきたねぇペンダント。

_____ .

c) お前が落としたので、オレ拾っといただけ。

_____ .

10. Change the address on the business card Nuria shows the taxi driver into Western style.

11. Choose three words from the box on the facing page, depending on what is asked.

a) 医者が病気を治すために患者にどんなことをしますか？

_____   _____   _____

b) 手紙を書く時は、どんなものが必要ですか？

_____   _____   _____

c) 買い物をしたいけど、どこへ行きますか？

_____   _____   _____

d) 今日は変なものを食べちゃった！どういう病気になるだろう？

_____   _____   _____

e) 郵便局で、手紙を送る時は、どんな送り方がありますか？

_____   _____   _____

f) 今日はたくさん写真をとりたい！何を忘れてはいけない？

_____   _____   _____

g) すごく寒いのに、服を着ずに外へ出ました。どういう病気になるでしょう？

_____　　_____　　_____

切手	書留	紙	風邪	胃炎	手術
消化不良	肺炎	注射	スーパーマーケット		
市場	検査	電池	インフルエンザ	普通	
商店街	速達	封筒	フィルム	食中毒	三脚

12. Find the word that doesn't belong in each one of these groups.

a) 湾 ／ 岬 ／ 島 ／ 神社 ／ 半島 ／ 海岸

b) 水族館 ／ 入場料 ／ 美術館 ／ 劇場 ／ 植物園 ／ 動物園

c) 入院 ／ 医者 ／ 患者 ／ 警察官 ／ 包帯 ／ 病院

d) 財布 ／ 心臓 ／ 腸 ／ 肝臓 ／ 肺 ／ 血管

e) 国番号 ／ テレホンカード ／ 商店街 ／ 携帯電話 ／ 公衆電話

f) 警察官 ／ 泥棒 ／ 盗む ／ 血圧 ／ 交番 ／ スリ

g) 住所 ／ 城 ／ ポスト ／ 絵葉書 ／ 切手 ／ 小包 ／ 郵便局

h) フィルム ／ レンズ ／ 写真 ／ 現像 ／ フラッシュ ／ 彫刻

13. Link each illness with a part of the body, and the type of doctor needed.

a) 消化不良	腸	眼科医
b) 中耳炎	目	内科医
c) 盲腸炎	胃	内科医
d) 貧血	血液	耳鼻咽喉科医
e) 下痢	肝臓	小児科医
f) 目の痛み	鼻	内科医

g) 肝炎	耳	内科医
h) 鼻炎	肺	外科医
i) 子どものぜんそく	腸	耳鼻咽喉科医

14. Choose the most suitable answer for each sentence.

a) 私の友達は仏教に興味があるので京都でたくさんの＿＿＿＿＿＿＿＿
   に行きました。
   1. 劇場　2. 動物園　3. 神社　4. お寺

b) 事故が起こりましたよ！けが人がいます！＿＿＿＿＿＿＿＿＿＿＿＿
   を呼んでください！
   1. 郵便局　2. 目撃者　3. 救急車　4. 泥棒

c) 今日は＿＿＿＿＿＿＿へ行きましたよ！いろいろな魚を見てみました。
   1. 水族館　2. 美術館　3. 映画館　4. 博物館

d) 神社にはお守りや絵馬や＿＿＿＿＿＿＿＿＿＿＿＿＿＿があります。
   1. おみまい　2. おみくじ　3. おみあい　4. おみもの

e) 最近、デジカメがあるので、＿＿＿＿＿＿＿＿＿はもう要らないね。
   便利ですね！
   1. フィルム　2. フラッシュ　3. レンズ　4. 三脚

f) 日本という国は＿＿＿＿＿＿＿＿＿＿＿＿＿＿＿＿＿＿です。
   1. 半島　2. 海岸　3. 島　4. 湖

g) あなたは熱があるかもしれません。＿＿＿＿＿＿＿＿を測りましょう。
   1. 包帯　2. 体温　3. 呼吸　4. 血圧

h) 今、＿＿＿＿＿＿＿＿＿＿＿＿＿がない若者はあまりいないですね。
   1. 携帯電話　2. 公衆電話　3. 国際電話　4. 電話帳

15. Fill in the blanks with an adverb from the box overleaf.

a) 私は母より＿＿＿＿＿＿＿＿＿背が高いです。私は１７０センチで、
   母は１６９センチです。

b) ピーターは１０００円で、ジョンは１１００円を持っています。

ジョンはピーターより＿＿＿＿＿＿＿＿＿＿＿＿＿＿お金を持っています。

c) あの１９歳の奥さんは８４歳のご主人より＿＿＿＿＿＿＿＿若いです。

d) この青い車は１２０万円ですが、あの赤い車は２００万円です。

あの赤い車はこの青い車より＿＿＿＿＿＿＿＿＿＿＿＿＿＿高いですね。

やや	ずいぶん	ずっと	少し

16. This conversation is out of order. Rewrite it in the correct order.

1) いらっしゃいませ！郵便局へようこそ。

2) ずっととは言えませんが、かなり高くなりますよ。どうなさいますか？

3) んん...しょうがないな...あまりお金がないので、船便で送ります。

4) そうですね。航空便って船便よりずっと高いですか？

5) おはようございます。実は、この小包みを送りたいんです。

6) カナダへ送りたいんですけど、かなり急いでいます。

7) この小包みですか？どちらへお送りになりたいのですか？

8) それでは、航空便で送った方がいいですね。

郵便屋さん：＿＿＿＿＿＿＿＿＿＿＿＿＿＿＿＿＿＿＿＿

お客さん：＿＿＿＿＿＿＿＿＿＿＿＿＿＿＿＿＿＿＿＿

郵便屋さん：＿＿＿＿＿＿＿＿＿＿＿＿＿＿＿＿＿＿＿＿

お客さん：＿＿＿＿＿＿＿＿＿＿＿＿＿＿＿＿＿＿＿＿

郵便屋さん：＿＿＿＿＿＿＿＿＿＿＿＿＿＿＿＿＿＿＿＿

お客さん：＿＿＿＿＿＿＿＿＿＿＿＿＿＿＿＿＿＿＿＿

郵便屋さん：＿＿＿＿＿＿＿＿＿＿＿＿＿＿＿＿＿＿＿＿

お客さん：＿＿＿＿＿＿＿＿＿＿＿＿＿＿＿＿＿＿＿＿

17. Complete this dialogue held at a hospital with the most suitable words.

Doctor: こんにちは。どうなさいましたか？

Patient: こんにちは。ちょっと気分が⁽¹⁾_____ です。

Doctor: そうですか？どんな症状<ruby>症状<rt>しょうじょう</rt></ruby>ですか？

Patient: ⁽²⁾_____が痛<ruby>痛<rt>いた</rt></ruby>いです。しかし、病院<ruby>病院<rt>びょういん</rt></ruby>に来る前に⁽³⁾_____を
測<ruby>測<rt>はか</rt></ruby>ったけれど、熱はありませんでした。

Doctor: 胃潰瘍<ruby>胃潰瘍<rt>いかいよう</rt></ruby>か胃炎<ruby>胃炎<rt>いえん</rt></ruby>ですかねぇ？

Patient: 痛<ruby>痛<rt>いた</rt></ruby>みはそれほど激<ruby>激<rt>はげ</rt></ruby>しくないですけど。

Doctor: わかりました。まず⁽⁴⁾_____になってください。

Patient: このベッドでいいですか？

Doctor: はい。それでは、シャツを脱<ruby>脱<rt>ぬ</rt></ruby>いで、⁽⁵⁾_____をしてください。

Patient: え？それは深<ruby>深<rt>ふか</rt></ruby>く呼吸<ruby>呼吸<rt>こきゅう</rt></ruby>することですか？

Doctor: そうです。(he touches him on the stomach) ここが痛<ruby>痛<rt>いた</rt></ruby>いですか？

Patient: はい、すごく痛<ruby>痛<rt>いた</rt></ruby>いです、そこは！

Doctor: 血液<ruby>血液<rt>けつえき</rt></ruby>を調<ruby>調<rt>しら</rt></ruby>べなければならないので、血液<ruby>血液<rt>けつえき</rt></ruby>⁽⁶⁾_____が必要<ruby>必要<rt>ひつよう</rt></ruby>です。

Patient: はい。何か悪い病気<ruby>病気<rt>びょうき</rt></ruby>ですか？

Doctor: まだ分かりませんが、⁽⁷⁾_____ことはないと思いますよ。

Patient: あ、よかった。何か薬<ruby>薬<rt>くすり</rt></ruby>を飲まなきゃなりませんか？

Doctor: そうです。⁽⁸⁾_____はありますか？

Patient: はい、ペニシリンに ...

Doctor: じゃ、この薬<ruby>薬<rt>くすり</rt></ruby>を２週間の間⁽⁹⁾_____ください。お大事に！

Patient: はい！ありがとうございます！

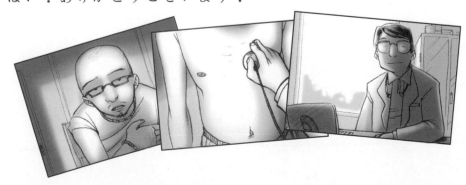

18. Identify what form of **keigo** each of the following sentences is: **sonkeigo** (S), **kenjōgo** (K) or **teineigo** (T). Then write each sentence in the -**masu** form, as in the example.

a) 先生はパソコンをお使いになっています。(S / K / T)

<u>先生はパソコンを使っています</u>　　　　　　　　。

b) あちらにいる方はとても有名な政治家でございますよ。(S / K / T)

＿＿＿＿＿＿＿＿＿＿＿＿＿＿＿＿＿＿＿＿＿＿＿＿。

c) 何かおっしゃいましたか、田中先生？(S / K / T)

＿＿＿＿＿＿＿＿＿＿＿＿＿＿＿＿＿＿＿＿＿＿＿＿。

d) 社長に大切な書類をお見せしたいのですが...(S / K / T)

＿＿＿＿＿＿＿＿＿＿＿＿＿＿＿＿＿＿＿＿＿＿＿＿。

e) あ、木村さん、こんにちは！どちらへ行かれますか？(S / K / T)

＿＿＿＿＿＿＿＿＿＿＿＿＿＿＿＿＿＿＿＿＿＿＿＿。

f) すみませんが、あなたのかばんの中を拝見してもよろしいですか？
   (S / K / T)

＿＿＿＿＿＿＿＿＿＿＿＿＿＿＿＿＿＿＿＿＿＿＿＿。

g) 先生はビールを飲まれないと私は存じております。(S / K / T)

＿＿＿＿＿＿＿＿＿＿＿＿＿＿＿＿＿＿＿＿＿＿＿＿。

h) 社長、青山さんとお会いしてもよろしいですか？(S / K / T)

＿＿＿＿＿＿＿＿＿＿＿＿＿＿＿＿＿＿＿＿＿＿＿＿。

19. Choose the sentence with the correct **keigo** and same meaning as the first sentence.

a) 私は先生の本を借りました。

　　1. 私は先生の本をお借りました　　2. 私は先生の本を借りられました

　　3. 私は先生の本を拝借しました　　4. 私は先生の本をお借りになりました

b) 社長は福岡に住んでいます。

　　1. 社長は福岡に住まれています　　2. 社長は福岡に住んでいたします

　　3. 社長は福岡にお住みしています　　4. 社長は福岡に住んでくださいます

c) 池田さんは死にました。あなたは知っていましたか？
　1. 池田さんは参りました。あなたはご存知でしたか？
　2. 池田さんは死なれました。あなたは存じていましたか？
　3. 池田さんはお死しました。あなたは存じていましたか？
　4. 池田さんはお亡くなりになりました。あなたはご存知でしたか？

20. Answer the following questions using comparative expressions.

a) エベストと富士山ではどちらが高い山ですか？
　<u>エベレストは富士山より高い山です</u>　　　　　。

b) 日本と中国ではどちらが人が多いですか？
　_____。

c) オレンジとりんごではどちらか大きいですか？
　_____。

d) 「人」という漢字と「龍」という漢字ではどちらやさしいですか？
　_____。

e) 一週間と七日間ではどちらが長いですか？
　_____。

21. Answer the following questions using comparative expressions.

a) エベストは富士山より高い山です。
　<u>富士山はエベレストほど高くない山です</u>　　　　　。

b) すいかはいちごより大きいです。
　_____。

c) タイのご飯は日本のご飯ほどおいしくないと日本人はいつも言っています。
　_____。

d) マリコちゃんはヒサコちゃんよりきれいな人です。
　_____。

22. Unscramble the following superlative sentences.

a) です | クラス | マリコちゃんは | の中で | きれいな | 女の子 | 最も

_____。

b) 一番 | 私の | 天ぷら | 料理は | です | 好きな

_____。

c) の中で | 人 | 一番 | 旦那は | エッチな | あたしの | だよ！ | 日本

_____。

d) 島 | 大きい | 最も | です | 世界で | オーストラリアは

_____。

23. Change these informal sentences into the polite Japanese -***masu*** form.

a) 何してんだよ、お前？早く行かなきゃ！

　あなたは何をしていますか？早く行かなければなりません　　。

b) 言っとくけど、あいつはめっちゃ頭いいのよ。

_____。

c) あのガキ、どっかへ行っちゃったぞ。

_____。

d) めっちゃたけえなぁ、フェラーリって車は ... オレには買えんぜ。

_____。

e) お前、オレのビール飲んじゃったの？飲んじゃいけないよ、それ！

_____。

f) 彼がお前にでかい車買ったげるって？マジの話なの、それ？

_____。

g) あっちでチャリに乗ってる奴のつら、おもしろいかもね！

_____。

h) あんた、もっとかいてくれよ、マンガ！すごいおもしろいんだ！

_____。

i) お金ねぇんだよ、オレ！これから働（はたら）かなきゃなんないよ。

_____。

24. Correct the mistakes in the following sentences.

a) A: あそこへ行きたくないの？| B: いいえ、行きたくないよ！

b) 電車は飛行機（ひこうき）ほど速いです。

c) 私はあの書類（しょるい）をご覧（らん）になりたいです。

d) あの人は猿（さる）のように男だね。

e) 先生はお話しいたしております。

f) 猫（ねこ）は象（ぞう）より大きい動物です。

25. Choose the most suitable answer for each sentence.

a) マユミさんはエミカさん_____やさしくないですね。

1. ほど   2. と同（おな）じぐらい   3. より   4. ずっと

b) 先生はここに_____か？

1. おります   2. いたします   3. いらっしゃいます   4. なさいます

c) 彼（かれ）はすごく金持ちなのに、お金を使いたくないみたいだね。_____
_____奴（やつ）だね！

1. すごい   2. せこい   3. やばい   4. ださい

d) A: 今夜（こんや）、ご飯を食べたいの？| B: _____、食べたくない。

1. はい   2. いいえ

e) 山本（やまもと）先生は新しい家を_____とおっしゃいました。

1. 買われる   2. 買える   3. 買えられる   4. 買わされる

f) センスがないね、彼女（かのじょ）。いつも_____服を着ているんだ。

1. すごい   2. せこい   3. やばい   4. ださい

g) 社長、私はあなたの娘_{むすめ}さんと＿＿＿＿＿＿＿＿＿＿＿＿＿＿＿です。

   1. お話したい　　2. お話になりたい　　3. 話されたい　　4. 申_{もう}し上げたい

h) A: 土曜日、映画を見に行かない？ | B: ＿＿＿＿＿＿＿＿、見に行かないよ。

   1. はい　　2. いいえ

i) 日本とロシア＿＿＿＿＿＿＿＿＿＿＿＿＿＿＿どちらが大きい国ですか？

   1. では　　2. は　　3. が　　4. のに

j) ロシアは日本＿＿＿＿＿＿＿＿＿＿＿＿＿＿＿＿＿＿＿大きい国です。

   1. ほど　　2. かなり　　3. と同じぐらい　　4. より

k) この本は ＿＿＿＿＿＿＿＿＿＿＿＿＿＿＿＿＿＿ので買えない。

   1. 高くすぎる　　2. 高くなすぎる　　3. 高すぎる　　4. 高いすぎる

l) 小泉_{こいずみ}社長は「明日_{あした}は休みだ」と＿＿＿＿＿＿＿＿＿＿＿＿＿＿。

   1. おっしゃいた　　2. おっしゃました　　3. おっしゃった　　4. おっしゃいますた

m) あの人は手塚治虫_{てづかおさむ}＿＿＿＿＿＿＿＿＿＿おもしろいマンガをかける。

   1. のように　　2. のようの　　3. ように　　4. ような

Kanji

病	院	京	都	旅	医	以	業	有	町	同
(139)	(182)	(233)	(234)	(235)	(258)	(189)	(189)	(190)	(181)	(191)
貸	借	員	研	究	注	意	世	界	止	急
(230)	(231)	(229)	(207)	(208)	(217)	(218)	(211)	(212)	(202)	(216)

26. Link each kanji with its ***kun'yomi*** reading.

都	と（ぐ）	世	か（りる）
急	みやこ	病	おな（じ）
業	たび	同	よ
旅	そそ（ぐ）	町	やまい
注	いそ（ぐ）	止	と（まる）
研	わざ	借	まち

27. Choose the correct kanji or kanji combination for each reading.

a) 「とうきょうの人いがい、ここに誰(だれ)も入ってはいけないよ」とちゅうい
   しました。

   とうきょう：1. 東京　2. 京者　3. 京都　4. 陳京

   いがい：1. 以外　2. 意内　3. 意外　4. 以内

   ちゅうい：1. 注以　2. 注意　3. 住以　4. 住意

b) あの若いいしゃはこのびょういんで働(はたら)いている。

   いしゃ：1. 意者　2. 以者　3. 医者　4. 病者

   びょういん：1. 病院　2. 病気　3. 病医　4. 病人

c) 昨日(きのう)、ビデオ屋さんへ行って、かいいんになって、ビデオをかりた。

   かいいん：1. 会院　2. 界院　3. 界員　4. 会員

   かりた：1. 究りた　2. 貸りた　3. 質りた　4. 借りた

d) 寺田(てらだ)先生は海野(うみの)先生とおなじ けんきゅうをなさっている。

   おなじ：1. 同じ　2. 伺じ　3. 同なじ　4. 伺なじ

   けんきゅう：1. 究明　2. 研究　3. 究研　4. 明究

e) 来週の北海道へのたびはちゅうしになりました。

   たび：1. 族　2. 旅　3. 旗　4. 施

   ちゅうし：1. 中上　2. 中止　3. 仲上　4. 仲止

28. Choose the correct reading for each kanji combination.

a) あの病人の借金は意外と少ないですね。

　病人：1. びょうじん　2. びょうしん　3. びょうひと　4. びょうにん

　借金：1. しゃっきん　2. しゃくきん　3. かりかね　4. かりがね

　意外：1. いぞと　2. いそと　3. いがい　4. いかい

b) 町長はとても高い料理を注文した。

　町長：1. ちょちょう　2. ちょうちょ　3. ちょうちょう　4. ちょちょ

　注文：1. ちゅうもん　2. ちゅうぶん　3. ちゅもん　4. ちゅぶん

c) ベネディクト１６世は京都に行きたいらしいです。

　１６世：1. じゅうろくせ　2. じゅうろくよ　3. じゅうろくせい　4. じゅうろくだい

　京都：1. きょと　2. きょうと　3. きょとう　4. きょうとう

d) 黒川（くろかわ）先生は研究所で難（むずか）しい作業をなさっていました。

　研究所：1. けんきゅじょ　2. けんきゅうじょう　3. けんきゅじょう　4. けんきゅうじょ

　作業：1. さぎょう　2. さくぎょう　3. つくりわざ　4. さくごう

29. Write the kanji for the given *furigana*.

a) あの＿＿＿＿＿＿（りょかん）の前で＿＿＿＿＿（と）まってくださいね。

b) 空手の＿＿＿＿＿＿（せかい）チャンピオンは＿＿＿＿＿＿（とうきょう）へ＿＿＿＿＿＿（りょこう）しました。

c) この＿＿＿＿＿＿（じいん）の水は＿＿＿＿＿＿（ゆうりょう）です。

d) この＿＿＿＿＿（まち）にはたくさんの＿＿＿＿＿＿（いがく）を勉強している学生が住（す）んでいる。

e) 車をすぐ＿＿＿＿＿（か）してください！＿＿＿＿＿（いそ）いでいますから！

f) この作文の＿＿＿＿＿＿（いみ）を教えてくださいませんか？

Lesson 56 • 第56課

The Conditional Form

In this chapter we will study in depth the four different constructions that are used to express the conditional form in Japanese.

🎧 The conditional form with と

The expression と is used to indicate a natural relationship based on habit or logic (if / when X happens, then Y usually happens). It is often used in sentences expressing events derived from natural phenomena, habits, etc. After a と clause, we never express will, or a wish, order or request. This kind of sentence usually has the nuance of "whenever," rather than "if."

Usage: と is placed directly after verbs and *-i* adjectives. *-na* adjectives and nouns require だ .

- １５日になると、給料が振り込まれる When the 15th comes, my wage is transferred (to my account).
- 毎日仕事が終わると、ビールを飲む Every day, when I finish work, I have a beer.

A different usage of と expresses "discovery":

- あの橋を渡ると、学校があります When you cross that bridge, there is a school.

🎧 The conditional form with ば

The expression 〜ば is used for sentences with the pattern "if X, then Y." It is similar to と in some ways, but has a stronger nuance of hypothesis or supposition. As with と, after a clause with 〜ば we never express will, or a wish, order or request.

Verbs have a special conjugation with 〜ば, so study the table opposite. For *-i* adjectives replace the last 〜い with 〜ければ: 甘い *amai* (sweet) ⇒ 甘ければ (if it is sweet). The negative is formed the same way: 甘くない (it is not sweet) ⇒ 甘くなければ (if it is not sweet). After *-na* adjectives and nouns, we use ならば: きれいならば (if she were pretty), 学生ならば *gakusei naraba* (if he were a student). In the negative, we need the verb です (ではない/じゃない), replacing the last 〜い with 〜ければ: きれいでなければ (if she weren't pretty), 学生じゃなければ (if he weren't a student).

- ワインを飲めば、気持ちよくなります If you drink some wine, you'll feel better.
- その本は安くなければ、買わないよ If that book isn't cheap, I won't buy it.
- 彼がもし親切ならば、助けに来ると思う If he were kind, he'd come to help me.

🎧 The conditional form with たら

The expression 〜たら is versatile and can be used in most conditional cases. If you always use 〜たら to form your conditional sentences, there is less possibility that you might make a mistake!

Unlike と and 〜ば, after 〜たら you can express will, a wish, an order or request.

Usage: Add ら after the past form of verbs (買ったら *kattara*, if I bought), -*i* adjectives (甘かったら if it were sweet). With -*na* adjectives and nouns, use だったら (きれいだったら, if she were pretty), (学生だったら, if he were a student).

• もし、ハワイに行ったら, お土産を買って来てね If you go to Hawaii, buy me a souvenir, OK?
• 行きたくなかったら、家に残ってもいい If you don't want to go, you can stay home.
• 彼が父親じゃなかったら、殴ったのに！ If he wasn't my father, I'd have hit him!

Note: In the first sentence we use the word もし, an adverb similar in meaning to "if." もし isn't strictly necessary, but is used to emphasize the condition.

🎧	Simple f.	Meaning	Rule	Conditional	Rule	Negative	Negative cond.
Group 1 Invariable	教える	to teach	ーるれば	教えれば		教えない	教えなければ
	起きる	to wake up		起きれば		起きない	起きなければ
Group 2 Variable	貸す	to lend	ーすせば	貸せば		貸さない	貸さなければ
	待つ	to wait	ーつてば	待てば		待たない	待たなければ
	買う	to buy	ーうえば	買えば		買わない	買わなければ
	帰る	to return	ーるれば	帰れば	**Negative form** すけさば	帰らない	帰らなければ
	書く	to write	ーくけば	書けば		書かない	書かなければ
	急ぐ	to hurry	ーぐげば	急げば		急がない	急がなければ
	遊ぶ	to play	ーぶべば	遊べば		遊ばない	遊ばなければ
	飲む	to drink	ーむめば	飲めば		飲まない	飲まなければ
	死ぬ	to die	ーぬねば	死ねば		死なない	死ななければ
Group 3 Irregular	する	to do	Irregular verbs: no rule	すれば		しない	しなければ
	来る	to come		来れば		来ない	来なければ

🎧 The conditional form with なら

The expression なら is used in conversation to reiterate what the other person has said, and then add data. なら can be used in to express will, or a wish, order or request. Its colloquial version is のだったら or んだったら. We will sometimes find の before なら; it adds the nuance of "in the case of." We place nothing between verbs, adjectives (*-i* and *-na*), nouns and なら. In the past form, nouns and *-na* adjectives need だった.

- A: 韓国に旅行したい | B: 韓国へ行く（の）ならビビンバを食べなきゃね
  A: I'd like to travel to Korea | B: If you are going to Korea, then you must eat bibimbap.
- 外に出るんだったら、ごみを捨ててきてね If you are going outside, then take out the garbage, OK?

	🎧 Conditional forms	
と	雨が降ると、カエルが鳴く If (when) it rains, frogs croak.	Since what is said in the first clause always comes true naturally then what is said in the second clause will come true, as well.
〜ば	雨が降れば、水不足が解決する If it rained, the drought would be solved.	If the condition in the first clause (to rain) comes true, the following action comes true too.
〜たら	雨が降ったら、試合は中止になる If it rains, the match will be canceled.	Provisionally, the match will be held, but if in the future the condition in the first clause (to rain) comes true, then, in that hypothetical future, the match would be canceled.
なら	雨が降るなら、家にいよう If (what happens is that) it rains, I'll stay home.	The speaker indicates a condition that he himself imposes: the second clause can be an intention.
雨が降る *ame ga furu* to rain; カエル frog; 鳴く *naku* to croak, chirp, mew; 水不足 *mizu buzoku* drought; 解決する *kaiketsu suru* to solve; 試合 *shiai* match; 中止する *chūshi suru* to cancel; 家 *ie* house; いる to be		

🎧 Hypothetical conditions: if / in case

For hypothetical conditions, we can use と, 〜ば, 〜たら or なら.

- 試験に合格すれば、卒業できます If I passed the exam, I'd be able to graduate.
- この本が好きだったら、あげるよ If you like this book, I'll give it to you.

In this kind of "pure" conditional sentence we can use 〜たら most times without making a mistake. **Note:** 〜ば is usually perceived as more formal than 〜たら.

🎧 Whenever

When the second action always and unavoidably follows the first one, as in the case of a naturally occurring event or the force of habit ("whenever" / "on . . . –ing"), <u>we use</u> と.

- 夏になると、蛍が出てきます Whenever summer comes, fireflies appear.
- 国の経済が成長すると、豊かになる Whenever the economy of a country develops, it becomes rich.

🎧 When / As soon as

When an action immediately follows the first one, but not necessarily in a natural or pre-determined way, we can use と or 〜たら.

- 彼女に会うと、いつも緊張する Whenever I come across her, I get nervous.
- 先生が呼んだら、すぐ行ってください When the teacher calls you, go at once.

🎧 Idiomatic usage

〜ば and 〜たら can be used idiomatically, without a conditional meaning.

- よかったら、今度家に来てください If you like, please come to my house sometime.
- 考えてみれば、私たちは長い付き合いだね Come to think of it, ours is a long relationship, isn't it?

Notice how in this case only, 〜ば can go before sentences expressing will, or a wish, order or request. **Note:** The conjugation of the adjective いい (good) is irregular: it becomes よかったら (〜たら form), and よければ (〜ば form).

🎧 When / As a result of / After

When something is learned or discovered as a result of a certain action, use と or 〜たら.

- 納豆を買いに行くと、もうなかった When I went to buy natto, there was no more left.
- 泳ぎに行ったら、プールには水がなかった When I went swimming, there was no water in the pool.

🎧 Regarding / As for

To introduce a specific topic in the conversation, use なら.

- 赤松さんなら、家に帰りましたよ As for Mr. Akamatsu, he's already gone home.
- 旅行なら、インドがいいな Talking about trips, I'd like (to go to) India.

🎧 You need to / You should

Use 〜ばいい. This expression is used to clarify doubts and things we are not sure about.

- この書類に記入すればいいんですね I only need to fill in this document, right?
- こんなこと、誰にきけばいいの？ Who should I ask about this?

🎧 Making suggestions

Use 〜たらどうですか？

- 疲れているなら、休んだらどうですか？ If you're tired, why don't you rest?
- 彼女を誘ってみたらどう？ Why don't you try inviting her?

🎧 Making soft proposals

Use 〜ば or 〜たら at the end of the sentence. Used in spoken language only.

- 寝ないでよ！ちょっと勉強すれば？ Don't sleep! How about a little more study?
- 疲れている？休んだら？ Are you tired? Why don't you take a rest?

🎧 Showing annoyance

Use ったら and ってば (といえば). Used in spoken language, mainly by women to children. **Note:** ったら is not conjugated: it goes directly at the end of a sentence.

- ぐずぐずしないでよ！勉強しなさいったら！ Quit idling! Get on with your study!
- 君！こっちに来てってば You! Come here, come on!

🎧 Explaining and requesting (idiomatic)

言えば : "This way" (explanation) / できれば : "If possible" (request).

- 簡単に言えば、彼はバカだ In short / in a few words, he is stupid.
- そう言えば、美紀が来ていないね Now you mention it, Miki hasn't come, has she?
- できれば、あなたと結婚したいんです If possible, I'd like to marry you.

🎧 A final usage for それなら and すると

- 疲れている？それなら、休んでよ Are you tired? If so, take a rest.
- 彼に会った。すると、彼は太っていた I came across him. That's when (I saw) he had put on weight.

🎧 漫画例 Manga Examples

The manga examples in this section will help you review and consolidate the conditional forms you've studied in this lesson.

Manga Example 1: The conditional *to*

As in this example, we often find と combined with a verb in the negative, with the negative conditional meaning of "if I don't do X, then Y." Other examples might be 食べないと大きくならないよ *tabenai to ookikunaranai yo* (If you don't eat, you won't grow); 行かないと死ぬ, *ikanai to shinu* (If I don't go, I'll die). We also often find と combined with だめだ or いけない, as in the sentences 食べないとだめだ or 行かないといけない. This construction has the same meaning as 〜なければならない and similar expressions studied in Lesson 32, that is "I must . . ." "I have to . . ." These sentences, then, would be "I must eat" and "I have to go," respectively. **Note:** 勝てそうにない (it doesn't look like we can win) is a kind of negation of the conjecture そうだ (2) (Lesson 43), linked to 勝てる, the potential form (Lesson 31) of the verb 勝つ (to win.)

Gabriel Luque

Jun: これはウチとやる時にはボクがフルタイム出場しないと勝てそうにないな

this TOP *"uchi"* CP *do time* TP TOP *full time participate not do (conditional) win not* EP

Seeing this, when we play against them, if I don't play full time, 1 don't think we will be able to win.

Manga Example 2: The conditional -*ba*

Here is an example of the 〜ば construction: うまくいけば literally means "if it goes well." 行けば *ikeba* is the conditional conjugation of the verb 行く (to go) (see table, page 283). For this conjugation, the last -*u* in the simple form of all verbs in all groups (including the irregular verbs) is replaced with an -*e* and then we add ば. Thus, *iku* ⇒ *ike* ⇒ *ikeba*. The only exception, as usual, are verbs ending in -*tsu*, which don't become -*tseba*, but change to -*teba*. **Notes:** もの means "thing" (we will study this in depth in the next lesson). Notice the usage of the conjecture はずだ (Lesson 43), which indicates a supposition that is almost a fact.

> **Lee:** そんなものがうまくいけばビルに飛行機は突っ込まないはずだ
>
> *that thing* SP *well go (conditional) building* PP *plane* TOP *crash look like*
>
> If that worked out, nobody would think of crashing planes into buildings.

Manga Example 3: The conditional *nara*

Here, the expression なら is used to reiterate a topic of conversation which has already been raised, and then add more information (see **Regarding/As for**, page 285). The sentence in the example is probably the answer to something like（彼女を）助けたほうがいいよ *Kanojo o tasuketa hō ga ii yo* (She had better be saved). The speaker reiterates this piece of information, transforms it into a conditional clause with the expression なら and then adds his own reply or opinion at the end. A more colloquial version of this sentence would be 助けたほうがいいんだったら助けよう. **Notes:** Review here the usage of the strong recommendation 〜ほうがいい (Lesson 49), and the "let's" form (Lesson 34) 助けよう (I'm going to save her), indicating purpose or intention.

> **Yūma:** 助けたほうがいいんなら助けよう！
>
> *save be recommended (conditional) save!!*
>
> If she had better be saved, then I'll save her!

Manga Example 4: An idiomatic usage of *yokattara*

We go back to 〜たら, used here combined with the adjective いい (good) to indicate "If you like," which is useful when you want to invite somebody or offer something. The past

conjugation of いい is irregular (よかった), so its 〜たら conjugation is よかったら.

Notice the adverb もし, translated as our conditional "if." In Japanese we don't need to place もし in every conditional clause; it is more often used when we want to emphasize a condition, or to introduce a conditional sentence. **Note:** The 〜てちょうだい construction means the same as 〜てください (Lesson 35).

Man: もしよかったら、今度ママとパパと三人でお芝居を観に来てちょうだいよ

if well, next time mom CP and dad CP the three theater DOP come to see please EP

If you like, come to the theater next time with mom and dad, please.

Manga Example 5: Another conjunction

There are several kinds of conjunctions—words that connect the clauses of a sentence—that are based on conditional expressions. Besides those we saw earlier in this chapter (それなら and すると), we also have そうしたら, そうすれば, だとしたら, and, as in this example, だとすれば.

Technically, だとすれば is not a conjunction, but the sum of だ (to be), the particle と (Lesson 41) plus すれば (the ば conditional of the verb する). Literally, it means "if (that) is done," i.e., "If that is the way it is," "in that case," "then . . ." **Note:** This manga has a clear example of a relative clause: 左足が動かない原因 (cause for the left leg not to move). (Lesson 50.)

Shōji: だとすれば左足が動かない原因は一つ

be CP do (conditional) leg left SP move cause TOP one

Then, there is one cause for the left leg not to move.

Manga Example 6: A "smart aleck" usage of the conditional *-ba*

Let's look at an amusing usage of the conditional 〜ば to give a "smart aleck" answer of the kind "I'm hungry" | "Then eat," or "I'm tired" | "Then sleep." It is simple to obtain the "smart aleck" effect of "then X" using the conditional 〜ば and an interrogative intonation, as in the following examples:

お腹がすいている **Onaka ga suite iru** I'm hungry
食べれば？ **Tabereba?** Then eat

眠いなぁ **Nemui naa** I'm tired
寝れば？ **Nereba?** Then sleep

Notes: 面倒を見る **Mendō o miru** (lit. "To look at a problem") means "to take care of." 父ちゃん and 母ちゃん are childish distortions of お父さん and お母さん.

Hina:	ふええ〜ん	Ken:	ふん　父ちゃんと母ちゃんにめんどう見てもらえば？
	hueeennn		*hum dad* CP *mom* IOP *problem look (receive)*
	Waaah!		Humph! Then, let mom and dad take care of you.

Exercises 練習

① Conjugate the conditional of the words 飛ぶ (to fly) and 元気な (healthy) in each of the four forms.

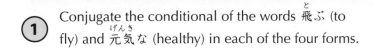

② Conjugate the verbs 歩く (to walk), 寝る (to sleep), 頑張る (to hang on), 来る (to come), and 泳ぐ (to swim) ～ば form of the conditional.

③ Conjugate the negative of the verb 運転する (to drive), the *-i* adjective 長い (long), and the noun 本 (book) in the conditional ～ば .

④ Translate: ドアを開けると、犬が入ってしまう。 (ドア door; 開ける to open; 犬 dog; 入る to go in)

⑤ Translate: 背が高くなければ、彼氏にはしない。 (背が高い tall; 彼氏 boyfriend)

⑥ Translate: もし 授業 が嫌だったら、廊下に出てください。 (授業 class; 嫌 dislike; 廊下 corridor; 出る to go out)

⑦ Translate: 学校へ行くなら、先生によろしく伝えてね。 (学校 school; 行く to go; 先生 teacher; よろしく伝える to give one's regards)

⑧ Translate: すみません、誰に 注文 すればいいんですか? (すみません excuse me; 誰 who; 注文 order)

⑨ Translate: もし、私が君ならこんなことをしないってば! (私 I; 君 you; こと thing)

⑩ Translate: ギリシャへ行きたいなぁ。今年の夏に行けば? (ギリシャ Greece; 行く to go; 今年 this year; 夏 summer)

— **Answers to all the exercises can be found online by following the link on page 7.** —

Lesson 57 • 第57課

Koto and Mono

In this lesson we will learn to distinguish between こと and もの, two different Japanese concepts which are both translated as "thing."

🎧 こと and もの

First let's clarify the difference between こと and もの. Although both mean "thing," their usage is different.

こと (sometimes written in kanji: 事) designates a non-physical thing, something intangible, like thoughts, concepts or words.

- 大事なことを君に言いたいんです I would like to tell you an important thing.
- とても悲しいことが起こりました A very sad thing happened.

こと is also used in noun + のこと constructions, which emphasize the noun.

- 君のことが大好きだよ I like you very much.
- 大学のことを忘れてくれよ Forget about university, come on.

As for もの (which can also be written in kanji: 物), it designates a physical "thing":

- そっちにある物を持ってきてくれない？ Can you bring me that thing over there?
- 今日、どんな物を買いたいの？ What kind of thing do you want to buy today?

Note: Don't mistake 物 (tangible thing) for 者, which has the same pronunciation but is a humble word for "person" or "member of," to refer to oneself or someone in the *uchi* group:

- はじめまして。星野という者です Pleased to meet you. I'm (somebody called) Hoshino.

🎧 こと as a nominalizer

In Lesson 40 we talked about "nominalizing": the process of transforming a verb, adjective, or a sentence into a noun phrase, so that it works exactly like any other noun. Japanese has two nominalizers: の and こと. Go back to Lesson 40 to review the nominalizer の. **Note:** Noun phrases (underlined in the examples) with の and こと are subordinate clauses, so their subject will never be marked with the topic particle は: always use が (Lesson 37).

- <u>彼が (no は) スキーをする</u>ことは皆が知っている Everybody knows <u>he skis</u>.

🎧 の as a nominalizer

Nothing is placed after the verb and *-i* adjective. After a *-na* adjective or noun, we place either な or である in the present tense, or だった in the past tense. Let's see a few examples now to refresh your memory:

- 映画を見るのは大好きです I like <u>watching movies</u> very much.
- 佐藤さんがゲイだったのはよく知っている I know very well <u>Mr. Sato was gay.</u>

こと is used just like の, in the same position and has the same usage with verbs, adjectives and nouns, with one exception: after *-na* adjectives and nouns in the present tense, we can only have である, **never** な.

- 映画を見ることは頭にいいです <u>Watching movies</u> is good for your brain.
- 佐藤さんがゲイであることはよく知っている I know very well <u>Mr. Sato is gay</u>.

🎧 Differences between the nominalizers の and こと

の and こと are often used to nominalize a sentence. We use の when the noun phrase expresses something subjective or something the speaker feels "close" to. We use こと when talking about something objective, or general, which doesn't imply any kind of emotion.

- 寝る前に本を読むこと / のは楽しいです <u>Reading books before sleeping</u> is fun.

With こと, we are simply stating that reading books before going to sleep is fun. Whereas, with の, we add emotion, implying it is fun for us and it affects us specially.

When to use の: Use の when the verb in the main sentence is either a verb of perception such as 見る *miru* (to see), 見える (to be able to see), 聞く *kiku* (to hear), 聞こえる (to able to hear), 感じる *kanjiru* (to feel), etc., or one of the following verbs: 待つ *matsu* (to wait), 手伝う *tetsudau* (to help), 邪魔する *jama suru* (to bother), やめる (to stop doing, to cease) or 止める *tomeru* (to stop).

- その時、あの人が死ぬのを見た At that time, I saw <u>that person's death</u>.
- 大学の宿題が終わるのを待ってね Wait till <u>I finish my university homework</u>, OK?
- あの子どもをいじめるのはやめてください Please stop <u>picking on that boy</u>.

When to use こと: Use こと when the main verb indicates verbal communication, for example, 話す *hanasu* (to speak), 命じる *meijiru* (to command), 伝える *tsutaeru* (to report), きく *kiku* (to ask), 約束する *yakusoku suru* (to promise), etc., or when the last verb after the nominalizer is です or だ. Don't mix it up with のです (Lesson 40).

- 息子が病気だったことを彼に伝えてください Tell him <u>my son was sick</u>.
- 私の一番好きな運動は走ることです <u>Running</u> is the exercise I like most.

🎧 Expressions with こと

こと and もの are used as components in some grammatical constructions in the Japanese language without their meaning as a tangible or intangible thing. Let's see some expressions with こと, of which we already know one: the potential ことができる (Lesson 32).

- 私はバイクを運転することができる I can drive motorcycles.

The first of the new expressions with こと that we will study is 〜たことがある, used frequently to indicate "I have the experience of having done X thing." **Usage:** Verbs and adjectives are always conjugated in the past. Nouns require だった.

〜たことがある can be conjugated in the negative (〜たことがない, not have the experience of), past (〜たことがあった, had the experience of), and past negative (〜たことがなかった, didn't have the experience of).

- 彼はエベレストに登ったことがある He has climbed Mount Everest.
- 僕はアメリカに行ったことがない I have never been to the United States.
- 私は十年前先生だったことがある 10 years ago, I was a teacher.
- 彼のギャグは面白かったことがなかった His gags were never funny.

An expression that is very easy to mistake for 〜たことがある is ことがある, which has the meaning of "now and then." Verbs, adjectives, etc., preceding こと are in the present infinitive. *-na* adjectives require な and nouns require の or である.

- 弟は働くことがある Sometimes, my younger brother works (he usually doesn't).
- スイカはバカ高いことがある Sometimes, watermelons are ridiculously expensive.

Note: When negative, は is used instead of が with this expression:

- 彼女が黙ることはない There are no occasions when she keeps quiet. | She never keeps quiet.

🎧 Decisions

The expression ことにする indicates "a decision taken by oneself or someone in the ***uchi*** group." It comes after verbs in the present infinitive (affirmative or negative).

- 日本語を学ぶことにします (I've decided that) I'm going to learn Japanese.
- 先生と話さないことにしたそうだ It looks like he's decided not to speak with the teacher.
- 来年、大阪へ行くことにしました I have decided that next year I'll go to Osaka.

The second expression is ことになる, which indicates "a decision which affects oneself or someone in the ***uchi*** group, but which has been made by someone or something external." It is often used for demands or commands. **Usage:** The same as ことにする.

- 私は英語を勉強することになっている I must (I've been told to) study English.
- パーティーはバーでしないことになった It has been decided that the party won't be held at the bar.
- 仕事をやめることになりそうだ Apparently, I'll have to (they're demanding that I) quit my job.
- 来年、大阪へ行くことになりました It's been decided that next year I'll go to Osaka.

The final sentence is very clear: with ことにする it is obvious that the decision to go to Osaka has been taken by the speaker himself, whereas with ことになる the speaker implies that the decision has been made by someone else.

🎧 Expressions with もの

The first もの we will see is used to give a kind of excuse. The effect is almost the same as "the thing is . . ." or "because . . ." in English and it is mainly used by children and women in colloquial Japanese. <u>Usage:</u> もの is always placed at the end of a sentence. Verbs and *-i* adjectives go in the infinitive, while *-na* adjectives and nouns need だ. The construction んだもの is very common. **Note:** もの can be contracted into もん.

- 今行けないの。とても忙しいもの I can't go now. The thing is I'm very busy.
- 幼稚園、行きたくないもん！ It's just that I don't want to go to kindergarten!
- どうして食べないの？ Why won't you eat it? | だって、まずいんだもん Because it's bad.

The second expression is ものですか, which we often see as ものか or even もんか. This construction, always at the end of a sentence, is quite rough and indicates a very strong refusal to do something. Although it ends with か, it is not a question. **Usage:** Verbs and **-*i*** adjectives go in the infinitive. **-*na*** adjectives and nouns need な and である, respectively.

• あの男と付き合うものですか！There's no way I'm going out with that man!
• お前に１００万円を払うものか I'm not paying you a million yen (not on your life).
• あんたとは旅行に行くもんかよ！I'm not going on a trip with you (under any circumstances)!

		🎧 **Expressions with *koto* and *mono***	
こと	こと（事）	Intangible thing (concept)	どんなことを言いたいの？ What kind of thing do you want to tell me?
	こと	Nominalizer: used to transform full clauses into nouns	運動をすることは体にいいです (The fact of) doing exercise is good for your health.
	〜たことがある	To have the experience of	ハワイに行ったことがあります I have been (I have the experience of going) to Hawaii.
	ことがある	Sometimes . . . Now and then X happens	彼は運動をすることがある He sometimes exercises (though he usually doesn't).
	ことにする	To decide something by oneself	ハワイに行くことにしました I decided to go to Hawaii.
	ことになる	Something external to the speaker makes a decision that affects the speaker	ハワイに行くことになりました It's been decided that I'll go to Hawaii.
もの	もの（物）	Tangible thing (object)	その物を持ってきてくれる？ Can you bring me that thing?
	もの（もん）	At the end of a sentence, childish or female expression implying "excuse"	今行けないの。忙しいんだもん！ I can't go now. The thing is I'm busy!
	ものか（もんか）	At the end of a sentence, it emphasizes a categorical refusal	ハワイに行くものか！ There's no way I'm going to Hawaii!

言う ***iu*** to say; 運動 ***undō*** exercise; 体 ***karada*** body; いい good; ハワイ Hawaii; 行く ***iku*** to go; 彼 ***kare*** he; 持ってくる ***motte kuru*** to bring; 今 ***ima*** now; 忙しい ***isogashii*** busy

 漫画例 Manga Examples

Let's go on now to illustrate with a few manga panels some of the language points we have covered in this lesson. The subject we are focusing on is the usage of こと and もの: both when they are used with their original meaning of "thing," and when they are part of set constructions.

Manga Example 1: *Mono* for tangible things and excuses

We start with a very peculiar example that is a great way to see two very different usages of the word もの. Look at the あなたのもの¹だもの² part (we have underlined and numbered both もの so that you can see them more clearly).

The first もの (物 in kanji) is a word designating our concept of "thing," but it refers to something palpable, physical. 私はあなたのものだ, then, means "I'm a thing of yours" (I'm yours): notice how the girl speaks about herself as if she were an object. Here, she does so because she is speaking in terms of her physical body.

We have just seen the second もの at the top of the facing page: it is always placed at the end of a sentence and it indicates a sort of excuse or is used to draw attention. This expression is almost always used by children and women, although now young men are also using it more and more. Often, we will see もの together with the emphatic のだ we studied in Lesson 40: のだもの (like in the example). The の can be contracted into ん (んだもん). Likewise, this expression often comes with だって at the beginning of the sentence. だって is an expression that could be translated as "the fact is." **Note:** The last でしょ is a shortened and colloquial version of でしょう/だろう, the tag meaning "am I not?," "isn't it?," etc., which we studied in Lesson 43.

だって私は
あなたのもの
だもの

〜でしょ？

Studio Kōsen

Ryanki: だって 私はあなたのものだもの　〜でしょ？

the fact is I TOP *you* POP *thing (emphasis) (excuse) be?*

The fact is I'm yours (your thing) . . . am I not?

Manga Example 2: The emphatic usage of *koto*.

This time we will study a special usage of こと, which means "intangible thing." The construction "noun + のこと" we find in this panel and which we studied on the first page of this chapter, is mainly used with personal pronouns: 私のこと **watashi no koto** (I), 君のこと **kimi no koto** (you), etc. It has no specific meaning, it just emphasizes the personal pronoun. In the example, 僕のこと(を)愛している (she loves me), could perfectly well be 僕を愛している, but the first sentence has a stronger meaning. **Note:** って is the contraction of という ("says that," Lesson 41), and そりゃ of それは ("that," Lesson 53).

Kazuki: 母ちゃんは僕のこと愛してるって

Mommy TOP I POP (thing) love do says

Mommy says she loves me.

Man: そりゃよかったね

that thing good EP

Isn't that great?

Manga Example 3: *Koto* for intangible things and nominalizers

This panel offers us two very different こと: the first one, in かわった<u>こと</u>, indicates an "intangible thing," like a thought, a concept, words, etc. かわったこと literally means "thing that has changed," talking about something abstract rather than something physical, which requires こと instead of もの. The second こと is a nominalizer: it transforms the previous clause into a noun phrase. In this case, the girl's sentence would finish with です if it hadn't been cut off: 大学生になったことです (the fact of becoming a university student). **Note:** Look at the いえば, which we saw at the end of Lesson 56 as an idiomatic usage of the conditional 〜ば. In the example, いえば is used to introduce an explanatory sentence.

Mariko: かわったことといえば、俊さんが大学生になったことくらい…

change thing say (conditional), Shun SP university student become NOM approx

Talking about changes, the only thing that has changed is that Shun has become a university student.

Manga Example 4: To have the experience of . . .

In the next three examples, we will slightly change subjects, and we will go on to comment on some grammatical expressions that use こと. Remember that sometimes, like in this panel, こと is written in kanji: 事.

Gabriel Luque

This manga example contains the expression 〜たことがある, which means "having the experience of having done something." We must bear in mind that this expression is only used with relatively uncommon actions (things we don't do every day): for example, we can't say 呼吸をしたことがある **kokyū o shita koto ga aru** (I have the experience of having breathed). The ある in 〜たことがある can be conjugated: in this example we find it in the interrogative -**masu** form.

Abeno:	あなたは人を傷つけた事がありますか？

you TOP *person* DOP *wound put (have the experience of)* Q?

Have you ever hurt anybody?

Manga Example 5: To decide something by oneself

This is a good example of ことにする, which means "to decide that" and is used when one makes a decision for oneself. In the example, it is the speaker himself who decides, on his own initiative, to make up with Professor Ozu; in theory, no one is forcing him to do it, he is doing it because he wants to. Notice how the sentence is dislocated (the correct order would

J.M. Ken Niimura

be 小津先生と和解することにしたんです: this is a typical characteristic of the spoken language (Lesson 53). **Note:** Notice how the speaker says 小津先生. The correct reading of these characters would obviously be おづせんせい (Professor Ozu). The provided reading, カレ, is for the kanji 彼 (he). This kind of strategy is used sometimes in written Japanese to indicate to the reader that the speaker says 彼 but he is really referring to 小津先生.

Ishibashi:	和解することにしたんです 小津先生と

reconcile with (decide) be that man CP

I've decided to make up with him (Professor Ozu).

Manga Example 6: An outsider makes a decision

Here we have こ と に な る, which indicates "it has been decided that" (the decision has been taken by someone else). This implies that somebody (or circumstances) determine something that affects the speaker (often in a negative way), for instance, in the sentence 僕はレポートを書くことになった **Boku wa repōto o kaku koto ni natta** (It has been decided that I will write a report). This denotes the idea that we are not too happy about it, but that there is a certain obligation to do it. Our example here is somewhat special. Although it can be interpreted as "The circumstances have prompted the decision that we

marry," the construction こ と に な る is also occasionally used in a "humble" way to refer to one's own decision and to downplay its importance.

Studio Kōsen

Hanako:	私この人と結婚することになりました
	I this person CP marry (it has been decided)
	I'm going to marry this man.

Manga Example 7: Categorical refusal

We will finish with a slightly complicated example. The expression も の か, as we studied earlier in the lesson, implies a categorical refusal to do something. It can be contracted into も ん か, and even into a simple か, as in the example. Confusing it with the interrogative particle か (Lesson 17) is very easy, and there is no way to distinguish them, except by

deducing it from the context. Don't worry, this か with the meaning of categorical refusal of も の か is not used too profusely. **Notes:** 赤児 is an archaic word for 赤ちゃん *akachan* or 赤ん坊 *akanbō* (baby). 斬る like 切る *kiru*, means "to cut," but the kanji 斬 implies "cutting with a sword" and, by extension, in the language of the 侍 (samurai), "to kill."

Gabriel Luque

Shigekatsu:	ふん 腹に赤児をもつ女なんか斬れるか
	humph belly PP baby DOP have woman (emphasis) cut (negative)
	Humph! I could never kill a woman with a baby in her belly.

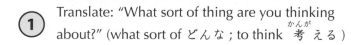

Exercises 練習

(1) Translate: "What sort of thing are you thinking about?" (what sort of どんな ; to think 考える)

(2) Translate: "Put this thing on the table, please." (to put 置く ; on 上 ; table テーブル)

(3) What two "nominalizers" are there in Japanese?

(4) Nominalize the clause 彼は行く, and use it to replace the ○ in: 私は○を命じた。 (彼 he; 行く to go; 私 I; 命じる to command)

(5) Translate: "I have never read (I don't have the experience of reading) Tezuka's manga." (to read 読む ; manga マンガ ; Tezuka 手塚)

(6) What is the difference between 美香は酒を飲んだことがない and 美香は酒を飲むことがない? (美香 Mika; 酒 sake; 飲む to drink)

(7) Translate: "It was decided that I will translate a novel." (I 私 ; to translate 翻訳する ; novel 小説)

(8) What is the difference between 美香は酒を飲むことにした and 美香は酒を飲むことになった?

(9) Translate: このバッグが欲しいんだもん！ What is the nuance of もん? (バッグ handbag; 欲しい to want).

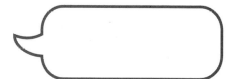

(10) Translate: "There's no way I'm going to drink sake!" in four possible ways.

— **Answers to all the exercises can be found online by following the link on page 7.** —

Grammar Scramble

Let's use this lesson to touch on a few useful grammatical constructions that will enhance your everyday Japanese, namely だけ, しか, ばかり, ところ, せい and おかげ.

🎧 The expression だけ

だけ means "only" and is simple to use:

- 昨日はコーラだけ（を）飲みました Yesterday I only drank cola.
- 関西といえば、大阪だけ（は）「都会」だと言えるだろう
  Regarding Kansai, only Osaka could be called a "big city."
- 僕にだけ教えてくださいよ Say it only to me, please.
- 毎日、図書館でだけ勉強している Every day, I study only in the library.

だけ comes directly after verbs, nouns -*i* adjectives and -*na* adjectives, usually in the same position as a grammatical particle. While it can precede を and は, it may also replace them completely. However, it may not replace other particles (に、で、の、へ, etc.), and they will remain in the sentence, preceding or following だけ. The phrase できるだけ means "as much as one can" / "as much as possible."

- できるだけ英語で話してください Speak in English as much as possible.

Xだけで（は）なく、Y（も）means "not only X, but also Y." **Usage:** As for だけ.

- 彼はハンサムなだけでなく、頭がいい He's not only handsome, but intelligent.
- 楽しいだけでなく、役にも立つホームページを作りたい
  I want to create a web page that is not only fun, but also useful.
- 能はおもしろいだけの芸能ではなく、歴史的でもある
  Noh (theater) is not only an interesting performing art, it is also historical.

🎧 The expression しか

しか also means "only" but with a different nuance to だけ. While だけ means "only" in a neutral way, しか has a more "negative" nuance, closer to "nothing but." **Usage:** しか is used only after nouns. The verb in the sentence must be in the negative. Regarding particles,

しか completely replaces が and を, and can replace に and へ. The particles で, の, と, から and まで remain in the sentence together with しか.

- こんなことは先生しか知らないと思う I think the teacher alone knows this.
- 龍彦はラーメンしか食べない Tatsuhiko only eats / eats nothing but ramen.
- 大学へはバスでしか行けないよ You can only go to university by bus (and by no other means).
- 昨日は吉田さんとしか会わなかった Yesterday, I met nobody but Mr. Yoshida.

The end-of-sentence expression しかない has to be mentioned separately as it has the meaning of "to have no choice but to." **Usage:** It always goes after a verb in the infinitive.

- これから勉強するしかないな From now on, I have no choice but to study.
- 岡山に行くしかないと思うよ I think we have no choice but to go to Okayama.

🎧 The expression ばかり

ばかり is a multipurpose expression of which we will study five usages. Although its basic meaning is "only," it has a nuance of excess.

ばかり meaning "only": The usage is similar to that of だけ and しか.
- 彼はビールばかり飲んでいる He drinks nothing but beer (excessively, I think).
- あの女は文句ばかり言う That woman does nothing but complain (and she's annoying).
- 図書館でばかり勉強している I only study in the library (and I study there a lot).

Notice that ばかり replaces the particles は, が and を. The particles へ and に are optionally replaceable, while other particles must go together with ばかり in the sentence.

ばかり meaning "not only, but also": The usage X ばかりで(は)なく、Y(も), is almost the same as X だけで(は)なく、Y(も), which means "not only X, but also Y,"

- 彼はハンサムなばかりでなく、頭がいい He's not only handsome, he's also intelligent.
- このロックバンドはいい音楽を作るばかりではなく、スタイルもすごい
  That rock band not only creates good music, it also has great style.

ばかり **meaning "do nothing but":** Placing ばかり in the middle of a gerund 〜ている (Lesson 35), we obtain 〜てばかりいる, "to do nothing but," with a negative nuance.

- その時、母は泣いてばかりいたよ That time, my mother did nothing but cry.
- 彼女は食べてばかりいて働かない She does nothing but eat and she doesn't work.
- 美根子ちゃん、遊んでばかりいると試験に落ちるぞ
  Mineko, if you do nothing but play (have fun), you will fail your exams.

ばかり **meaning "to have just finished doing":** The expression 〜たばかりだ, that is, ばかり after a verb conjugated in the past, means "to have just finished doing something."

- 今、ご飯を食べたばかりだよ I have just finished eating lunch now.
- 授業が終わったばかりだよ The class has just finished.

ばかり **meaning "more or less":** After a counter (Lesson 25), ばかり means "more or less" or "about," quite like ぐらい/くらい (Lesson 40), but more formal.

- バナナを１０本ばかりください Give me about 10 bananas, please.
- 彼は車を３台ばかり持っているかもしれません He might have 3 cars more or less.

🎧 The expression ところ

ところ, like ばかり, is a multipurpose expression.

ところ meaning "place":

- おばのところへ行ってきます I will go visit my aunt (at her place).

ところ meaning "state" or "moment":
ところ can mean "state" or "moment" when it modifies a verb, adjective or noun. It goes directly after verbs, *-na* and *-i* adjectives. With *a* noun, it requires の.

- ２人でラブラブしていたら、一番盛り上がっているところに母が部屋に入ってきた The two of us were making out when, at the most exciting moment, Mom came into the room.

- お忙しいところお邪魔してしまって、本当にごめんなさい
  Please excuse me for bothering you when you are so busy (in such a busy state).

ところ **meaning "just about to do something":** Infinitive + ところだ

- 手_て紙_{がみ}を書_かくところだ I'm just about to (start writing) write a letter.

ところ **meaning "to be in the process of doing something":** 〜ているところだ

- 手_て紙_{がみ}を書_かいているところだ I'm in the middle of writing a letter.

ところ **meaning "to have just finished doing something":** 〜たところだ means "to have just finished doing something." ばかり (page 303) has a similar usage.

- 手_て紙_{がみ}を書_かいたところだ I have just finished writing a letter.

🎧 The expressions せい and おかげ

せい or せいで (で is optional) means "because of" with negative nuances. It comes directly after verbs and *-i* adjectives. With *-na* adjectives, it needs な and, with nouns, の.

- 太_た郎_{ろう}のせいで試_し合_{あい}に負_まけた It is because of Taro that we lost the match.
- 友_{とも}達_{だち}が死_しんだのは彼_{かれ}のせいだよ It was his fault that my friend died.
- 昨_{ゆう}夜_べ、あまり眠_{ねむ}れなかったせいで、今_{きょう}日は仕_し事_{ごと}に集_{しゅう}中_{ちゅう}できない
  Because I couldn't sleep much last night, today I can't concentrate on my work.

おかげ or おかげで has the opposite meaning, "thanks to." We use it just like せい.

- 太_た郎_{ろう}のおかげで試_し合_{あい}に勝_かった Thanks to Taro we won the match.
- 石_{いし}原_{はら}さんに数_{すう}学_{がく}を教_{おし}えてもらったおかげで、高_{こう}校_{こう}を卒_{そつ}業_{ぎょう}できた
  Thanks to Ishihara teaching me math, I could graduate from senior high school.

🎧 A couple of conjunctions: ところで and ところが

ところで can be translated as "by the way" or "now then."

- ところで、哲_{てつ}治_{はる}は来_きてない？ By the way, hasn't Tetsuharu arrived?

ところが is like けれども (Lesson 49), meaning "but," "however," "nevertheless," etc.

- お母_{かあ}さんは東_{とう}京_{きょう}では元_{げん}気_きだった。ところが、尾_{おの}道_{みち}に帰_{かえ}ると、重_{おも}い病_{びょう}気_きに
  なった Mom felt well in Tokyo. But on going back to Onomichi, she fell seriously ill.

		🎧 **Grammar scramble**	
だけ	だけ	Only	私の猫は魚だけ食べる My cat only eats fish.
	だけでなく	Not only X, but also Y . . . (similar to ばかりでなく)	私の猫は魚を食べるだけでなく、 肉も食べる My cat not only eats fish, it also eats meat.
しか	しか＋ neg.	Only / Nothing but . . .	私の猫は魚しか食べない My cat eats nothing but / only eats fish.
	Inf. + しかない	To have no choice but . . .	今は魚を食べるしかないね Now, we have no choice but to eat fish, don't we?
ばかり	ばかり	Only (similar to だけ)	私の猫は魚ばかり食べる My cat only eats fish.
	ばかりでなく	Not only X, but also Y . . . (similar to だけでなく)	私の猫は魚を食べるばかりでなく、 肉も食べる My cat not only eats fish, it also eats meat.
	〜てばかりいる	To do nothing but X	私の猫は魚を食べてばかりいる My cat does nothing but eat fish.
	Past + ばかりだ	To have just finished doing X (similar to Past + ところだ)	今、食べたばかりです I have just finished eating now.
	ばかり	More or less / about (similar to ぐらい, Lesson 40)	私の猫は毎日、魚を五匹ばかり食べる My cat eats about five fish every day.
ところ	ところ	Place	ここは食べるところです This is the place to eat.
	Inf. + ところだ	To be just about to do X	今、食べるところです I'm just about to start eating now.
	Ger. + ところだ	To be in the process of doing X	今、食べているところです I'm eating now.
	Past + ところだ	To have just finished doing X (similar to Past + ばかりだ)	今、食べたところです I have just finished eating now.
せい	せい（で）	Because of . . .	私の猫は食べすぎたせいで、 太ってしまった Because my cat ate too much, it got fat.
おかげ	おかげ（で）	Thanks to . . .	私の猫は魚を食べるおかげで、 とても元気だ Thanks to the fact that my cat eats fish, he's very healthy.

私 *watashi* I; 猫 *neko* cat; 魚 *sakana* fish; 食べる *taberu* to eat; 肉 *niku* meat; 今 *ima* now;
毎日 *mainichi* every day; 匹 *hiki* counter for small animals; 太る *futoru* to get fat;
元気な *genki-na* healthy

🎧 漫画例 **Manga Examples**

So far in this lesson, we have seen a great number of new expressions, some of them very easy to confuse with each other. So there is nothing better than analyzing a few manga examples to get a clearer idea of some of these constructions!

Manga Example 1: Usages of *tokoro*

From the first manga example we can get quite a lot of information, even though this may not seem likely at first glance. The most obvious point to highlight is, of course, ところが, a sentence connector we have just studied (page 305), and which has the meaning of "however." Something less obvious, as it is concealed in its kanji form is 所, the word meaning "place" or "spot," whose synonym is 場所 (***basho***). In fact, 所 and 場所 can be used equally in any sentence without any change in nuance; notice how 所 and the second kanji in 場所 are the same, and they are only pronounced in a different way because of the 音読み ***on'yomi*** and 訓読み ***kun'yomi*** readings (Lesson 3).

J.M. Ken Niimura

Finally, it is worthwhile mentioning that the ほど in the example means "more or less" or "about," like ぐらい/くらい (Lesson 40) and ばかり (page 303): this excerpt could be １０キロぐらい or １０キロばかり. Bear in mind that ほど is perceived as more formal than ぐらい but less so than ばかり. **Note:** The translation of the sentence in this panel has been adapted to sound more "natural." Perhaps a more literal translation, more in keeping with what it really says, will help you understand the meaning better: "However, in this house that is in a place about 10km away from there . . ."

Jun'ichi: ところが そこから１０キロほど 離れた 所にある この 家では…

however there from 10 km approximately separate place PP *be house* PP *TOP*

However, in this house situated about 10km from there . . .

Manga Example 2: *Tokoro* as "state"

Let's continue analyzing the usages of ところ. In this case we have an instance of the usage we saw on page 304: as a verb, adjective or noun modifier with the meaning of "state" or "moment." In the case of 機関車の答えにおかしいところはない, the expression ところ is modifying the *-i* adjective おかしい (unusual, strange). A more literal translation of the sentence in the example would be "In the response of the locomotive there is nothing (no state / point) unusual." **Note:** In colloquial registers, the word 所 *tokoro* (place) and the expression ところ are usually contracted into とこ, so that this sentence would become 機関車の答えにおかしいとこはない.

Gabriel Luque

Mina: 機関車の答えにおかしいところはないわ　機能はすべて完全よ

locomotive POP answer PP unusual place TOP there is EP function TOP all perfect EP

There's nothing unusual in the locomotive's response. All its functions are perfect.

Manga Example 3: *Tokoro* for "about to"

Here we have yet another usage of ところ. Be careful with this one, because it is the easiest to confuse, since, depending on the conjugation of the verb preceding ところ, the meaning of the sentence changes.

In the example ジャマするところだった, the verb する is in the infinitive, which

Studio Kōsen

indicates the usage shown at the top of page 305 (to be about to do something). Thus, ジャマするところだった means "I was about to intrude." If we had found ジャマしているところだった, that is, with the verb in the gerund, the sentence would have mean "I was in the process of intruding" (page 305). Last of all, if we had found ジャマしたところだった, then its meaning would have been "I had just intruded" (page 305). **Note:** As we saw in Manga Example 5, Lesson 57, sometimes the author takes the license of imposing the reading of some kanji. Here, 他人 (another person) is read ヒト (person, 人).

Naoya: あやうく他人の恋路をジャマするところだった！

dangerously others POP romance DOP intrusion do (about to) be!

I have been about to intrude in someone else's love life!

Manga Example 4: To have no choice but . . .

After all these ところ expressions, we will move on to look at a different one: しか (nothing but). In this panel we have an example of one of the variations of しか: the end-of-sentence expression しかない. As we saw earlier in the lesson, this expression means "to have no choice but" and its usage merely consists of placing it at the end of a sentence; simple and effective. **Notes:** やっぱり is the colloquial version of やはり, an adverb without direct translation and with the nuance of "I knew it" or "just as I thought," although it has very different usages and its meaning changes depending on the context.

Take the opportunity as well to review the usage of the expression 〜てもらう ("to receive a favor," Lesson 45).

Shin'ichi: やっぱり医者（いしゃ）に見（み）てもらうしかないかなァ

after all doctor by see receive (nothing but) EP

After all, I will have no choice but to go and have a doctor see me.

Manga Example 5: An emphatic "only"

The expressions だけ and しか mean "only," and despite both having slightly different nuance and usage, they can be used together emphasize the negative: 山歩きに行くとだけしか言っていない (I have told her nothing but that I was going hiking.). The word order is always だけしか, and the verb must be in the negative. The sentence could be expressed neutrally (with だけ only): 山歩きに行くとだけ言っている (I have only told her that I was going hiking); or with a negative nuance (with しか only): 山歩きに行くとしか言っていない (I've told her nothing but that I was going hiking.)

Man: 妻（つま）にはただ山歩（やまある）きに行（い）くとだけしか言（い）っていない

my wife TOP only mountain walk go SBP only only say

I've told my wife nothing but that I was going hiking.

Manga Example 6: The usage of *bakari*

We will now look at ばかり, an expression with lots of meanings depending on the context, as you saw earlier in the lesson. In this particular panel we have an instance of a very similar usage to that of だけ or しか (meaning "only"), but with a slight nuance of "excess." **Notes:** In the colloquial register, ばかり is usually pronounced ばっかり, and there are some who even use ばかし or ばっかし. Take the opportunity to review the expressions "noun + のこと" (織田さんのこと) and だって ("the thing is") in Lesson 57.

Studio Kösen

Rena: だって、あなた　いつも織田さんのことステキってばかり言ってる

the thing is, you always Oda SUF POP thing adorable SBP only say

The thing is you do nothing but say that Mr. Oda is adorable.

Manga Example 7: Thanks to . . .

Here we have an example of the expression おかげ (thanks to). The 投票してくれたおかげだ part is "Thanks to them voting for me." The opposite is せい, which has the negative meaning of "because of" and lays blame on someone or something. If we change the sentence a little into 投票してくれたせいだ, this acquires the negative nuance of "Because of them voting for me (something bad happened)." Both expressions are very useful and easy to use. **Notes:** We add 〜中 (be careful, here it is read じゅう, and not ちゅう as usual) after some words indicating time or place to give them the meaning of "throughout": 国中 *kunijū* (throughout the country), 家中 *iejū* (throughout the house), 一年中 *ichinenjū* (all year round), 冬中 *fuyujū* (all winter), etc. The suffix 〜たち indicates plural after some nouns: ロボットたち (the robots), 君たち *kimitachi* (you, plural), 学生たち *gakuseitachi* (the students), 美穂たち *Mihotachi* (Miho and friends), etc.

J.M. Ken Niimura

Daneel: 国じゅうのロボットたちがぼくに投票してくれたおかげだ

country all POP robots (plural) SP I IOP vote do (favor) thanks be

This is thanks to all the robots in the country voting for me.

Exercises 練習

(1) What are the three expressions that convey the meaning "only"? What are their differences in nuance and how do we use them?

(2) Translate: "I only read novels." Give two versions, one with だけ and one with しか. (to read 読む; novel 小説)

(3) Translate: 私は女が好きなだけではなく、お金も好きだ。(私 I; 女 woman; 好きな that one likes; お金 money)

(4) Translate: 山本くんはゲームをやってばっかりいるぞ。(山本 Yamamoto; ゲームをやる to play videogames)

(5) Translate: "I have just turned the TV off." (to turn off 消す; TV テレビ) Give two possible versions.

(6) Translate: この映画の一番おもしろいとこはどれですか? (映画 movie; 一番 the most; おもしろい interesting, fun)

(7) Translate: "Now, I'm just about to watch a movie." (now 今; movie 映画; to watch 見る)

(8) Translate: "Now, I have just seen a movie" and "Now, I'm watching a movie."

(9) Translate: "Because my motorcycle broke down, I couldn't go." (motorcycle バイク; 壊れる to break down; to go 行く)

(10) Translate: ところで、街じゅうにいた猫たちは大丈夫ですか? (街 town; 猫 cat; 大丈夫な to be well)

— **Answers to all the exercises can be found online by following the link on page 7.** —

Lesson 59 ● 第59課

Dialects and Proverbs

Japanese has hundreds of dialects, among which the Kansai dialect stands out the most. In this lesson we will see the characteristics of the best known dialects.

🎧 The Kansai dialect

The region of 関西 **Kansai**, which has the official name of 近畿 **Kinki** is, together with the 関東 **Kantō** region around Tokyo, a driving force of the Japanese economy. The most important cities in 関西 are 大阪 **Ōsaka**, 神戸 **Kōbe** and 京都 **Kyōto**. A very distinct dialect called 関西弁 **Kansai ben** (弁 means dialect) is spoken in the region, with slight differences from place to place. We will study some 大阪弁 **Ōsaka ben** in this lesson.

• 儲かりまっか？ | ぼちぼちでんなぁ Are you making a profit? | Well, more or less.

It is a widely held belief in Japan that this is an everyday greeting and response in 関西. The truth is that it is not used at all nowadays, but you can use it when joking!

• 大阪弁はよう分からんわ！（大阪弁はよく分からないぞ！）I don't understand the Osaka dialect very well!

• 何や、めっちゃ上手やで、あんた！（何だ、とても上手だよ、君！）What! You are great at it!

🎧 Kansai dialect: Vocabulary		
Kansai ben	**Standard**	**Meaning**
あほ	ばか	stupid
ええ	いい	good
おおきに	ありがとう	thank you
おもろい	おもしろい	funny
けったいな	変な	odd, peculiar
しゃあない	しょうがない	can't be helped
しんどい	つかれる	tired
ちゃう	違う	you are wrong
なんぼ？	いくら？	how much?
べっぴん	美人	beautiful woman
ほかす	捨てる	to throw
ほな	それじゃ	well, then
ほんま	本当	truth / really
まいど	こんにちは	hello / welcome
えらい	とても	very / much
ごっつい	すごく	very / much
めっちゃ	ちょう〜	very / much

The Osaka dialect has particular intonation, vocabulary (take a look at the table on the facing page) and grammar (see table on page 314). Using や instead of the verb だ and the negative verb ending 〜へん or 〜ん instead of 〜ない are the two most prominent features. There are different end-of-sentence particles, like で instead of よ or ぞ and ねん instead of んだよ. The particle わ, only used by women in standard Japanese, is in 関西弁 used by men with a similar meaning to the standard よ. The Kansai-ben counterpart to the profusely used ね is な at the end of a sentence, with many different nuances, from invitation to surprise.

We will now see a sample conversation. Referring to the vocabulary and grammar tables in this chapter, "translate" it into standard Japanese. You will find the solution in the online **Answers to the Exercises** by following the link on page 7.

- 浩二はん、来られへんかった？ Koji couldn't come?
- はい、ミナミの方で仕事があったさかい Yes (no), he had a job down south.
- 残念やわ！ほな、ビール買うとこか What a pity! Well, shall we buy some beer?
- あかん、あかん！お酒飲めへんわ No, no! I can't drink alcohol!
- ほんまに？なんでやねん？けったいやなぁ！ Really? Why's that? How strange!
- コーラでええで。えらいうまいもん I'm fine with cola. The fact is it's delicious!
- しゃあないなぁ！ほな、おごるわ Well, then! Come on, I'm buying.
- おおきに！なんぼやろ、これ？ Thanks a lot! How much will that be?

Other dialects

Let's look at other Japanese dialects, using this general guide that covers some of the main sub-dialects and variations. We'll use this sentence as our model:

- 彼は毎日、村へ洗濯に行っているよ He goes into town every day to do the laundry.

Tōhoku ben 東北弁: Tohoku covers the north of Honshu. The main cities include 仙台 ***Sendai*** and 秋田***Akita***. 東北弁 is the most different dialect from standard Japanese: ***t*** and ***k*** sounds become ***d*** and ***g*** respectively, and せ is pronounced しぇ. Instead of the direction particles へ and に (Lesson 38), さ is used. The end-of-sentence particle べ is used with a similar meaning to よ.

- 彼は毎日、村さ洗濯に行ってるべ

🎧 Kansai dialect: Grammar				
Standard	**Standard example**	**Kansai ben**	**Kansai ben example**	**Translation**
だ (verb です)	行かないだろう？	や	行かへんやろう？	You're not going, are you?
〜ない	大阪へ行かない	〜へん 〜ん	大阪へ行かへん 大阪へ行かん	I'm not going to Osaka.
んだよ	彼女はきれいんだよ	ねん	彼女はきれいやねん	She is beautiful (really).
よ/ぞ	彼女はきれいだぞ	で	彼女はきれいやで	She is beautiful (really).
〜あった	車を買ったぞ！	おう	車を買うたで！	I bought a car!
いる	彼女、いる？	おる	彼女、おる？	Is she (here)?
〜ていらっしゃる	どこへ行ってらっしゃる？	〜はる	どこへ行ってはる？	Where are you going?
〜てしまった	車を買ってしまった	〜しもた	車を買うてしもた	I bought a car.
さん	香里さんはいない	はん	香里はんはおらん	Kaori is not (here).
から/ので	忙しいから、行かないよ	さかいに	忙しいさかいに、行かへんで	Since I'm busy, I'm not going.
だめ	これを使ったらだめだよ	あかん	これを使うたらあかんで	You can't use this.
行く *iku* to go; 彼女 *kanojo* she; きれいな beautiful; 車 *kuruma* car; 買う *kau* to buy; 忙しい *isogashii* busy; 使う *tsukau* to use; 香里 Kaori				

Kyūshū ben 九州弁: Kyushu is the furthest west of the main Japanese islands. Major cities include 福岡 ***Fukuoka*** and 長崎 ***Nagasaki***. This dialect uses な instead of the particle は, and じゃ instead of だ (to be). It also uses 〜ちょる instead of the gerund 〜ている.

• 彼な毎日、村へ洗濯に行っちょるばい

Okinawa ben 沖縄弁 or ***Okinawa go*** 沖縄語 *Okinawa go*: Specialists can't agree if what is spoken in Okinawa, in Japan's tropical south, is a separate language or a dialect. Expressions include ***mensooree*** (welcome), ***mata yaasai*** (goodbye), ***nifee deebiru*** (thank you).

Ainu go アイヌ語: The ancient settlers of Japan, the Ainu, have their own language. Nowadays, there are very few Ainu left and most of them live in Hokkaido. Some expressions: ***irankarapte*** (hello), ***apunno paye yan*** (goodbye), ***iyayraykere*** (thank you).

🎧 Proverbs

Many Japanese proverbs (ことわざ, or in kanji, 諺) come from ancient China or from Buddhism. The table below lists ten common ones. Here are some examples of daily use:

- 娘さんも医者になりたいそうですね It seems your daughter wants to be a doctor too.
- そうよ。カエルの子はカエルだもんね That's right. "Like mother, like daughter."

In Japanese there are four-character sayings, called 四字熟語 *yojijukugo*, most of which were borrowed from China many centuries ago. Some have a literal meaning, such as 東西南北 ***tōzainamboku*** (east-west-south-north = in all directions), but many are far from obvious. In the table below you have the ten most frequent 四字熟語. An example of usage:

- 臼井さんはチョコレートが嫌いって！ Mr. Usui says he doesn't like chocolate!
- ま、十人十色だよね Well, "so many men, so many minds."

🎧 Proverbs and sayings			
ことわざ (諺) Proverbs		**四字熟語 *Yoji-jukugo***	
猿も木から落ちる	Even monkeys fall from trees (Nobody is perfect)	一石二鳥	One stone, two birds (To kill two birds with one stone)
カエルの子はカエル	The frog's child is a frog (Like father, like son)	弱肉強食	Weak meat is food for the strong (The law of the jungle)
花より団子	Dumplings rather than blossoms (Bread is better than the songs of birds)	自業自得	One does, one earns (One reaps what one sows)
後の祭り	The day after the festival. (The doctor after death)	自由自在	Freedom-freedom (With perfect freedom)
ウソも方便	A lie is also expedient (White lie)	日常茶飯	Every day, tea and rice (An everyday affair)
郷に入っては郷に従え	When you enter a village, obey the village (When in Rome, do as the Romans do)	十人十色	Ten people, ten colors (So many men, so many minds)
出る釘は打たれる	The nail that sticks out gets hammered (A tall tree catches much wind)	一期一会	One's lifetime, one meeting (A chance in a lifetime)
仏の顔も三度まで	Buddha (gets mad if you touch) his face 3 times (There are limits to one's endurance)	花鳥風月	Flower, bird, wind, moon (The beauties of nature)
鬼のいぬ間に洗濯	To do the laundry while the ogre is out (When the cat's away, the mice will play)	順風満帆	Favorable wind, full sail (Smooth sailing)
能ある鷹は爪を隠す	The clever hawk hides its talons (He who knows most, speaks least)	天下無双	No twin under the heavens (Unique in the world)

Cultural Note:
The Language of the Samurai

All languages in the world evolve and, of course, 日本語 **nihongo** is not an exception, in fact the Japanese language has evolved at a frenzied pace, proof of which lies in literature. The language has changed so much since the 平安 **Heian** period (794–1192), when the ひらがな and カタカナ syllabaries were invented, that there are many (very thick!) 古語辞典 **kogo jiten** ancient-language dictionaries.

There are several interesting things about ancient Japanese: for example, there are two kana which are not used nowadays: the hiragana letter ゐ (romanized **wi**, but pronounced **i**,) and the katakana letter ヰ (romanized **we**, but pronounced **e**). Other changes are that は was read **wa** (hence the present pronunciation of the topic particle は), ひ was read **i**, and を was not only used as direct object particle, but also in words, such as をとこ (男 **otoko** "man").

Matsumoto Castle is a great example of samurai architecture
(Photo: M. Bernabé)

The type of archaic Japanese you will mostly come across, especially when reading books and マンガ or watching movies and TV series set in the 江戸 **Edo** period (1603–1867), will be the dialect used by the 武士 **bushi**, usually called 侍 **samurai**. Although the dialect of the ancient 武士 is not radically different from present-day Japanese, you will find some aspects that may surprise or perplex you, such as:

• Usage of first person pronouns (I) such as 拙者（せっしゃ）, 某（それがし） or 我（われ）.

• Usage of the verbs なり and, especially, でござる instead of です.

• Extensive usage of the honorific suffixes 〜様（さま） and 〜殿（どの） (e.g., 徳川殿（とくがわどの） Lord Tokugawa).

• Today's negative 〜ない was 〜ぬ (e.g., 行かない（い） not to go ⇒ 行かぬ).

• Today's 〜ないで used to link sentences was 〜ず (e.g., 行かないで ⇒ 行かず)

• **An example:** 拙者（せっしゃ）は忍（しの）びの者（もの）でござる I am a fellow of stealth (I'm a 忍者（にんじゃ）).

Finally, some numbers were also written in a different way, for instance, 壱 (**ichi**), 弐 (**ni**), 参 (**san**), 伍 (**go**), 拾 (**jū**). And they are still sometimes used . . . Take a look at the 10,000 yen note: it says 壱万円 **ichi man en**!

🎧 漫画例 **Manga Examples**

We hope the following manga examples will deepen your understanding of the diversity of Japanese dialects and give a broader idea of what Japanese constitutes.

Manga Example 1: Osaka dialect

This example has someone talking in a dialect of Kansai: Osaka dialect (大阪弁 *Ōsaka ben*), to be precise. Notice the negative 〜へん (せえへん=しない), the emphatic particle で and the や instead of だ. やせたる is a typical 大阪弁 contraction of やせてやる (Lesson 53). This sentence, in standard Japanese, would be 今からぜったい間食しないよ！ぜったいやせてやるんだ！

　大阪弁 is often used by merchants, yakuza and comedians. Why? Osaka has long been known as a city of merchants, where money always comes first (hence the greeting 儲かりまっか？ *Mōkarimakka?* you saw on page 312). Certain areas of the city are reputed to be swarming with yakuza and other organized criminals. Osaka is also the capital of 漫才 *manzai*, a kind of popular stand-up comedy. All these clichés are exploited in novels, comic books, movies and TV series. Mastering some 大阪弁 will help you enjoy all this!

J.M. Ken Niimura

Sakie:　もー 今からぜったい間食せえへんで！ぜったいやせたるんや

(exclamation) now from swear snack do EP! swear lose weight be

Grrr! From now on, no more snacks! I'm definitely going to lose weight!

Jirō:　何で関西弁になるの？

why Kansai dialect become Q?

Why are you speaking in the Kansai dialect?

Manga Example 2: Kansai dialect for business

あかん
あかん
シバでは
そんな高い
もん
必要おまへんわ！

This example exploits the "commercial" or even "criminal" aspect of 大阪弁 *Ōsaka ben*. The man talking is the president of Shiba, a company that has murky dealings with the local mafia.

Here you can see the word あかん (だめ in standard Japanese); the negative ending 〜へん (おまへん is the equivalent of ない, the negative of ある); and the emphatic particle わ, which is used by both men and women in Kansai.

Gabriel Luque

Man: あかん あかん シバではそんな高いもん必要おまへんわ！

no no Shiba PP TOP as that expensive thing need there is EP!

No way! No! In Shiba we don't need anything as expensive as that!

Manga Example 3: Kyoto dialect

This example shows us a woman speaking in 京都弁 *Kyōto ben*. As you can see, she uses the negative ending 〜へん, a feature you find all over Kansai, although in Kyoto 〜ひん is sometimes used. Notice, too, the どす, the equivalent of the verb です. Generally, 京都弁 is perceived as soft and melodic. The most typical phrase in this sub-dialect is おいでやす (welcome).

今私が好き
なのは島さん
しかいてしまへん
これも真実どす

Studio Kōsen

Ai: 今 私が好きなのは島さんしかいてしまへん　これも真実どす

now I SP like NOM TOP Shima only there is this too truth be

Now I like nobody but Mr. Shima. This is also true.

Manga Example 4: Does the Hokkaido dialect exist?

The northern Japanese island of 北海道 *Hokkaidō* was practically ignored until the beginning of the 明治時代 *Meiji jidai* Meiji era (1868–1912), when the repopulation of the island started. Most settlers came from the 関東 *Kantō* area (Tokyo and its surroundings), so the language spoken in 北海道 nowadays is similar to standard Japanese. However, over the years, traces of the old 北海道弁 *Hokkaidō ben* have permeated 東北弁 *Tōhoku ben*, for example the emphatic particle べ, or words like こっこ (egg; child) or めんこい (handsome; beautiful).

Studio Kōsen

Kimie: 「シンちゃんのこっこがほしいべぇ…」
*"Shin **SUF POP** egg **SP** want **EP** . . ."*
"I want a child by Shin . . ."

Manga Example 5: A *yoji-jukugo* proverb

Gabriel Luque

Here is an example of a 四字熟語 *yojijukugo*, a kind of compact proverb with four kanji, in this case 海千山千, literally "sea-thousand-mountain-thousand." Apparently, this comes from a popular Chinese saying "a snake who lives a thousand years in the sea and a thousand years in the mountain ends up becoming a dragon." 海千山千 is used, then, to describe someone with a lot of experience and wisdom, hardened in all aspects of life; in English we might say a "sly old fox." **Note:** This panel uses an example of the construction "ほど + neg." (Lesson 54) meaning "not as . . . as."

Midori: あたし、若い女性ってほどでもありませんから　海千山千ですから
I, young woman say not so much be as sea-1000-mountain-1000 be because
I'm not what you would call a young woman. I'm a sly old fox.

Manga Example 6: The language of the samurai

Finally, an example of the language of the ancient samurai. Notice the use of the first person pronoun 拙者 and the verb でござる (the modern です), two stereotypical characteristics of what is supposed to be the warriors' ancient dialect. The other social classes in the ancient feudal system of the 士農工商 *shinōkōshō* ("warriors-farmers-artisans-tradesmen," by order of importance) did not use the speech patterns of the samurai class, nor could they carry swords. We say that the usage of 拙者 and でござる is stereotypical because there is a tendency to use them in works of fiction. The samurai dialect was actually more complex, but it is now simplified to make its comprehension easier.

Xian Nu Studio

Maruo: 拙者は今も昔も変らないでござるよ

I TOP now too before too change be EP

I haven't changed, I'm the same now as in the past.

Exercises　練習

1 What is 関西弁 (かんさいべん) and in which region is it used?
What are the main sub-dialects of 関西弁 (かんさいべん)?

2 What is the set answer to the greeting 儲 (もう) かりまっか What clichés are there about 大阪弁 (おおさかべん)?

3 Translate into standard Japanese and into English:
しんどい仕事 (しごと) はめっちゃ嫌 (いや) やなぁ。（仕事 work; 嫌 disliked)

4 Translate into standard Japanese and English:
キタは人 (ひと) がごっつい多 (おお) いさかいに、歩 (ある) かれへんで。（人 peoplc; 多い many; 歩く to walk)

5 Change this sentence into 大阪弁 (おおさかべん):
光彦さんがまだいないので、行ってはだめだよ。
（光彦 Mitsuhiko; まだ still; 行く to go)

6 To what dialect does this sentence belong, and what does it mean? 行かへんやろう？

7 What does the following proverb mean?
郷 (ごう) に入 (い) っては郷 (ごう) に従 (したが) え？

8 What is a 四字熟語 (よじじゅくご)? What does the expression 一石二鳥 (いっせきにちょう) mcan?

9 Translate into modern Japanese and English:
某 (それがし) は織田殿 (おだどの) のところへ行 (い) かぬ。
（織田 Oda; ところ place; 行く to go)

10 Does 北海道弁 (ほっかいどうべん) exist? If so, could you name its main characteristics?

— **Answers to all the exercises can be found online by following the link on page 7.** —

The Passive and Causative Forms

Welcome to the last lesson in of our two-volume course! We are going to end by taking a look at two of the most complicated constructions in Japanese: passive and causative sentences.

🎧 What is the passive verb form?

The passive verb form is used to show the point of view of the recipient of an action. That is, the subject receives the action of the agent, taking no part in performing the action. In the sentence "Paul was fired by the president," we are showing the action from the point of view of Paul (the subject), although he doesn't take part directly in the firing process. The person performing the act of firing is the president (the agent). The table on page 324 shows the conjugation of passive verbs in Japanese. As a general rule for Group 1 verbs, the last る is replaced by られる: 見る *miru* (to see) ⇒ 見られる (to

be seen). For Group 2 verbs the last *-u* is replaced by *-a*, and we add れる: 抱く *daku* (to embrace) ⇒ 抱かれる (to be embraced). Group 3 verbs are irregular.

To make the passive form in English, we might change a sentence as follows: *The woman scolded Meg ⇒ Meg was scolded by the woman*. Let's do the same in Japanese:

- あの女性はメグをしかった That woman scolded Meg.
- メグはあの女性にしかられた Meg was scolded by that woman.

As you can see, the process is similar to English, in the way that both place the recipient of the action as the subject. Thus, Meg (the direct object marked with を in the regular sentence), becomes the topic of the passive sentence and is marked with は. The agent (performing the action) is almost always marked with the particle に.

- 警察は老人に棒で叩かれた The policeman was hit with a stick by the old man.
- 洋子ちゃんは彼氏にとても愛されている Yoko is much loved by her boyfriend.

Passive sentences without a specific agent also exist in Japanese:

- このビルは５０年前に造られました This building was built fifty years ago.
- この間、あの犯人は投獄にされた The other day, that criminal was jailed.

The construction によって is used instead of the particle に in passive sentences of a "historical" kind, where the action of somebody important is described.

- 「源氏物語」は紫式部によって書かれた *The Tale of Genji* was written by Murasaki Shikibu.
- アメリカはコロンブスによって発見された America was discovered by Columbus.

🎧 The "victim" passive

In Japanese the passive form is sometimes used to describe an action that affects the subject and is performed by someone else. Almost always the effect is negative, so this construction is called the "victim passive." For example, in the first sentence the passive indicates that my brother drinking the cola I considered mine affected me in a negative way.

- 私は兄にコーラを飲まれた (Lit: I had my cola drank by my elder brother). My elder brother drank (my) cola (and I didn't like that at all).
- (私は)隣の人にタバコを吸われたよ The person next to me smoked (and I don't like it).
- (私は)娘に秘密を知られた My daughter discovered my secret (and I wasn't pleased).
- 百合子は犬に死なれそうだよ Yuriko's dog is about to die.

For Group 1 verbs, the passive conjugation is the same as the potential (Lesson 32) and the the formal *sonkeigo* form (Lesson 52). We can usually infer the meaning from the context:

- 社長は窓を閉められた This sentence can be potential (The president could close the window), respectful (The president closed the window), or victim passive (Someone closed the window [and the president didn't like that]).

🎧 What is the causative verb form?

The causative is used to express "making" or "letting" someone do something. The table on page 324 shows the conjugations of causative verb forms. As a general rule, for Group 1 verbs, replace the last る with させる. 見る *miru* (to see) ⇒ 見させる (to let / make see). For Group 2 verbs, replace the last *-u* with *-a*, and add せる. 抱く *daku* (to embrace) ⇒ 抱かせる (to let / make embracc). Group 3 verbs are irregular and must be learned by heart.

	Simple f.	Meaning	Passive	Causative	Causative-passive
Group 1 Invariable	教える	to teach	教えられる	教えさせる	教えさせられる
	見る	to look	見られる	見させる	見させられる
Group 2 Variable	貸す	to lend	貸される	貸させる	貸させられる
	待つ	to wait	待たれる	待たせる	待たせられる
	買う	to buy	買われる	買わせる	買わせられる
	帰る	to return	帰られる	帰らせる	帰らせられる
	書く	to write	書かれる	書かせる	書かせられる
	急ぐ	to hurry	急がれる	急がせる	急がせられる
	遊ぶ	to play	遊ばれる	遊ばせる	遊ばせられる
	飲む	to drink	飲まれる	飲ませる	飲ませられる
	死ぬ	to die	死なれる	死なせる	死なせられる
Group 3 Irregular	する	to do	される	させる	させられる
	来る	to come	来られる	来させる	来させられる

When using the causative to indicate permission, the particle に is usually used to mark the one receiving permission.

- お母さんは子どもにプールへ行かせた The mother let the boy go to the pool.
- 徹は犬に公園でいっぱい走らせた Toru let his dog run a lot in the park.

In a sentence of obligation, the particle を is usually used to mark the person being forced to perform the action.

- 先生は学生たちを走らせた The teacher made the students run.
- 母は私をむりやり勉強させた My mother made me study.

However, if the verb is transitive and the sentence has a direct object marked with を, we use に for the person who is forced or allowed to do something: thus we avoid having two を in the sentence. These sentences are ambiguous and their meaning must be inferred from the context.

- ベロニカは弟にケーキを食べさせた Veronica let my brother eat the cake.
- 母は私にお風呂の掃除をさせた My mother made me clean the bath.

- 私は森さんにメッセージを聞かせた I let / made Mr. Mori listen to the message.
- 社長は社員に酒を飲ませた The president let / made his employees drink sake.

The first two sentences are clear, but the latter two are ambiguous, and their meanings must be inferred from the context. **Note:** When an object or an inanimate being takes part in the sentence, を must always be used.

- 僕は車を愛媛まで走らせた I made the car go to Ehime / I drove the car to Ehime.
- 社長はあの土地を遊ばせている The president is letting that land lie idle.

The causative form can be combined with 〜てください or 〜ていただく to form sentences such as "let me do X" and "you let me do X," often used in formal contexts.

- この映画を見させてくださいよ Let me watch that movie, please.
- この会社を辞めさせていただきたいです I want to leave this company. (Lit. I want to be allowed to leave this company.)

🎧 The causative-passive

The causative-passive is used to mean "being forced to do something (that one doesn't like)." That is, the causative is combined with the victim passive. The table on page 324 shows the conjugation of causative-passive verb forms. As a general rule for all verb groups, the last る of the causative form is replaced by られる: 抱く *daku* (to embrace) ⇒ 抱かせる (to let / make embrace) ⇒ 抱かせられる (to be made to embrace). Take a look at these examples:

- 学生たちは先生に走らせられた The students were forced to run by the teacher.
- 私は母にお風呂の掃除をさせられた I was forced to clean the bath by my mother.
- 僕は会社を辞めさせられた I was forced to leave the company (I was fired).
- 彼は彼女に告白させられそうだね He seems to feel forced to declare his love to her.

Note: Causative-passive sentences only have the connotation of "obligation," never that of "permission" as in causative sentences.

🎧 Other constructions

Let's finish with three new expressions について, ずつ and こそ.

について **meaning "about":** This expression is the Japanese version of our "about" or "concerning." It is extremely easy to use and, needless to say, very useful in any context or situation. It is worthwhile remembering.

- 日本の歴史について話してください Talk about Japanese history, please.
- あの男について何か知っていますか？ Do you know anything about that man?
- 禅について書くことが大好きです I love writing about Zen Buddhism.
- 彼について言えば、とても親切な人です Concerning him, I'll say he is a very kind person.

ずつ **meaning "each":** This expression is used to indicate that something is distributed in an equal way (similar to "each" or "X by Y" in English). ずつ can only go after counters (Lesson 25) and some adverbs. Take a look at the examples and you will get a clearer idea:

- オレンジを 2 個ずつ食べてください Eat two oranges each, please.
- 各家にパソコンが 1 台ずつあればいいのに It'd be nice if there was a computer in every house.
- 漢字を毎日六つずつ覚えることにした I decided to memorize six kanji a day.
- 俳句が少しずつ上手になってきた Little by little I have improved in (the composition of) haiku.

こそ **for emphasis:** This expression is quite common in written and spoken Japanese, and is used to emphasize the word preceding it. There is no exact translation in English, so take a look at the example sentences to understand how it works.

- 真理子はきれいだね | 違う、公江こそきれいだよ
  Mariko is beautiful, isn't she? | No, Kimie is the one who is beautiful.
- 今年こそ東大に入るぞ！ This is the year I'll get in to the University of Tokyo!
- 今度こそダイエットしてやせるぞ！ I swear next time, for sure, I'll go on a diet!
- どうもありがとうございました | いいえ、こちらこそ
  Thank you very much. | No, I'm the one (to thank you).

🎧 漫画例 Manga Examples

The passive, causative, and causative-passive conjugations are very easy to confuse due to their similarity, as you have probably realized. But don't worry, with practice, you will get used to them. Let's now see a few examples (the last in the book!) to clarify the concepts we have been studying.

Manga Example 1: Victim passive

We start with an example of one of the so called victim passive sentences, a very particular usage of the Japanese passive that you will find quite often. The part we will take into consideration is 自分の名前が歌われる. The verb 歌われる is the passive form of 歌う, (to sing). Remember the rule for the conjugation of verbs in Group 2: the last *-u* is replaced with *-a*, and we add れる. With verbs ending in *-u*, the conjugation is somewhat special, because, for example, the passive form of 歌う is not 歌<u>あ</u>れる, but 歌<u>わ</u>れる. The same happens with other verbs ending in *-u*, like 買う *kau* (to buy) ⇒ 買われる (to be bought).

The so called "victim" passive is used to indicate an action performed by someone else which affects (negatively most of the time, hence the name "victim") the subject of the sentence. 自分の名前が歌われる, then, would literally mean "my name is sung (and this affects me)." In this specific case, we can't say the effect is a negative one, although the usage of ビックリする (to be surprised) right after, denotes that the fact of hearing his name "being sung" has affected the speaker. **Note:** The usage of the conditional 〜たら in トイレに行ったら (when I went to the toilet) is the one we saw on page 285, Lesson 56: to learn or discover something as a result of a certain action ("when," "as a result of," "after").

Studio Kōsen

Yama: ちょうどトイレに行ったら自分の名前が歌われてビックリしましたよ
just toilet DP go (conditional) I POP name SP sing surprise do EP
When I went to the toilet, I heard my name being sung and I was surprised.

Manga Example 2: The passive

In this panel we have an instance of a "normal" passive sentence, where a subject (ワタシ) receives the action (殺す) from an agent (こんな男) without taking part in it. The usage of grammatical particles is noteworthy: the passive subject is marked with the topic particle

は or the subject particle が, while the agent is followed by に. The literal translation of this sentence would be "I won't be killed by a man like this," although we propose a more natural translation in English, below. **Note:** There is an example of the usage of ～たり to make a non-exhaustive list of actions (Lesson 46). 殺されたりしない literally means "I won't be killed (or anything like that)."

J.M. Ken Niimura

Yoshiko: ワタシはこんな男に殺されたりしないわ

I TOP *this kind of man* SBP *kill or something do* EP

A man like him won't kill me.

Manga Example 3: The causative for obligation

Let's see an example of the causative (used to give the idea of "making" or "letting" do something). Here, the verb is 爆発する (to explode.) Since する is an irregular verb, we must learn the conjugation by heart: the causative form of する is させる.

Thus, we have 爆発させる (to make explode), here conjugated in the *-ō* form (爆発させよう, Lesson 34), giving the nuance "let's make it explode." Although the sentence doesn't show who or what is receiving the obligation, we will imagine it is a 戦車 *sensha* (tank) that, being an inanimate object, must be marked with を. Therefore, we would have 戦車を爆発させよう (Let's make the tank explode.).

Gabriel Luque

Sally: かっこよく大爆発させようぜ

nice big explosion do EP

Let's blow it to smithereens!

Manga Example 4: The causative for permission

While in the previous panel we saw the causative of "obligation" (the tank is made to explode), we now have an instance of the causative of "permission." The verb here is 出す, a transitive verb (Lesson 44) that means "to take out." The causative form is, then, 出させる (to let take out). 犠牲者を出す has the meaning of "causing victims," therefore 犠

牲者を出させない would literally be "not to allow to cause victims." In this case, there is no agent specified but, if there was one, it would be introduced with に, because there can't be two を in the sentence. An example: ジョンに犠牲者を出させない (Not to allow John to cause victims).

Kishida: もうこれ以上犠牲者は出させない！
any more this more victim TOP take out!
I won't allow there to be any more victims!

Manga Example 5: Causative + *morau*

In formal contexts we often find a combination of the causative with the 〜ていただく or 〜てもらう constructions (Lesson 45). In this case, やらせてもらう comes from やる (to do), which is conjugated in the causative form (やらせる), which in its turn is conju-

gated in the -*te* form (やらせて) so that it can link to もらう. The literal translation of やらせてもらう would be "To receive the favor of being allowed to do." This form, like in the sentence 日光へ行かせていただきたいのです *Nikkō e ikasete itadakitai no desu* ("I would like to be allowed to go to Nikko" or "I want to go to Nikko"), is used to make sentences of request or action that sound humble and indirect at the same time.

Kumasaka: 第一外科の熊坂俊介だ
num. 1 surgery POP Kumasaka Shunsuke be
I'm Shunsuke Kumasaka, from the first section of surgery.
君たち2人の指導医をやらせてもらう事になっている
you 2 POP supervisor doctor DOP do receive (it has been decided)
I have been appointed as the medical supervisor for both of you.

Manga Example 6: The causative-passive

Let's look at the causative-passive. In the example we have やめさせられた, which comes from the verb 辞める *yameru* (to leave a job). To obtain a causative-passive form, we must first conjugate a verb in the causative and then in the passive, for example: 辞める (to leave a job) ⇒ 辞めさせる (causative, to force to leave) ⇒ 辞めさせられる (causative-passive, to be forced to leave). Compare the following sentences:

1. 信夫は千草にお酒を飲ませた *Nobuo wa Chigusa ni osake o nomaseta.*
   Nobuo made / let Chigusa drink sake
2. 信夫は千草にお酒を飲まれた Nobuo had his sake drunk by Chigusa = Chigusa drank Nobuo's sake (and Nobuo didn't like that)
3. 信夫は千草にお酒を飲ませられた Nobuo was forced by Chigusa to drink sake.

Jack: やあ伊東先生 あなたは病院をやめさせられたんですってね
いとう せんせい　　　　びょういん

hey Itō-professor you TOP hospital DOP abandon be say EP

Hi, Dr. Ito. I've been told that you have been forced to leave the hospital . . .

Manga Example 7: The usage of *koso*

And we finally arrive at the last example in the lesson and, by extension, in the course. Here we see an example of the usage of こそ, an adverb used to emphasize the word preceding it. In this case, 今こそ has the meaning of "now is indeed . . ." An example: Imagine you are on a diet, and you can't eat chocolate. You finally reach your ideal weight: this is the moment to say 今こそチョコレートが食べられるぞ! *Ima koso chokoretto ga taberareru zo!* (Now, indeed, I can eat chocolate!) **Notes:** ラジコン is the contraction of ラジオコントロール, that is, "device controlled by radio," although the word in Japanese designates "radio-controlled toys." 活躍する *katsuyaku suru* is a difficult verb to translate: we could say it indicates "to be active," "to take active part in."

Emika: 今こそあなたのラジコンがかつやくするときよ
いま

now yes you POP radiocon SP activity do moment EP

Now is indeed the moment to get your models to perform.

Exercises 練習

1 Conjugate the passive form of the verbs 踊る (to dance), 招く (to invite), 食べる (to eat), and 払う (to pay).

2 Translate: "Ken was praised by the teacher." (Ken 健 ; to praise ほめる ; teacher 先生)

3 Translate: 私 は里奈に泣かれた。 What is the nuance of the passive conjugation here? (私 I; 里奈 Rina; 泣く to cry)

4 Conjugate the causative form of the verbs in question 1.

5 Translate: "The editor made the writer go to a hot spring." (editor 編集者 ; writer 作家; to go 行く ; hot spring 温泉)

6 Translate: 先生 は俺にマンガを描かせた。 (先生 teacher; 俺 I; マンガ comic book; 描く to draw)

7 Conjugate the causative-passive form of the verbs in question 1.

8 Translate the following sentence: 私 は彼女に指輪を買わせられた。 (私 I; 彼女 she; 指輪 ring; 買う to buy)

9 Translate: 日本について作文を一人ずつ書いてください。 (日本 Japan; 作文 composition; 一人 one person; 書く to write)

10 Translate: 読者がいたからこそ、この本ができた。 (読者 reader; 本 book)

— **Answers to all the exercises can be found online by following the link on page 7.** —

あ、この壺か？2000円でええで。

2000円だって？それは高すぎるよ。もっと安くしてくれないの？こんなに高い壺は買ったことがないよ。

どの壺や？これかい？

いいえ、それじゃなくて、隣の方です。

おはようございます。すみませんが、あの壺はいくらですか？

そうやな…なんぼ払うの、あんた？

500円。

500円やて？そりゃほんまに安すぎるで。あかん、あかん。

じゃ、700円でどう？

もし、この壺を買うたら、この茶碗もあげるで。1500円でどう？

ま、「郷に入っては郷に従え」っていうんだもの。

それなら、お願いします。

おおきに！しかし、あんた、上手やなぁ、日本語！

けどな、こんな茶碗は一つしかあらへんで。もう一つあったけ、盗まれたんや。他の茶碗でどう？えらいお得やで!!

茶碗を一つだけでなく、二つ売ってくれれば、考えてみるよ。お母さんとおばあさんのプレゼントになるので、一石二鳥だね。

いらっしゃいませ！

この荷物をスペインまで送りたいのです。

中身は何ですか？

壺と茶碗です。

壊れやすいものですね。気をつけます。

ありがとう。

航空便でお願いします。

少し急いでいるので、航空便がございます。どちらで送ればいいですか？

最も早い方法はEMSですが、それはもう少し高くなります。

いいえ、普通の航空便でいいです。いくらですか？

あ、大切なことを忘れるところでした！この三枚の絵葉書も送りたいです。

2400円です。

絵葉書は80円ずつですから、全部で2640円です。

どうぞ。

関西国際空港に到着です。関西国際空港、

ヌリアさん？谷村です。お元気ですか？

はい、元気です！今、関西空港にいるんだけど…

美奈話通信

りんりんりん

そういえば、美奈にひどいことを言っちゃったな…彼女はいつも優しくしてくれたし、彼女のおかげで東京でいい写真をとれたのに…あたしって、本当にバカだった。帰る前に電話してみようかな…

私もですよ。ヌリアさんの荷物がやっと届いたので、持って来ました。

本当ですか？どこにいるの、今？

三階の喫茶店です。こちらへ来ませんか？

はい、行きます！

それじゃ…

終わり

Review for Lessons 56–60

Answers to all the review exercises can be found online by following the link on page 7.

🎧 *KAGE* – New vocabulary 新しい単語

壷 (つぼ)	jar, pot	方法 (ほうほう)	method, way
イライラする	to be annoyed		

1. According to what you have read in the sixth episode of **Kage**, how much does the street vendor first ask Nuria for the object she wants to buy, and how much does Nuria end up paying? Does she only buy the object she has asked about?

2. As you have probably noticed, the vendor at the street market speaks in a Japanese dialect; what region does it belong to, and what is it called?

3. At the post office, how does Nuria choose to mail her package, by airmail or sea mail? Special delivery or standard?

4. In the end, Nuria decides to call Mina. Why?

5. Why is Mina at Kansai airport?

6. Where in the airport is Mina? Does she go to meet Nuria, or is it the other way around?

7. In Nuria's conversation with the market vendor, there are two conditional sentences. Find them and give their translation into English.

8. Translate the following sentences from the text of **Kage**, which have several idiomatic uses of the conditional.

a) どちらで送ればいいですか？ _____

b) そう言えば、美奈(みな)にひどいことを言ったね _____

c) 三階(がい)にある喫茶店(きっさてん)です。来ませんか？ _____

9. Translate these sentences, which differ only in the conjugation of the verb.

a) パソコンが壊れるところだった　　　_____

b) パソコンが壊れているところだった　_____

c) パソコンが壊れたところだった　　　_____

10. Change the following sentences from **Kage** into polite Japanese (**-masu** form).

a) なんぼ払うの、あんた？

　　_____.

b) そりゃほんまに安すぎるで。あかん、あかん。

　　_____.

c) こんな茶碗は一つしかおらへんで。

　　_____.

11. The verbs 謝らせてください and 気付かせられる appear in the text. In what form has each verb been conjugated? Give the translation of both sentences.

12. A proverb and a **yoji-jukugo** appear in the text. Find them and explain their meanings in English.

13. Translate the following sentences written in Kansai dialect into standard Japanese, as in the example.

a) あしたは京都で買い物をするんやで！
　　あしたは京都で買い物をするんだぞ！_____。

b) これをほかすなよ！なんぼやと思っとるんや？

　　_____。

c) たこ焼きを食べへんか？ほんまに？

　　_____。

d) ミナミへ行ったんやけど、けったいな外人に会^あってしもたわ！

_____。

e) あのべっぴんはほんまにやばいで！話したらあかんで！

_____。

f) まいど、元気かい？ところで、この間買^こうてくれたバッグ、大好きやねん！

_____。

g) 今日はしんどかったなぁ...ええ仕事をできへんかったし...

_____。

h) 青木^{あおき}さんはおらへんわ。「買い物をしてくる」って言いはったんや。

_____。

14. Fill in the blanks in the following sentences with the most appropriate 四字熟語^{よじじゅくご} from the box below. (Watch out, two of them cannot be used!)

a) A: 彼^{かれ}はいつも女性^{じょせい}に失礼^{しつれい}だね。お尻^{しり}に触^{さわ}ったりするし...

   B: そうだけど、この間ミホちゃんに殴^{なぐ}られたよ。＿＿＿＿＿＿＿＿だよ！

b) A: ミサエさんは納豆^{なっとう}が大好きで、チョコレートが嫌^{きら}いって。信^{しん}じられない！

   B: ま、＿＿＿＿＿＿＿＿＿＿＿＿＿＿＿だもんね。

c) A: 彼^{かれ}は金持ちの女と結婚^{けっこん}したし、会社でえらくなったし、ポルシェも買ったし...

   B: そうだね、彼^{かれ}の人生は＿＿＿＿＿＿＿＿＿＿＿＿みたいだね。

d) A: マンガが好きで、翻訳^{ほんやく}することも大好きだよ、オレ。

   B: そうだよね！じゃ、マンガの翻訳家^{ほんやくか}になれて、＿＿＿＿＿＿＿だったね！

| 一石二鳥^{いちごいちえ} 一期一会^{いちごいちえ} 十人十色^{じゅうにんといろ} 順風満帆^{じゅんぷうまんぱん} 自由自在^{じゆうじざい} 自業自得^{じごうじとく} |

15. Choose the most suitable answer for each sentence.

a) 「＿＿＿＿＿＿＿＿＿＿＿＿＿＿＿」というのは夏用の着物のような服ですね。

1. Ｔシャツ　2. 動物　3. 浴衣　4. 下駄

b) ハハハ！日本語の先生が間違えたよ！「緊張している」と言いたかったのに、「浣腸している」と言ってしまったよ！「＿＿＿＿＿＿＿」んだよね！

1. ウソも方便　2. 猿も木から落ちる　3. 鬼のいぬ間に洗濯　4. 花より団子

c) 彼はドイツ語が話せないのに、よくドイツへ＿＿＿＿＿＿＿＿＿＿＿しようとしているね。

1. 見学　2. 留学　3. 数学　4. 大学

d) 私は辛い料理が好きだから、＿＿＿＿＿＿＿＿＿をたくさん入れてください。

1. こしょう　2. だし　3. きゅうり　4. ごま

e) 下着をはいたまま、＿＿＿＿＿＿＿＿＿＿＿＿って無理だよ、アホ！

1. ナンパする　2. びびる　3. むかつく　4. エッチする

f) 遅くまで遊んだので＿＿＿＿＿＿＿＿＿＿＿に間に合わなかった。タクシーで帰るしかなかった。

1. 駅　2. 運賃　3. 終電　4. 始発

g) A: 川内さんはあまりかっこよくないけど、すごい美人と結婚したよね。

B: そうだね、「＿＿＿＿＿＿＿＿＿＿＿＿」というのは本当だろうね。

1. 出る釘は打たれる　2. 後の祭り　3. 能ある鷹は爪を隠す　4. 花より団子

h) 日本の夏はすごく暑いので、ホテルの部屋に＿＿＿＿＿＿＿＿＿＿がないとだめだね。

1. 冷房　2. たんす　3. 暖房　4. 鍵

i) マドリッドのプラド美術館へ行けば、レンブラントの＿＿＿＿＿＿＿が見られるぞ。

1. 写真　2. 歌　3. 浮世絵　4. 絵画

j)　この手紙を早く届けさせたかったら、＿＿＿＿＿＿＿で送った方がいいよ。

　　1. 速達　2. 郵便局　3. ポスト　4. 書留

k)　日本人はよく「＿＿＿＿＿＿＿＿＿＿」というスープを飲みますね。

　　1. 醤油　2. サラダ　3. あんこ　4. 味噌汁

l)　「ありがとう」というのは関西弁で＿＿＿＿＿＿＿＿＿と言います。

　　1. おおきに　2. サンキュー　3. ありごう　4. まいど

16. Fill in the blanks in the following sentences, choosing from だけ, しか or ばかり.

a)　昨日のパーティーに来たのは黒沢＿＿＿＿＿＿＿＿＿＿だったよ。

b)　あいつは歌を歌って＿＿＿＿＿＿＿で、何も仕事をしないんだよ！

c)　彼は日本語が上手な＿＿＿＿＿＿＿＿でなく、中国語も上手だ。

d)　今、お風呂に入った＿＿＿＿＿＿＿＿だから、家を出られないよ。

e)　この間、ＤＶＤを５枚＿＿＿＿＿＿＿＿買ってしまいました。

f)　昨日のパーティには黒沢先生＿＿＿＿＿＿＿＿来ませんでしたよ。

g)　クラスの中で、オレ＿＿＿＿＿＿がポルシェを持っているよ！ハハハ！

h)　お母さんに呼ばれたから、今は家に帰る＿＿＿＿＿＿ないね。ごめん！

i)　あいつは授業中に寝て＿＿＿＿＿いるよね！本当にだめなやつだなぁ！

17. This conversation is out of order. Rewrite it in the correct order.

1)　それほどでもありませんよ ... 上手になったかもしれないけど、関西弁はまだですよ。

2)　「郷に入っては郷に従え」ってどういう意味ですか？

3)　こんにちは！お元気ですか、おばさん？

4)　そうですね。普通の日本語と大阪弁を両方習えて、一石二鳥ですものね！

5)　関西弁を習った方がええで！「郷に入っては郷に従え」やもん！

6)　大阪に来たなら、大阪の話し方を習わなあかんという意味やわ。

7)　ハハハ！ほんまや！よう言ったな、あんた！ほな、大阪弁、がんばりや！

8) はい、元気やで。あんた、日本語が上手<ruby>上手<rt>じょうず</rt></ruby>になったなぁ、外人さんやのに！

外国人： _____

おばさん： _____

外国人： _____

おばさん： _____

外国人： _____

おばさん： _____

外国人： _____

おばさん： _____

18. Complete this dialogue with the words from the box on page 344, bearing in mind that seven of the words in the box cannot be used.

Minako: マリーさん、こんにちは。何を ⁽¹⁾ _____ いるの？

Marie: あ、美奈子<ruby>美奈子<rt>みなこ</rt></ruby>ちゃん、こんにちは。これは ⁽²⁾ _____ だよ。

Minako: 手紙<ruby>手紙<rt>てがみ</rt></ruby>に使うために？たくさんの手紙<ruby>手紙<rt>てがみ</rt></ruby>を書くの？

Marie: そうじゃないよ、これは ⁽³⁾ _____ だけだよ。

Minako: あ、そうか？私は派手<ruby>派手<rt>はで</rt></ruby>な服を買うことが大好き。同<ruby>同<rt>おな</rt></ruby>じようなことなの？

Marie: はい、そうだね。ところで、何をしにきたの？

Minako: ちょっと ⁽⁴⁾ _____ なので、どこかへ行きたい。一緒<ruby>一緒<rt>いっしょ</rt></ruby>に行こうよ！

Marie: 私？すみません、今はかなり ⁽⁵⁾ _____ ので、出来ないよ。

Minako: 残念<ruby>残念<rt>ざんねん</rt></ruby>だね！じゃ、あたし一人で行くわ。

Marie: どこへ行くの？渋谷<ruby>渋谷<rt>しぶや</rt></ruby>？

Minako: うん、渋谷<ruby>渋谷<rt>しぶや</rt></ruby>！⁽⁶⁾ _____ に乗<ruby>乗<rt>の</rt></ruby>っていくつもりよ。

Marie: じゃ、ここから３０分 ⁽⁷⁾ _____ かかるよね。

Minako: うん！で、渋谷<ruby>渋谷<rt>しぶや</rt></ruby>でかっこいい男に ⁽⁸⁾ _____ されちゃおう！

Marie: ええ？かっこいい男の人がいるの？

Minako: そうよ！たくさんいるよ！マリーさんも来れば！？

Marie: じゃ...かっこいい男がいるなら、あたしも行くわ！

Minako: よし！二人で渋谷へＧＯ！

忙しい（いそが）	えんぴつ	趣味（しゅみ）	切手（きって）	飛行機（ひこうき）	暇（ひま）	集めて（あつ）	悲しい（かな）
集まって（あつ）	つまらない	やや	ナンパ	電車	ぐらい	チャリ	

19. Complete the following table as in the example.

食べる（た）	食べれば	食べたら	食べさせる	食べられる	食べさせられる
動く					
転ぶ（ころ）					
行く（い）					
死ぬ（し）					
走る					
洗う（あら）					
持つ（も）					
来る					
落とす（お）					
教える（おし）					
飛ぶ（と）					
住む（す）					

20. Combine the two sentences, using the conditional form indicated in the brackets.

a) あした、彼は行かない。僕らも行かない。（〜ば）

あした、彼が行かなければ、僕らも行かない_____。

b) このラーメンはおいしい。お姉さんにも食べてもらいたい。（〜たら）

_____。

c) ８月１５日になる。日本人は田舎へ行きたがっている。（と）

_____。

d) チエコさんがエアコンを買いたくない。あなたが買ってください。（〜たら）

_____。

e) あなたは旅行をしない。部屋の掃除をしてください。（なら）

_____。

21. Fill in the blanks with the most suitable word from the box below.

a) すみません、赤川さんに会いたいけど、どこへ行け_____ですか？

b) こら！ここで遊ぶんじゃない_____！

c) お腹がすいたって？じゃ、あそこにあるケーキを食べ_____？

d) _____赤川先生に会いたいのですが...やはり、無理ですか？

e) マンガを買ってほしいの？じゃ、どのマンガを買え_____ですか？

f) 先生、電車が嫌なら、車で来_____？

g) 東京に住みたいの、あんた？じゃ、住_____？

h) あしたは休みなの？そう_____、先生も同じことをおっしゃいましたね。

```
┌─────────────────────────────────────────────────────────────┐
│  〜ってば     〜めば     出来れば          言えば            │
│                                                               │
│    〜たらどうですか     〜ばいい   〜たら      〜ばいい      │
└─────────────────────────────────────────────────────────────┘
```

22. As in the example, write the verb in parentheses in the past tense of the given form (except f, which goes in the infinitive). Also, translate the resulting sentence.

a) あの家は有名な漫画家に (買う passive) ___買われた___ 。

    <u>That house was bought by a famous manga artist</u>   。

b) 彼女は子どもにボールを (取る causative) _____。

_____。

c) この映画は小津安二郎監督によって (作る passive) _____。

_____。

d) 私は彼女に２時間も (待つ passive) _____。

_____。

e) あの家に行けば、掃除を (する caus-pas) _____のので、行きたくない。

_____。

f) あの人はかわいそうな犬を何時間も (走る causative) _____。

_____。

g) オレは彼女に高いプレゼントを (買う causative-passive) _____。

_____。

h) 冷蔵庫にあった私の牛乳が全部 (飲む passive) _____。

_____。

23. Fill in the blanks in the following sentences with こと or もの , as appropriate.

a) 昨日、スーパーマーケットへ行って、いろいろな_____
を買いました。

b) 私はアクション映画を見る_____はあまり好きじゃない。

c) 無理だ！あなたと結婚する_____ですか！

d) 彼は富士山に登った_____があるらしいよ。

e) すみませんが、来週からアメリカへ行く_____になりました。

f) A: どうして宿題をしなかったの？｜B: だって、難しいんだ＿＿＿＿＿＿＿！

g) はじめまして。私は諸星アタルという＿＿＿＿＿＿＿＿＿＿＿＿＿＿です。

h) あしたからダイエットをする＿＿＿＿＿＿＿＿＿＿＿にしたよ、あたし。

i) 彼女は掃除をする＿＿＿＿＿＿＿＿＿＿＿＿＿＿＿＿＿＿＿がある。

24. Conjugate the verb into its infinitive, gerund, or past form, as appropriate.

a) このりんごはおいしそうだね。今＿＿＿＿＿ところだった。（食べる）

b) このりんごはおいしい！今、＿＿＿ところだから、分かる。（食べる）

c) このりんごはおいしかった！今、＿＿＿＿＿ところだ。（食べる）

d) 今、マンガを＿＿＿＿＿ところだ。５０ページぐらい読みましたけど、まだ１５０ページぐらい残っている。終わったら、行くね。（読む）

e) A: ジョンさん、いる？｜B: 今、＿＿＿＿＿＿＿ところなので、いないよ。（出る）

f) うぉっ、やばいな！うんこを＿＿＿＿＿＿＿＿＿ところだった！（踏む）（うんこ：poop）

g) A: 宿題、終わった？｜B:いいえ、まだだ。今、＿＿＿＿＿＿＿＿ところだ。（やる）

25. Correct the mistakes in the following sentences.

a) 彼は日本語しか出来るよ。

b) あの人にバイクを運転することを教えば、すぐ覚えると思いますよ。

c) 本田さんは新しい本を書くものにしました。

d) おじいさんは君のおかげで死んだよ！許せない！

e) 私はお父さんに田舎に住めらせされた。

f) マサコさんはお金がないのに、高いものを買ってだけいるよ！

26. Choose the most suitable answer for each sentence.

a) ここにえんぴつやペンや紙がある。一つ＿＿＿＿＿＿＿取ってください。

　　1. もの　2. ところ　3. こそ　4. ずつ

b) 先生、お忙しい＿＿＿＿＿＿＿を邪魔して、すみません。今、少し時間がありますか？

　　1. もの　2. こと　3. ところ　4. もし

c) 彼はスペイン語を先生に＿＿＿＿＿＿＿ので、今、彼はスペイン語が出来る。

　　1. 教えられた　2. 教えさせた　3. 教えさせられた　4. 教えれば

d) アフリカへ行きたい＿＿＿＿＿＿＿＿＿、航空券を買ってください。

　　1. ければ　2. なら　3. ったら　4. と

e) アフリカへ行きた＿＿＿＿＿＿＿＿＿、航空券を買ってください。

　　1. ければ　2. なら　3. ったら　4. と

f) アフリカへ行きたか＿＿＿＿＿＿＿＿＿、航空券を買ってください。

　　1. ければ　2. なら　3. ったら　4. と

g) ＿＿＿＿＿＿＿、パーティーに誰もいなければ、映画館へ行きますか？

　　1. すると　2. もし　3. こそ　4. ところに

h) 先生の＿＿＿＿＿＿＿＿＿、試験に合格した。ありがとう、先生！

　　1. おかげで　2. ところ　3. せいで　4. ところで

i) この本は１００年前に＿＿＿＿＿＿＿＿＿＿＿＿＿＿＿＿。

　　1. 書かせられた　2. 書きられた　3. 書かれた　4. 書かせた

j) このボタンを押す＿＿＿＿＿＿＿＿＿＿＿＿、窓が開くんだ。

　　1. ければ　2. なら　3. ったら　4. と

k) 彼はロック＿＿＿＿＿＿＿＿＿＿＿＿＿＿＿＿＿聞かないね。

　　1. しかだけ　2. だけ　3. だけしか　4. しかし

l) A: なんで怒っているの？ | B: だって、自転車が＿＿＿＿＿＿んだもん！

　　1. 盗められた　2. 盗みられた　3. 盗まれた　4. 盗れた

m) 君はいい学生だから＿＿＿＿＿＿＿、この練習帳を全部終わることが
できたよ！

　1. こそ　2. ぐらい　3. ばかり　4. ずつ

Kanji

試	験	問	題	答	回	転	族	親	主	住
(209)	(210)	(213)	(214)	(215)	(221)	(222)	(236)	(237)	(238)	(239)
考	死	別	計	英	集	歌	切	去	運	建
(240)	(241)	(242)	(243)	(197)	(245)	(246)	(248)	(249)	(253)	(256)

27. Link each kanji with its *kun'yomi* reading.

住	はか（る）		集	かんが（える）
試	き（る）		運	あつ（まる）
切	おも		問	と（う）
計	さ（る）		考	た（てる）
主	す（む）		建	はこ（ぶ）
去	こころ（みる）		答	こた（える）

28. Choose the correct kanji or kanji combination for each reading.

a) <u>きょねん</u>、サチコさんはご<u>しゅじん</u>に<u>えいご</u>を教えていました。

　きょねん：1. 去年　2. 法年　3. 年去　4. 年法

　しゅじん：1. 住人　2. 王人　3. 主人　4. 玉人

　えいご：1. 映語　2. 英語　3. 央語　4. 瑛語

b) 「<u>ししょく</u>」という言葉は「<u>ためし</u>に何かを食べること」という意味です。

　ししょく：1. 式食　2. 試食　3. 式飲　4. 試飲

　ためし：1. 試し　2. 式し　3. 試めし　4. 式めし

c) この<u>しつもん</u>の<u>せいとう</u>は何ですか？

　　しつもん：1. 質問　2. 質間　3. 貸問　4. 貸間

　　せいとう：1. 止合　2. 正合　3. 正答　4. 止答

d) この荷物（にもつ）はここに書いている<u>じゅうしょ</u>に<u>うんそう</u>しなければならない。

　　じゅうしょ：1. 主所　2. 玉所　3. 王所　4. 住所

　　うんそう：1. 蓮逆　2. 運逆　3. 蓮送　4. 運送

e) この<u>もんだい</u>は<u>とくべつ</u>にやさしくしますね！

　　もんだい：1. 門題　2. 問題　3. 間題　4. 閉題

　　とくべつ：1. 特別　2. 持別　3. 待別　4. 侍別

29. Choose the correct reading for each kanji combination.

a) その<u>時計</u>とあの<u>自転車</u>は<u>英国</u>で作られた物でございます。

　　時計：1. ときけい　2. とけい　3. じけい　4. とうけい

　　自転車：1. じてんしゃ　2. じどうしゃ　3. してんしゃ　4. しどうしゃ

　　英国：1. えいぐに　2. えいごく　3. えいこく　4. えいくに

b) ヒデオくんの<u>父親</u>と一緒に<u>回転</u>寿司（ずし）の店へ行きました。

　　父親：1. ちちおや　2. ふしん　3. ちちしん　4. ふおや

　　回転：1. がいでん　2. かいてん　3. がいてん　4. かいでん

c) あなた！<u>運動</u>のために郵便局（ゆうびんきょく）まで歩いて<u>切手</u>を買ってきてくださいね。

　　運動：1. うんど　2. れんどう　3. うんどう　4. れんど

　　切手：1. せっしゅ　2. きりしゅ　3. せって　4. きって

d) 来週、<u>考古学</u>の<u>集会</u>があるので、たくさん勉強しなければなりません。

　　考古学：1. ここがく　2. ここうがく　3. こうこがく　4. こうこうがく

　　集会：1. しゅかい　2. しゅうかい　3. じゅかい　4. じゅうかい

30. Write the kanji for the given *furigana*.

　　　　　　し　けん　　　　　　　　　　　　　　　しゅう　ちゅう
a) ＿＿＿＿＿＿＿のために勉強に＿＿＿＿＿＿＿＿＿＿しなければならない。

　　　　　　　　　　　　　　か　しゅ　　　　　　し
b) 昨日、あの有名な＿＿＿＿＿＿＿＿は＿＿＿＿＿にました。
　　きのう

　　　　　　　たて　もの　　　　　　　　　　　　　　か　ぞく　　　　　す
c) この＿＿＿＿＿＿＿＿にはマサオさんのご＿＿＿＿＿＿＿が＿＿＿んでいる。

　　　　　　おや　こ　　　　　　　　　　　　　もん　だい
d) あの＿＿＿＿＿＿はかわいそうだ...＿＿＿＿＿＿ばかりあるんだよね...

　　　　　　おも　　　　　　　はこ
e) この車は、＿＿＿＿＿に物を＿＿＿＿＿ぶのに使われている。

　　　　　　　　　えい　ご　　　　　　うた　　　　　うた
f) おねがい！＿＿＿＿＿＿＿の＿＿＿＿＿を＿＿＿＿＿ってくださいよ！

31. There are some mistakes in these words, either in the kanji or in the matching hiragana. Can you correct them?

試めす　ためす	別れる　かわれる	親友　おやとも
休験　たいけん	考思　しこう	運行　うんこ
話題　だいわ	口転　かいてん	住食　しゅしょく

"Books to Span the East and West"

Tuttle Publishing was founded in 1832 in the small New England town of Rutland, Vermont [USA]. Our core values remain as strong today as they were then—to publish best-in-class books which bring people together one page at a time. In 1948, we established a publishing outpost in Japan—and Tuttle is now a leader in publishing English-language books about the arts, languages and cultures of Asia. The world has become a much smaller place today and Asia's economic and cultural influence has grown. Yet the need for meaningful dialogue and information about this diverse region has never been greater. Over the past seven decades, Tuttle has published thousands of books on subjects ranging from martial arts and paper crafts to language learning and literature—and our talented authors, illustrators, designers and photographers have won many prestigious awards. We welcome you to explore the wealth of information available on Asia at www.tuttlepublishing.com.

Published by Tuttle Publishing, an imprint of Periplus Editions (HK) Ltd.

www.tuttlepublishing.com

Originally published as JAPONÉS EN VIÑETAS: VOLUMES 2 and 3
Copyright © 2023 by Marc Bernabé / Represented by NORMA Editorial S.A. Translation rights arranged by Sandra Bruna Agencia Literaria SL.

Library of Congress Control Number: 2022940733

ISBN 978-4-8053-1694-8

First edition, 2023

26 25 24 23   7 6 5 4 3

Printed in China   2311CM

TUTTLE PUBLISHING® is a registered trademark of Tuttle Publishing, a division of Periplus Editions (HK) Ltd.

Distributed by

North America, Latin America & Europe
Tuttle Publishing
364 Innovation Drive
North Clarendon,
VT 05759-9436 U.S.A.
Tel: 1 (802) 773-8930
Fax: 1 (802) 773-6993
info@tuttlepublishing.com
www.tuttlepublishing.com

Japan
Tuttle Publishing
Yaekari Building, 3rd Floor,
5-4-12 Osaki, Shinagawa-ku,
Tokyo 141 0032
Tel: (81) 3 5437-017
Fax: (81) 3 5437-0755
sales@tuttle.co.jp
www.tuttle.co.jp

Asia Pacific
Berkeley Books Pte. Ltd.
3 Kallang Sector #04-01
Singapore 349278
Tel: (65) 6741-2178
Fax: (65) 6741-2179
inquiries@periplus.com.sg
www.tuttlepublishing.com